# PERSONALITY AND HYPNOSIS

Josephine R. Hilgard, M.D.

# Personality and Hypnosis

A Study of Imaginative Involvement

*The University of Chicago Press*
*Chicago and London*

Standard Book Number: 226–33441–4
Library of Congress Catalog Card Number: 77–95656
The University of Chicago Press, Chicago 60637
The University of Chicago Press, Ltd., London
© 1970 by The University of Chicago. All rights reserved
Published 1970. Printed in the United States of America

# Contents

# Preface

Some individuals have the capacity for deep involvements in reading, in music, in religion, in the enjoyment of nature, and in adventure. It turns out that this capacity is related to hypnotizability, and interviews with hundreds of students prior to their experience of hypnosis have been used not only to predict how hypnotizable the students will be but to see how these involvements develop and what they mean to the individual. The research is directed not so much to the hypnotic practitioner as to those interested in the development of personality, in the contagion of enthusiasms from parent to child, and in the role of imagination as shaping the experiences that the individual is prepared to enjoy.

This investigation seeks to find what the precursors to hypnosis are in the experiences of childhood and in the characteristics the young adult brings to the hypnotic situation. The long-term study was carried on within the Laboratory of Hypnosis Research, Department of Psychology, Stanford University. An earlier account of the program, with emphasis upon the experimental and psychometric findings, has already appeared (E. R. Hilgard 1965); in that book a single chapter gave a preliminary account of the clinical interviews, and this book is a further report that was promised.

The combination of psychometric measurements with clinical assessment, both prior to hypnosis and following it, provides an integration of methods useful at this stage of our knowledge.

A study of this kind is possible only in the team setting of a large laboratory, and I wish to express my gratitude to the many workers who made it possible. Were it not for the susceptibility scales developed by André M. Weitzenhoffer and my husband,

ix

Ernest R. Hilgard, we should have lacked the anchorage required to define individual hypnotizability; without the other studies of hypnosis going on in the laboratory, we would not have had access to the large number of students for interviewing (a total of 822 students and 1,398 interviews) over the period of study. Numerous assistants aided in the statistical work that was necessary in coding interview material for quantitative study. If, then, this book chiefly presents the work of a staff of interviewers, it was made possible only by the supplementary work of hypnotists and data analysts within the laboratory. While I conducted a full share of the interviews myself, I was ably assisted by skilled social workers. Martha Newman was a devoted colleague for over five years, Ursula Moore for two years, and Nancy Kautz for two years. Others served for shorter periods. In analyzing the data and arriving at interpretations, I drew heavily on the help of Arlene H. Morgan and Ernest R. Hilgard.

The opportunity to talk with a large number of normal college students, both men and women, about their childhood relationships with their parents and about their interests and activities as they were growing up proved rewarding in itself. I wish it were possible to express to each of them my gratitude for their willingness to talk frankly about themselves. In the effort to understand hypnosis we were forced to raise questions about child rearing, discipline, and identification that modified our views about normal personality development. To preserve privacy, all names and identifying characteristics have been modified in the text.

The work of the Laboratory of Hypnosis Research, of which this study was an integral part, was made possible by a number of grants, the original one from the Ford Foundation, later ones from the Robert C. Wheeler Foundation, the San Mateo County Heart Association, the National Institute of Mental Health (Grant MH–3859), and the U.S. Air Force Office of Research (Contract AF 49[638]–1436). To these granting agencies, to Stanford University, and to private donors, those of us working in the Laboratory of Hypnosis Research are deeply grateful.

Josephine R. Hilgard, M.D.,Ph.D.

Department of Psychiatry
Stanford Medical School

Department of Psychology
Laboratory of Hypnosis Research
Stanford University

# PERSONALITY AND HYPNOSIS

# 1

## Involvement as a Manifestation of Personality: The Relevance of Hypnosis

Reflective men have always wondered about themselves—what it is that makes man unique, how it comes about that the human mind can ask questions about its own experiences, what is the deeper meaning of human life. But men do not spend all of their time in reflection: they satisfy their curiosity and seek areas of enjoyment, alone or in the company of others. If they are men of energy and vitality, they become engrossed in what they do.

Psychology as a science might do well to concern itself with such matters, and occasionally psychologists do. Unfortunately, however, the experimentalist, preoccupied with making a conventional science out of his discipline, often turns to less crucial problems because for them his tools are appropriate; and the applied psychologist is often so occupied with solving an immediate problem that he too is little concerned with some of the deeper problems of human consciousness.

There are many signs that this is changing. The popularity of existential psychology, with its emphasis upon "being," the vogue of the strongly value-oriented humanistic psychologies, the attempts to expand consciousness through various kinds of sensitivity training or through psychedelic drugs—all these are manifestations of a desire to cope with what is central, even if mysterious, in man.

Our studies on hypnosis began ten years ago, before some of these movements were so prominent. We felt that psychology had been moving away from its natural focus on human experience toward peripheral concerns capable of objective measurement. Even the concept of personality structure was giving way to the picture of a collection of habits, which had been the way of

3

describing a person fifty years earlier. The study of hypnosis appeared to be an excellent way in which to focus on the problems of awareness. It is an area of study where central psychological problems in normal human beings are inescapable: distortions of perception, hallucinations, dreams, regressions, temporary memory losses, disturbances of voluntary movement, increased control over autonomic processes. These familiar hypnotic phenomena are at the very heart of what we mean by *the mental,* and we felt that psychology ought again to come to grips with them. During the nineteenth century, when most of the phenomena were discovered and widely attested, psychology was not ready to make orderly scientific use of them. In the twentieth century, the era of behaviorism, a good start was made by Clark L. Hull (1933), but the "subjective" phenomena were out of style: a behaviorist could study them without doing violence to his methodological commitments, but he was little likely to become interested in them.

We had no sooner started our studies at Stanford than we became impressed by the persistent individual differences in hypnotizability among eager and willing student subjects. As a clinical psychiatrist I was interested in these differences and in what they might mean for personality. There are few behavioral situations to which individuals can readily be exposed that yield such consistent evidence of different individual styles of experiencing and responding as we were able to show in hypnosis. It became an intriguing goal to find out, if we could, what lay behind these differences. Many others had attempted to do this, and their failure to come up with anything consistent made the task all the more challenging. Hence we set up a program of interviews prior to hypnosis to see if we could tell in advance which subjects would be hypnotizable; then we hypnotized them in a uniform manner so as to obtain a quantitative estimate of how hypnotizable they actually were; and finally, in many cases we conducted another interview to see how nearly correct our advance conjectures had been and where we had gone wrong.

Prediction of hypnotizability, of course, was only a methodological aim, not a practical one. We knew all along that the best way to assess a person's hypnotizability, was to try to hypnotize him. To understand *why* one person is hypnotizable and another not, it was important to attempt prediction: by this means we avoided the kind of retrospective rationalizing that can always find something in a complicated history to explain a later course of events.

What we found out was that the hypnotizable person was capable of a deep involvement in one or more imaginative-feeling areas of experience—reading a novel, listening to music, having an aesthetic experience of nature, or engaging in absorbing adventures of body or mind. This involvement is one of the things the existentialist is talking about when he speaks of the breaking down of the distinction between the subject and the object of his experience; it is what those seeking expansion of consciousness mean by their all-embracing experiences; it is something like Maslow's (1959) peak experiences. There need be nothing abnormal or extreme about it, and we shall point out that our readily hypnotizable subjects are more likely to be normal than neurotic. If we were to define this involvement, to distinguish it from its nearest relatives such as enjoyment of, or interest in, an activity, we would have to stress the quality of almost total immersion in the activity, with indifference to distracting stimuli in the environment. The often observed narrowing of attention in the hypnotized subject implies something like this, but concentrated attention is not the whole story. The child glued to the TV screen, who fails to hear himself being called, whether by mother or by friends, is not only attending but is having a vivid experience through involvement, an experience some adults are also capable of.

The concept of involvement is related to earlier efforts to indicate what the hypnotic experience is like. Gill and Brenman (1959) make much of the regressive nature of hypnosis, using regression in the psychoanalytic sense of a more primitive (primary process) type of thought. The regression they speak of is a partial one, the "regression in the service of the ego" that Kris (1952) talked about in describing the approach of an artist to his work: he permits a welling-up of unconscious processes for a time and later reworks them in a more disciplined fashion. To the extent that the regressive phase is characterized by impulse and feeling, rather than by critical thought, it has something in common with the immersion we call involvement. Sarbin (Sarbin 1950; Sarbin 1954; Sarbin and Lim 1963; Sarbin and Andersen 1967) both earlier than Gill and Brenman and more recently, has stressed role enactment as characterizing the hypnotically susceptible person. Shor (1962), somewhat critical of Sarbin's position, believes it better to use the expression role involvement, which includes both the capacity to take a role (stressed by Sarbin) and the involvement in the role which gives it the involuntary flavor of hypnotic participation. Shor's position comes nearer to ours. While we do not feel that what we shall have to report is contradictory to these earlier statements, we believe that we have gone on to be more specific about what the involvements are like and what their history is in the life of the individual.

As we began to look into these imaginative involvements, and tried to understand their nuances so as to distinguish those deeply involved from those superficially interested, we felt that we were entering an almost uncharted chapter of psychology. We were no longer studying merely some of the indicators of hypnotic susceptibility, but something deeply coloring the lives of those who had the capacity for involvement. This book turns out to be as much about involvement and personality as about hypnosis. As we went along hypnosis came to be the indicator of personality dimensions that we were trying to understand.

In addition to studying the nature of these involvements, and what they mean for the individual today, we became interested in their childhood origins. It was soon evident that relationships with parents who themselves were capable of involvement was an important background, but these relationships were by no means simple. We were forced to reexamine some of our concepts of identification as we noted how important were non-sex-typed aspects of parents, such as temperament, enthusiasm, and enjoyment of carefree recreation. A son or daughter might be appropriately sex-typed, and fully identified with the appropriate parent, so far as work and social behavior were concerned, but might be much closer to the other parent in the kinds of deeply involved experiences which gradually came to interest us. In addition, unexpected relationships emerged between childhood discipline, especially punishment, and later hypnotizability.

What, then, does this book set out to do? It attempts to recount, through the statistical analysis of coded interview material, reflected against measured hypnotic susceptibility, some of the personality correlates of hypnosis. But through both statistical material and case studies it also tells what we have learned about involvement as an important aspect of personality, how these involvements develop, and what they mean in satisfaction to the persons capable of them.

The message that emerges is one of potential significance in child rearing, education, and psychotherapy. If there can be rich personality fulfillment through involvement, and if involvement can be encouraged through known types of affiliative experiences, what we have learned goes beyond hypnosis. In fact, some psychotherapeutic experiences growing out of our findings have resulted in experiments where an affiliative relationship was used most advantageously with disturbed adolescents (Hilgard and Moore 1969).

In the present period of emphasis on creativity, the fulfilling of human potential, the discovering and celebrating of values, we need new studies on the deeper meaning of human experiences.

# 2

# Interviewing and Rating Procedures

In the autumn of 1957 workers in the Laboratory of Hypnosis Research at Stanford undertook the revision of standard hypnotic susceptibility scales. The progress was routine until one subject reported an unusual reaction following hypnosis. I was called in as a psychiatrist to see if I could explain what had occurred. For two nights after going to bed she had been troubled by an imaginary fly buzzing around (a fly which she could not get rid of because she recognized it as hallucinatory—the same fly she had hallucinated in one of the items of the hypnotic test); she also heard her name called when no one was there to call (this too had been one of the hypnotic suggestions). The attempt to understand why she had these experiences, which were most unsual for our subjects, and how she was able to identify the experiences as hallucinatory and related to hypnosis, suggested the importance of finding out more about the nature of hypnosis *from the point of view of the hypnotized person.*

This led to the first attempt to do some exploratory interviewing with a number of students of known hypnotic susceptibility, a total of twelve male students and sixteen female students of whom half were high in hypnotic susceptibility and half low.

It is very easy to develop plausible ideas about why one person is readily hypnotized and another not, but in practice these ideas seldom show more than a trivial relation to hypnotizability. These initial interviews took into account fantasy life (reveries, daydreams, night dreams); studies and activities; recreational practices, drinking, relaxation, interpersonal relationships with peers; early childhood experiences, including discipline, and relationship with parents. It appeared that hypnosis as an interpersonal rela-

7

tionship of deference to, and comfort with, authority might well be related to the problems of self-image and relationships with others. The interviews often revealed a good deal of material that appeared relevant in explaining the individual case, but it was evident that there were many internal contradictions and that much more care would have to be exercised if plausibility were to be converted to proof.

By this time the project had become formally interesting; although the results were baffling, it was evident that a great deal of material could be obtained in a short interview with these normal subjects who were ready to contribute to science and were not (in this setting) preoccupied with their own troubles. The decision was made to take advantage of the experiments then going on within the project for standardizing the Stanford Hypnotic Susceptibility Scales. These experiments required large numbers of subjects covering the whole range of hypnotizability, and this population could be made available for the interview project.

**Exploratory Interviews following Hypnosis**

We decided to embark upon the long-term study in several steps. First we would do further exploration with interviews conducted after hypnosis so as to detect, if we could, some of the relevant variables. Following this we would use the trained interviewing staff to interview in advance of hypnosis and attempt to predict hypnotizability from the interview; then to reinterview after hypnosis in order to either reaffirm the basis for prediction or correct where errors had been made. Once these experiences were behind us, we would enter upon a more formal program, with more fully standardized procedures.

The first planned, semistructured interview program was carried out during the year 1958–59, with the subjects constituting the standardization sample for forms A and B of the Stanford Hypnotic Susceptibility Scale (Weitzenhoffer and Hilgard 1959).[1] The interviewing was done following hypnosis, for at this stage the formalities of attempted prediction seemed to us less important than getting leads from the subjects who had just experienced an attempted induction. We would have them tell us why they thought they were able to be hypnotized or why not. The questions, based on the experience of the preceding year and going further, included such background items as major in college,

1. Reference to scores on these forms and on form C will be made hereafter as SHSS-A, SHSS-B, and SHSS-C.

grades, vocational plans, activities, and items reflecting personality such as ascendance-submission (leader-follower) or observer-participant, as in dramatics or athletics. To round out the developmental picture the subject was asked to describe his or her mother, father, and siblings and how they all interacted. Something of a personal biography was called for, as well as present-day self-characterizations. The kinds of leads that came out of these interviews were summarized in a number of case studies which, while interesting, fell short of being conclusive in their characterization of the more or less hypnotizable person (Hilgard and Hilgard 1962).

During the year 1959–60 essentially the same program was carried out, but with more questions exploring the possible connection between hypnosis and sleep, as in dreaming, nightmares, sleepwalking, and sleeptalking. By this time it became evident that many of the ideas explored in the interview had been too general and that differentiations would have to be made to get at the subtle differences reflected in hypnotic susceptibility. Thus we gradually found that we had to break down the identification with parents into different kinds, of which sex-role identification was only one; we had to examine recreational interests for degrees of involvement, as we shall see later on. In any case, it now seemed that we should be ready for a more formal study, in which our ideas would be tested by their predictive power. That is, hereafter the interviewing would be done *before* hypnosis as a test of the power of our hypotheses. Some interviews would be done following hypnosis, to provide a better understanding of what was going on, but the correlational data would now be limited to prehypnotic interview data. In our successive samples during 1960–61 and 1961–62, the predictions by the interviewers, made in advance of hypnosis, yielded the correlations of table 1. By 1960–61 the standardization of the Stanford Hypnotic Susceptibility Scale, form C, was under way (Weitzenhoffer and Hilgard 1962), and we began to use its scores as the criterion of hypnotic susceptibility because the scale is somewhat richer in content than form A.

These correlations, while low, still added up to a positive relationship, and it appeared that refinement of our interviews on the basis of this experience would lead us to firmer conclusions about the foundations of hypnotic susceptibility. To improve the interview, we felt it desirable to assess the reliabilities of the separable ratings that entered into the global prediction of hypnotic susceptibility and so proceeded with a major reliability study in the summer of 1962.

TABLE 1

*Prediction of Hypnotic Susceptibility from Interviews in Advance of Hypnosis, 1960–1962*

| Subject Group | Period of Study | Correlation Between Interviewer Prediction and Later Hypnotic Susceptibility Score | | |
|---|---|---|---|---|
| | | N | r | p |
| Female University Students | Autumn 1960; Winter 1961 | 99 | .30 | < .01 |
| Male University Students | Autumn 1961; Winter 1962 | 98 | .35 | < .01 |

## A Reliability Study

Developing ratings on the basis of a semistructured interview raises difficult problems, for the rating of any one item may require drawing upon information obtained in reply to another; this not only affects the reliability of the individual rating but through a "halo" effect may distort other ratings in the series. The interviewers themselves, while recording the replies given to a variety of questions, were attempting to assess positive and negative factors so as to produce an overall rating of hypnotizability. They of course had access not only to recorded replies but to unrecorded nuances of expression and gesture. Still, if any analysis was to be made of the detailed replies of the interviews it would be necessary to separate out special items and ultimately to correlate them with the criterion of hypnotic susceptibility. Unless the replies could be coded and rated with some measure of reliability, later correlations could not be interpreted with any assurance.

We chose to work with two sets of interviews, one sample of fifty-one female subjects obtained in the winter of 1961 and the other a sample of fifty-one male subjects in the winter of 1962. The interviews during this exploratory period had been changed somewhat, but there was a common core of questions asked both times. Three judges participated in the study, and for each interview we had an independent analysis by two of them.[2] Before the judges could perform their tasks they had to become thoroughly familiar with the nature of the interviews and had to agree among themselves on the kinds of ratings possible. Hence ten interviews

2. Gratitude is expressed to the judges—Peter M. Bentler, Evelyn Lee-Teng, and Mary R. Roberts—and to Lillian W. Lauer, who supervised the project.

were selected at random from each of the interview periods for training and practice. They discussed these among themselves and agreed on the handling of most points. These interviews were then discarded from the reliability samples, which consisted of the forty-one interviews remaining from each of the two quarters under review.

A summary of the results by these judges appears in Table 2. While a number of the items yielded reliabilities between .70 and .90, others had reliabilities so low that either more information had to be obtained on the topic to increase the reliability, or the item abandoned. It was evident that too much information was being sought in too short an interviewing period, and the next steps were determined accordingly. At the same time, the reliabilities were high enough that significant correlations could be obtained with the criterion if there were underlying relationships of substantial importance.

TABLE 2

*Interjudge Reliabilities of Rating Derived from Interviews (Female Sample, Winter 1961, N = 41; Male Sample, Winter 1962, N = 41)*

| Common to Both Interviews | | |
|---|---|---|
| | Female Sample | Male Sample |
| Expectation of hypnotizability | .83 | .90 |
| Attitude toward hypnosis | .53 | .85 |
| Mother's warmth | .72 | .76 |
| Mother's temperament | .73 | .77 |
| Mother's involvement with hobbies | .48 | .71 |
| Mother's relation to outsiders | .65 | .61 |
| Father's warmth | .44 | .60 |
| Father's temperament | .77 | .71 |
| Father's involvement with hobbies | .36 | .41 |
| Father's relation to outsiders | .86 | .82 |
| Subject's achievement striving | .48 | .32 |
| Involvement in reading | .75 | .61 |
| Excitement or novelty seeking | .79 | .77 |
| Ability to concentrate | .84 | .57 |
| Ability to relinquish control | .59 | .31 |
| Ability to give adequate self-description | .55 | .61 |
| Role as primary participant or as observer | .77 | .83 |
| Satisfaction with current life situation | .43 | .37 |

TABLE 2—*Continued*

| Female Interview Only* | | Male Interview Only | |
|---|---|---|---|
| Mother's community | | Father's seriousness | .78 |
| orientation | .85 | Father's reading | .48 |
| Mother's reading | .73 | Father's use of | |
| | | rationality | .74 |
| Father's community | | Father's work | |
| orientation | .75 | organization | .79 |
| Playful activities of | | | |
| parents | .75 | Mother's seriousness | .90 |
| Punitiveness in discipline | .74 | Mother's use of | |
| Love-oriented discipline | .76 | rationality | .82 |
| Rationality in discipline | .73 | Mother's work | |
| Control by dominant | | organization | .86 |
| disciplinarian | .67 | | |
| Consistency of childhood | | Physical "space traveler" | .47 |
| discipline | .57 | Mental "space traveler" | .36 |
| Parental agreement on | | Involvement in movies | |
| discipline | .58 | or TV | .71 |
| Effectiveness of discipline | .48 | Music listening | .45 |
| | | Music performance | .56 |
| Frequency of home duties | .83 | | |
| Subject's acceptance of | | Willingness to accept | |
| family standards | .63 | responsibility | .43 |
| Current nervousness- | | Organization in work | .74 |
| neuroticism | .56 | Moodiness | .79 |

*Differences in female and male questionnaires owing to exploratory nature of the interviews, not to hypotheses about sex differences.

To achieve any depth at all, it was essential to get appropriate information and to pass over in the interview those items on which the subject was vague or had little to offer; and here a problem arose. For example, determining whether or not a subject classified as a physical or mental "space traveler" was easy for the few for whom such a question was appropriate, but difficult for the many whose fantasy lives or lives of adventure were, even to the subjects, notably unclear. Subjects do not readily admit that they have no imagination or desire for novelty, but these unclear subjects make reliability ratings uncertain, even when the information on the minority of space travelers, say, is abundantly clear.

A dilemma now appeared. Because we had not yet been able to purify our study sufficiently to select a few decisive variables, we preferred to try to modify some of the items of low reliability rather than to reject them, but, once they were modified, a new reliability study would ordinarily be called for. We made an unusual decision, which weakens somewhat the quantitative nicety of our study—a decision to redesign our questionnaire annually on the basis of all the information available and then to go ahead without new reliability studies. As a consequence, when significant positive relationships between ratings and the criterion occur we may assume that reliabilities are satisfactory. Hence we are not misled in our positive findings. What we sacrifice is the other side of the coin: when we do *not* find a relationship with a variable, unless we know its reliability we cannot assert with any confidence that no relationship exists between that variable and our criterion. This sacrifice we felt ready to make, in view of the technical difficulties of obtaining appropriate reliability measures with changing forms, and appropriate reliability measures for ratings made by interviewers who had more information before them than the judges of written interviews could have. We trusted that what we had learned from our earlier reliability study would warn us against trying to distill too much information from too few questions.

### Conclusions from Exploratory Interviews

The work of these preliminary years resulted in a rich collection of interviews but not much in the way of material appropriate for careful quantitative study. This lack of precise quantification came about in part because of the frequent changes in the interview as we sought to find some approach that would have a greater predictive significance, and because the interviewers were oriented more toward a global prediction of hypnotizability than toward a delineation of special variables subject to separate rating and analysis. Our experience with a large number of interviews during these years is summarized in table 3.

We recognized that university students, particularly those coming primarily from elementary psychology classes and fulfilling part of their course requirements by serving as subjects, were not ideal representatives of the broader society. They had some advantages for our purposes, in that we could obtain similar samples year after year and thus build upon our prior experiences. We did, however, make a few excursions outside the regular samples and interviewed some volunteers from the student community (who turned out to differ from the psychology-class samples), and a few others, as shown in table 4. We shall meet the volunteer students

TABLE 3

Interviews Conducted: Preliminary Explorations

| Academic Year | Number of Subjects | | | Number of Interviews | | |
|---|---|---|---|---|---|---|
| | Male | Female | Total | Prior to Hypnosis | Following Hypnosis | Total |
| 1957–58 | 12 | 16 | 28 | 0 | 28 | 28 |
| 1958–59 | 65 | 60 | 125 | 0 | 216 | 216 |
| 1959–60 | 84 | 55 | 139 | 0 | 169 | 169 |
| 1960–61 | 0 | 99 | 99 | 99 | 119 | 218 |
| 1961–62 | 98 | 0 | 98 | 98 | 110 | 208 |
| Total | 259 | 230 | 489 | 197 | 642 | 839 |

in chapter 9, the drama students in chapter 4, and the creative writers in chapter 7. The student nurses had been selected in the hope of finding a pool of highly susceptible subjects. Because their scores did not differ from our Stanford students' scores, we shall not report separately upon them.

TABLE 4

Interviews Following Attempted Hypnotic Induction:
Special Samples

| Academic Year | Characterization of Sample | Number of Interviews | | |
|---|---|---|---|---|
| | | Male | Females | Total |
| 1960–61 | Volunteer students | 28 | 20 | 48 |
| 1961–62 | Volunteer students | 28 | 17 | 45 |
| 1961–62 | Student nurses from area hospitals | — | 20 | 20 |
| 1961–62 | Drama students | 16 | 14 | 30 |
| 1961–62 | Creative writers | 2 | 1 | 3 |
| Total | | 74 | 72 | 146 |

By this time we knew that it was not going to be easy to find simple correlates of hypnotic susceptibility; our successes were not great enough, even though we had covered a wide area of inquiry. As we shall see later, we were misled by our guiding idea, which was to try to balance off positive indications (traits judged favorable to hypnosis) against negative ones (traits judged unfavorable to hypnosis). We had not yet hit upon the notion of alternate paths, wherein one set of positive indicators might overcome a number of apparently negative ones. We had learned, however, not to judge everything in terms of a global prediction of hypnotizability but to make a sharper distinction between the antecedent variable—subject to rating on its own, independent of hypnotizability—and the consequent variable, the hypnotic susceptibility being predicted. We did later on what we wish we had done earlier, which was to forget all about hypnotizability while rating the background factors and to permit later analysis to tell us how it was related to ultimate hypnosis scores. Still, we could not have begun that way, for we had to know something about the relationship to hypnosis in order to know what background variables to examine in greater detail.

### The Final Interview Program

With this background we were ready to construct an interview that would consolidate our experience and provide individually assessed variables that could be correlated with subsequent hypnosis. These interviews became the basis for the remaining tables in this volume, which present quantitative results. While during the year 1962–63 we still attempted a global prediction of hypnosis, the result was not better than before, despite our abundant experience; in fact, for a sample of $N = 103$ it dropped somewhat to $r = .23$. We recognized that this was not the way to go about our task, and in 1963–64 we no longer attempted to make a global prediction. Hence for those two years we settled upon the pattern of assessing as many pertinent variables as possible, with the interviewer paying attention to each variable independently of the relationship it might have to hypnosis. The ultimate relationship can then be established by correlations computed after the hypnotic scores come in.

The purpose of the quantitative material is to establish a nonchance relationship; once this is established, the "purer" cases that turn up in the interviews provide insights that help us to understand what is going on. Note that this is a different matter from using the quantitative scores for prediction: a quantitative relationship that does not account for enough variance to be useful in prediction may still help to validate the inferences from a few cases which exhibit the relationship in great clarity. It is as though a chemical analysis might detect the presence of a mineral in minute quantities in an area, while a lump of the mineral (like a nugget of gold), which is only rarely found, substantiates the analysis.

Because most of what follows (except for the excerpts from earlier cases) is based on the interviews of the years 1962–64, some of the procedures will now be described in greater detail. The total samples for these years are given in table 5.

TABLE 5
Interview Samples Used in Subsequent Data Analysis, 1962–64

|  | Number of Subjects | | | Number of Interviews | | |
|---|---|---|---|---|---|---|
| Academic Year | | | | Prior to | Following | |
|  | Male | Female | Total | Hypnosis | Hypnosis | Total |
| 1962–63 | 51 | 53 | 104 | 204 | 77 | 285 |
| 1963–64 | 64 | 19 | 83 | 83 | 45 | 128 |
| Total | 115 | 72 | 187 | 291 | 122 | 413 |

**The Criterion: Hypnotic Susceptibility**

One of the difficulties in personality studies is finding some criterion to serve as an anchorage—a dependent or consequent variable —against which to reflect the predictive power of the independent or antecedent variables. For the purposes of this study we fortunately had available the standardized scores of the Stanford Hypnotic Susceptibility Scales, particularly form C (Weitzenhoffer and Hilgard 1962). These scales consist of a brief attempted induction of hypnosis, followed by a number of simple tests of the kinds of behavior characteristic of hypnotized subjects. The person who performs more of these behaviors (that is, passes more of the tests) is judged to be more hypnotizable than the person who passes fewer of them. The distribution of scores is sufficiently normal for them to enter into correlations. The items of the Stanford Hypnotic Susceptibility Scale, form C, are listed in table 6 along with the criterion of passing. Hypnotic susceptibility as measured by SHSS-C is more satisfactory than many criteria used in personality studies; it has a reliability of $r = .85$ by the Kuder-Richardson method (formula 20), and it is valid because it correlates $r = .72$ with form A, with considerably different content (.62 with those items which differ entirely between the two scales).

Hypnotic susceptibility has been found to furnish a fairly satisfactory criterion, although an imperfect one. Another problem is, can hypnotic susceptibility be changed by training? There is some evidence that modification with training is very difficult (Ås, Hil-

TABLE 6

*Items of Stanford Hypnotic Susceptibility Scale, Form C (SHSS-C)*

| Item | Criterion of Passing |
|------|----------------------|
| 0. Eye closure during induction | (Noted, but not scored) |
| 1. Hand lowering (right hand) | Lowers at least 6 inches in 10 seconds |
| 2. Moving hands apart | Hands 6 inches or more apart after 10 seconds |
| 3. Mosquito hallucination | Any acknowledgment of effect |
| 4. Taste hallucination (sweet, sour) | Both tastes experienced *and* one strong or with overt movements |
| 5. Arm rigidity (right arm) | Less than 2 inches of arm bending in 10 seconds |
| 6. Dream | Dreams well; experience comparable to a dream |
| 7. Age regression (school fifth and second grades) | Clear change in handwriting between present and one regressed age |
| 8. Anosmia to ammonia | Odor of ammonia denied and overt signs absent |
| 9. Arm immobilization (left arm) | Arm rises less than 1 inch in 10 seconds |
| 10. Hallucinated voice | Subject answers voice realistically at least once |
| 11. Negative visual hallucination (sees two of three boxes) | Reports seeing only two boxes |
| 12. Posthypnotic amnesia | Subject recalls three or fewer items before "Now you can remember everything" |

Source: Weitzenhoffer and Hilgard 1962.
Note: Possible score = 12. For standardization sample ($N$ = 307), Mean = 5.19; $SD$ = 3.09.

gard, and Weitzenhoffer 1963; Shor, Orne, and O'Connell 1966; Cooper et al. 1967), but the evidence is not all on one side, and some striking gains have been reported in some circumstances (Wiseman and Ryher 1962; Blum 1963; Sachs and Anderson 1967). The best way to summarize this is as follows: Under the ordinary conditions of everyday life, a person has had experiences which stabilize his hypnotizability, so that, without intervention, scores obtained at intervals of months will correlate highly with each other. This is the kind of stability counted upon in this study. With special training, however, those with moderate or high scores can increase their scores; those with very low scores appear to be refractory to change. The final scores tend to correlate with the original ones, but because they are higher they introduce some change in level of scoring compared with the scores of those who have not had the special experiences. Since the experiences of everyday life may already have introduced such changes more for one subject than for another, we see here a limitation upon prediction despite the demonstrated stability of hypnotic scores.

## The Content of the Interviews

The most complete program of interviewing prior to hypnosis was carried out in the year 1962–63, during which two one-hour sessions were devoted to the interviewing of each subject prior to any attempted hypnosis. The complete questionnaire used during that year is reproduced in the Appendix. The range of information covered can be inferred from the following headings used in the interview forms:

*First hour*

1. Present status (age, year in college, major, vocational plans)
2. Prior experiences of and attitudes toward hypnosis
3. Composition of the family (parental)
4. Health history of subject and family
5. Developmental or family crises
6. Participation in activities: Special interests and hobbies
7. Attitudes toward play activities (absorption, involvement, adventuresomeness, curiosity, etc.)
8. Religion as an interest or activity
9. Peer relationships
10. Leadership-followership
11. Personal characteristics (assets and liabilities, humor, ease of relinquishing control, etc.)

*Second hour*

1. Parent with whom subject has most in common
2. Relationship to father
3. Relationship to mother
4. Identification

we could not go into depth, it was surprising how interview was possible with a majority of the college
en they knew they were coming for scientific purposes
nfidentiality would be observed. Out of respect for
ity, all names have been changed and identifying mate-
en altered, but there has been no distortion of major
asionally material from one case has been combined
ial from a similar case. The cases described have been
m the larger body of interviews and are not limited to
s presented statistically.

**or Presentation of Data**

presents the data in support of the conception of hyp-
developed in the course of the investigation, as set forth
r 1. This does not mean that data have been selected to
thesis, and other data rejected; on the contrary, the
and doubtful cases will be presented along with those
pport the major contentions. We have, however, become
ced that hypnosis is related to a variety of deep involve-
at in the next seven chapters we shall discuss one major
ent after another: reading, drama, religion, sensory and
appreciation, imagery, imaginary companions, and ad-
omeness. Each of these chapters (chaps. 3–9) begins with
ta showing the statistical basis for accepting the involve-
elation to hypnosis and then goes on to specific cases which
te the type of involvement and its relationship to hypnosis
ding the cases in which the involvement appears to be
although hypnotic susceptibility is low. Chapter 10 is de-
o some involvements unrelated to hypnosis.
chapter 11, the specific involvements reported in the earlier
rs are summarized according to their intercorrelations and
ing to the theory of personality that results from their study.
he involvements are not the whole story of hypnotizability;
were, correlations with hypnotic susceptibility would be
substantial than they turn out to be. The remaining chapters
der some other matters, related but separable, such as nor-
versus neuroticism, identification with parents, punishment
mode of discipline, and some relationships between motiva-
and hypnotizability.
The final chapter reflects upon the findings and their bearing
eories of hypnosis and on theories of personality.

5. Personal problems
6. Childhood discipline and duties

The first hour was concerned particularly with characterizing
the subject himself, in his development and present status; the
second hour tried to assess the influences of parental figures in
line with our developmental interpretation of hypnotic susceptibility. The most searching questions—those on personal problems
—were left to the end on the assumption that by then maximum
interviewer rapport would have been established.

Because of the semistructured nature of the interview, with
digressions and probes, it was felt that much of the quantitative
coding could best be done by the interviewer in the form of ratings
of the aspects of behavior and personality that lay behind the questions and represented their objectives. In the interview proper, the
replies to questions were recorded as nearly verbatim as possible
(without an actual taped transcript); following the interview the
interviewer immediately filled out a rating form, a copy of which is
also included in the Appendix.

To show how the interview was conducted, and how it served
as a basis for ratings, let us consider the approach to an estimate
of absorption in reading, the results of which become the subject
for the next chapter.

The somewhat open-ended entering question was stated in
general terms:

> Now we are especially interested in the things that interest
> you. What are your special interests and hobbies? (Note
> duration; note source of intense interests.)

The statements in parentheses in the interview form are reminders to the interviewer to be alert for certain items not necessarily reflected in the way in which the question is put. If the subject did not spontaneously offer relevant answers when given only
the more general question, some "probes" on reading were called
for. These appear as reminders to the interviewer on the interview
form:

> Reading (adventure, fiction, science fiction, mysteries, biog-
> raphy, history; absorption through high school; and now).

The interviewer continued with this part of the discussion
until satisfied that enough material was recorded to permit the
ratings that the interviewer knew would be called for. After the
interview was terminated, the interviewer, with the replies before
her, filled in the accompanying rating form. The relevant rating
scales with respect to reading were as follows:

| Participation in reading (various kinds) | Little | 1-2-3-4-5-6-7-x | Much |
| Absorption in reading | | | |
| through high school | Little | 1-2-3-4-5-6-7-x | Much |
| Absorption in reading now | Little | 1-2-3-4-5-6-7-x | Much |

Every effort was made to put the ratings on the numerical scale, but the x was allowed for those cases where rating seemed impossible because the evidence was lacking or self-contradictory.

Another kind of rating was also called for during the year 1962–63, when we were still attempting global ratings of hypnotizability. Periodically throughout the interview, the interviewer was asked to estimate the hypnotizability of the subject *on the basis of the evidence obtained in that portion of the interview*. For example, after the section on activities and interests, the interviewer was asked for the following rating:

Hypnotic susceptibility as estimated from activities and interests:

$$0-1-2-3-4-5-6-7-8-9-10-11-12-x$$

The predicted susceptibility ratings were placed on a twelve-point scale because the predicted scores on the Stanford Hypnotic Susceptibility Scale, form C, were also on that scale. It may be noted that these were extremely difficult judgments for the interviewer to make, but they permitted some internal analysis of bias, halo effect, and the like. The separation of the seven-point and the twelve-point scales emphasized the importance of keeping the descriptive ratings of activities and interests separate from the prediction of hypnotizability, even though the rated activities might enter into that prediction.

The final step of the rating process was a general hypnotic-susceptibility prediction arrived at in a group conference of the interviewers. As noted earlier, this type of prediction was abandoned in 1963–64, and so it does not enter into the subsequent two-year data analyses. This much explanation is offered because the full interview used in 1962–63 is given in the Appendix and includes these scales with global ratings of hypnosis.

Conducting the interviews prior to the subject's first experience of hypnosis (except in those very rare cases in which hypnotic experiences occurring prior to the subjects' coming to the laboratory were reported) assured independence between the predicting variables and the criterion variable.

The interviews following hypnosis tended to be less routine than those preceding because they were often held for the purpose of gaining specific information related to the responsiveness of the individual subject within the hypnotic session.

The full program o... nosis, and the use of rat... tics and for predictions... scribed in 1962–63 but w... year the interview, model... was reduced to a single... were sufficiently similar to... bining the data for those it... As noted before, the ratings... ability were dropped. The s... to hypnosis were going on... a shortened version of the... bility Scale, form C, was use... the items (items 3 and 10 in... ten instead of twelve. A table... the basis of the score distribu... vidual scores are reported on... those of the second year (1963–... scale. These inelegancies in de... cumstances under which we w... ously handicapping. For some... altered slightly from year to yea... nificant had to meet satisfactory... ering of reliabilities of the ratings... two years.

## Summary on Interviewing Methods

We have combined the clinical n... quantitative methods of the test or... interviewing and the variety of the... for our interpretations. The quantita... cautious, for trends that seem evider... ally fail to meet statistically accepta... material is the main substance of this... this background, we believe it would... additional studies of greater quantita... must caution researchers that the work... such as the Minnesota Multiphasic Per... the California Psychological Inventory... sonality Inventory (MPI), or projective... Apperception Test) have not borne muc... of exciting correlations (E. R. Hilgard 19...

One additional comment may be ma...

# 3

## Reading Involvement as a Pathway for Hypnosis

A college-student population is, by definition, a population of readers, but this does not mean that all students read with an equal degree of involvement, as involvement has been defined in the preceding chapter. If reading is purely for expository purposes—as, for example, in mathematics or some aspects of science—the book codes information which the attentive student learns. He may be attentive, and in that sense instructed by what he learns, without becoming emotionally involved, transformed, or transported by what he reads. The hypothesis to be explored is that there is a special kind of involvement in reading, in which the very "being" of the person is swept emotionally into the experience described by the author, and that those who are capable of such experiences are the ones more likely to prove hypnotizable. For them, the reading experience provides the background for their hypnotic experience, as other involvements may provide the background for other persons. Hence we speak of reading involvement as one of the pathways into hypnosis.

While we might have come to this hypothesis through an examination of the similarities between being lost in reading and lost in hypnosis, the connection was in fact brought strongly to our attention by some of the persons we interviewed. A few of our subjects spontaneously described their experiences within hypnosis as related to what they experienced in reading. One of the first to bring this to our attention was Julie, who was highly hypnotizable. A few quotations from her interview will help to show how we learned from her. As we touched upon reading, among other interests, Julie saw a relationship immediately and unequivocably:

"Hypnosis was like reading a book. . . . It's stronger in a way than reading. When I get really involved in reading, I'm not aware of what is going on around me. I concentrate on the people in the book or the movie and react the way they react. The intense concentration is the same in a book or a movie or in imagination as it is in hypnosis. Reading a book can hypnotize you."

Having affirmed the relationship, she went on to make clearer how she felt and to give examples of what she meant.

"After each book, I'm completely washed out. After hypnosis it was the same. I was completely washed out and couldn't keep my eyes open. I lacked the ability to communicate.

"I identify with characters that think the way I do. You can see yourself in the character. . . . Then there's the kind where I'm not so much part of the character, but I can understand why the character feels or acts the way he does." She illustrated this point by choosing the story of a man who was an isolate, with an amazing ability to shut out the world. "I'm not that way, but I've experienced that kind of experience a few times, and so I could identify. The whole movie was brought to immediate focus by this character." It is interesting how Julie moved back and forth between reading and movies as she attempted to describe her feelings in reading; her imagery is so rich that the experiences are, in fact, very much alike, and she said that she hates to see a movie based on a book she has read, because the characters do not look as she has pictured them for herself.

For Julie the involvements in reading and hypnosis were very similar, including a perseverant period afterward in which she had difficulty in readjusting to the realities surrounding her. Reports such as hers led us further into the relationship between reading and hypnosis.

Despite the plausibility of a relationship between reading and hypnosis, a global rating on "participation in reading" did not correlate significantly with hypnotic susceptibility in the 1962–63 sample of 104 cases; the trends, however, were in the appropriate direction. We found it necessary to be more subtle in the interpretation of reading involvements in a group of generally high readers, as represented by successful university students. So in the next year (1963–64) we made seven ratings of reading, as follows:

1. Amount of reading in grammar and high school
2. Amount of reading during the last two years
3. Preference for reading that emphasizes plot or story
4. Preference for reading that develops characterization
5. Absorption (i.e., concentration) independent of involvement

6. Emotional involvement in story during or after reading

7. Special interest in science fiction, etc.

It turned out, coherent with evidence gradually accumulating from other directions, that it was the rating of *emotional involvement in reading* that led to a correlation with hypnotic susceptibility. It must be kept in mind that all of these ratings were made prior to the subject's experience of hypnosis. The relationship between the rated emotional involvement in reading and the later-tested hypnotic susceptibility is shown in table 7, yielding a chi-square significant at the .05 level.

TABLE 7

*Susceptibility to Hypnosis as Related to Rated Involvement in Reading, 1963–64*

| Involvement | Susceptibility (SHSS-C) | | | |
|---|---|---|---|---|
| | Low (0–3) | Medium (4–7) | High (8–12) | Total |
| High (6–7) | 2 | 6 | 5 | 13 |
| Medium (4–5) | 8 | 8 | 13 | 29 |
| Low (1–3) | 18 | 16 | 6 | 40 |
| Total | 28 | 30 | 24 | 82* |

Significance test: $\chi^2 = 9.61$, $df = 4$, $p = .05$.
*One case not ascertained.

We thus have sufficient statistical support to give greater cogency to the relationships that were becoming evident through individual case studies.

## The Involved Reader

The kinds of reading which provide fertile soil for the highly involved experience are those in which human beings engage in mental and physical activities and the reader participates in this action through some sort of fantasy, with appropriate emotion. The participation may or may not be an identification with the characters; he need not become the hero or heroine, but he must at least empathize with them. The kinds of literature most conducive to these experiences include biography, autobiography, tales of historical events, novels, mysteries, adventure stories, science fiction. The kinds less conducive are impersonal scientific treatises, mathematics, and analytic or discursive tomes with little of human excitement in them. There are borderline types, such as inspirational books, which may in some cases serve very much as fiction does to stir up emotion and to permit one to feel oneself in the role of another.

Can anything more specific be said about the kind of involvement which develops in this type of reading? It is useful to distinguish *character identification* and *empathic identification*. By the first we mean a kind of participation in the action and feeling as though one were indeed one of the characters; by the second we mean a participation in the feeling of the story even though the separation of the self from the character is maintained. From another viewpoint, it is as though an empathic identification is with the emotion that the author has intended to portray even when the subject cannot, in fantasy, be the character. Some readers can shift back and forth between these types of involvement.

The *character-identification* type of involvement is illustrated by the following quotations from two hypnotizable subjects, John and Waldo. In reviewing his involvement in books, John cited his experience with Orwell's *1984*:

"I identify myself with the character in *1984*, with Winston Smith, who was tortured at the end, fearing rats. His head was in a cage and he felt he would have to submit. I *felt* the fear that he felt as it came closer, closer. Walking back from the Union after finishing the book I had a problem relating myself to my present environment, to the stuff around me, for I was so entangled in the story that I had become exhausted." In *Death of a Salesman* he identified with Willy, and said that he had cried at the end. "I identified him with my father and myself, afterward felt the same way." He said that he was sitting somewhere, watching the rain out of the window for quite awhile after finishing the book, not really thinking of anything, but somehow in a depression relating to the story and how what happened might also happen to him.

Waldo says that he identifies strongly with the characters in a story but interrupts occasionally to criticize or evaluate them. "I don't read: I live the character. I *become* that character. I put myself in his place rather than putting him in my place. I became Rufus in *Death in the Family*, Becket in *Murder in the Cathedral*, Ivan in *The Brothers Karamazov*." He sometimes interrupts this intense identification; for example, he stopped to evaluate Rufus's situation in *Death in the Family*, but then "I went ahead and became him again."

The illustrations suffice to show that some subjects feel themselves to be living the lives of the characters in the story. This, however, is not always the case. We turn now to other aspects of reading involvement.

What we have termed *empathic identification* is illustrated by the cases of William, Beverly, and Raymond, all of whom were hypnotiźable.

William made it quite clear that he savored the scenes in the book he was reading as though he were there as an observer, not as a character. "It's almost as if I'm two people. One, I'm me, reading the book, physically here and aware of my present environment; but, two, I'm another me who is sitting next to the first me, aware of the environment of the book, feeling the warmth, smelling the dry air." William here is describing the coexistence of the observing and participating egos. William said he was a slow reader when he got involved because he didn't want to miss anything in the book. He wanted to get the whole book, the whole idea of the surroundings around the characters, a visual impression of the landscape and a sensory picture, for example, of the desert or whatever he was reading about, what everything *felt* like.

Beverly shows clearly how an involved reader can follow the author without identifying with the characters. For example, *L'Assommoir* is a French novel which depicts the downfall and decline of a family. "It would be difficult to identify with the washerwoman or with her daughter, who becomes a prostitute, or with the father, who degenerates and neglects the family. Few people who read it liked it, but I enjoyed it because it portrayed a literary philosophy and had a fascinating character study which the author was making." She described *Lord of the Flies* similarly. "I felt sympathy for Piggy and felt an impatience toward Ralph, the leader of the group. I was quite involved and concerned over the fact that the children were running wild. Once you get the author's point of view it's frightening, how on this island a microcosm of people, left to their own devices, become animals and all this is a reflection of the war that is going on in the rest of the world." She went on to say: "In reading, you suspend yourself, your background, you don't have a personality of your own. You're not using your judgments of right and wrong and standards of value; you're dealing with the author on his home ground. I become more involved with the author than with the characters."

Raymond put it this way: "I don't tend to imagine myself as a character but I tend to *be there* myself, watching what's going on. I guess it's passive participation. When I'm reading a book on Spain, I'm detached from the main character yet involved in what happens." He pointed out that he was outside the characters, although related very closely to them: "I'm aware of what they're feeling and thinking, but it's happening to someone else."

It is thus possible to be deeply involved in two ways: to belong more to those who identify with the characters themselves (character identification with feeling) or to belong to those who feel with the characters, but remain outside them (empathic identification).

The intelligent human subject always resists classification into any narrowly conceived "type." Thus the distinction between the character-identifier and the empathic-identifier is one worth making, but not all involved readers fit into these classifications: some occasionally belong to the one class, occasionally to the other, or to both at once.

Paul for example says, "It takes a book with an outstanding character to make me feel I'm the hero. I can picture the situation, all the descriptive material in detail. I want a complete image of what the author is trying to describe, what he wants me to see as he is seeing it, and that's what I'm trying to do." He gave as an illustration Hemingway's The Sun Also Rises, which is a story about a reporter, written through the reporter's eyes. "I felt I was there, and looking out through the character's eyes." "I'll feel that I'm missing things if I hurry too much." Note how he identifies both with the character, and empathically, with the author's portrayal of the whole setting.

Or Virginia. She describes her reaction in Lord of the Flies. Toward the end when Ralph was being chased by the rest of the boys and they met a naval officer, she was suddenly aware that she had been the height of a young boy, that she had been running with the boys, and that "all of a sudden, when the young naval officer appeared, I felt I grew a couple of feet." While here her character identification stands out, her whole experience is not readily put into this framework. "I don't know if I identify. When I finish a book I feel I've lived through something. Do I identify with all the characters rather than with one? Am I also experiencing the different insights the author talks about?"

## The Development of Reading Involvement

We are dealing in our sample only with successful students, successful enough, that is, to meet the stringent entrance requirements of Stanford University and to survive in its competitive atmosphere. Why, then, in our sample, are we able to find such differences in reading involvement? During the last year of ratings, interviews with eighty-two students turned up only 16 percent in our highest categories (ratings of six or seven), with 35 percent rated at four or five and the rest (49 percent) below that.

5. Personal problems

6. Childhood discipline and duties

The first hour was concerned particularly with characterizing the subject himself, in his development and present status; the second hour tried to assess the influences of parental figures in line with our developmental interpretation of hypnotic susceptibility. The most searching questions—those on personal problems —were left to the end on the assumption that by then maximum interviewer rapport would have been established.

Because of the semistructured nature of the interview, with digressions and probes, it was felt that much of the quantitative coding could best be done by the interviewer in the form of ratings of the aspects of behavior and personality that lay behind the questions and represented their objectives. In the interview proper, the replies to questions were recorded as nearly verbatim as possible (without an actual taped transcript); following the interview the interviewer immediately filled out a rating form, a copy of which is also included in the Appendix.

To show how the interview was conducted, and how it served as a basis for ratings, let us consider the approach to an estimate of absorption in reading, the results of which become the subject for the next chapter.

The somewhat open-ended entering question was stated in general terms:

> Now we are especially interested in the things that interest you. What are your special interests and hobbies? (Note duration; note source of intense interests.)

The statements in parentheses in the interview form are reminders to the interviewer to be alert for certain items not necessarily reflected in the way in which the question is put. If the subject did not spontaneously offer relevant answers when given only the more general question, some "probes" on reading were called for. These appear as reminders to the interviewer on the interview form:

> Reading (adventure, fiction, science fiction, mysteries, biography, history; absorption through high school; and now).

The interviewer continued with this part of the discussion until satisfied that enough material was recorded to permit the ratings that the interviewer knew would be called for. After the interview was terminated, the interviewer, with the replies before her, filled in the accompanying rating form. The relevant rating scales with respect to reading were as follows:

| Participation in reading (various kinds) | Little | 1-2-3-4-5-6-7-x | Much |
| Absorption in reading through high school | Little | 1-2-3-4-5-6-7-x | Much |
| Absorption in reading now | Little | 1-2-3-4-5-6-7-x | Much |

Every effort was made to put the ratings on the numerical scale, but the x was allowed for those cases where rating seemed impossible because the evidence was lacking or self-contradictory.

Another kind of rating was also called for during the year 1962–63, when we were still attempting global ratings of hypnotizability. Periodically throughout the interview, the interviewer was asked to estimate the hypnotizability of the subject *on the basis of the evidence obtained in that portion of the interview.* For example, after the section on activities and interests, the interviewer was asked for the following rating:

Hypnotic susceptibility as estimated from activities and interests:

$$0-1-2-3-4-5-6-7-8-9-10-11-12-x$$

The predicted susceptibility ratings were placed on a twelve-point scale because the predicted scores on the Stanford Hypnotic Susceptibility Scale, form C, were also on that scale. It may be noted that these were extremely difficult judgments for the interviewer to make, but they permitted some internal analysis of bias, halo effect, and the like. The separation of the seven-point and the twelve-point scales emphasized the importance of keeping the descriptive ratings of activities and interests separate from the prediction of hypnotizability, even though the rated activities might enter into that prediction.

The final step of the rating process was a general hypnotic-susceptibility prediction arrived at in a group conference of the interviewers. As noted earlier, this type of prediction was abandoned in 1963–64, and so it does not enter into the subsequent two-year data analyses. This much explanation is offered because the full interview used in 1962–63 is given in the Appendix and includes these scales with global ratings of hypnosis.

Conducting the interviews prior to the subject's first experience of hypnosis (except in those very rare cases in which hypnotic experiences occurring prior to the subjects' coming to the laboratory were reported) assured independence between the predicting variables and the criterion variable.

The interviews following hypnosis tended to be less routine than those preceding because they were often held for the purpose of gaining specific information related to the responsiveness of the individual subject within the hypnotic session.

The full program of two hours of interviewing prior to hypnosis, and the use of rating scales both for descriptive characteristics and for predictions of hypnotizability, was carried out as described in 1962–63 but was modified in 1963–64. During the latter year the interview, modeled on the interviews of the year before, was reduced to a single hour, but the ratings that were retained were sufficiently similar to those of the year before to permit combining the data for those items which both years had in common. As noted before, the ratings making global predictions of hypnotizability were dropped. The subjects brought for interviewing prior to hypnosis were going on to an experiment in hypnosis in which a shortened version of the standard Stanford Hypnotic Susceptibility Scale, form C, was used, a version which eliminated two of the items (items 3 and 10 in table 6). The possible score became ten instead of twelve. A table of conversions was worked out on the basis of the score distributions of both years; therefore individual scores are reported on the twelve-point basis, even though those of the second year (1963–64) were obtained on the ten-point scale. These inelegancies in design were unavoidable in the circumstances under which we worked, but they did not prove seriously handicapping. For some items, reliability may have been altered slightly from year to year, but any results that proved significant had to meet satisfactory statistical criteria despite any lowering of reliabilities of the ratings, owing to changes between the two years.

## Summary on Interviewing Methods and Data Analysis

We have combined the clinical method with the more strictly quantitative methods of the test or laboratory. The volume of our interviewing and the variety of the areas explored give us a basis for our interpretations. The quantitative material chiefly makes us cautious, for trends that seem evident to an interviewer occasionally fail to meet statistically acceptable standards. The interview material is the main substance of this book. With the advantage of this background, we believe it would be profitable to undertake additional studies of greater quantitative precision, although we must caution researchers that the work with various test procedures such as the Minnesota Multiphasic Personality Inventory (MMPI), the California Psychological Inventory (CPI), the Maudsley Personality Inventory (MPI), or projective tests (Rorschach, Thematic Apperception Test) have not borne much fruit, either, in the way of exciting correlations (E. R. Hilgard 1965, 1967).

One additional comment may be made in regard to the interview. While we could not go into depth, it was surprising how intimate an interview was possible with a majority of the college subjects when they knew they were coming for scientific purposes and that confidentiality would be observed. Out of respect for confidentiality, all names have been changed and identifying material has been altered, but there has been no distortion of major trends; occasionally material from one case has been combined with material from a similar case. The cases described have been selected from the larger body of interviews and are not limited to the samples presented statistically.

### The Plan for Presentation of Data

This book presents the data in support of the conception of hypnosis that developed in the course of the investigation, as set forth in chapter 1. This does not mean that data have been selected to support a thesis, and other data rejected; on the contrary, the negative and doubtful cases will be presented along with those which support the major contentions. We have, however, become so convinced that hypnosis is related to a variety of deep involvements that in the next seven chapters we shall discuss one major involvement after another: reading, drama, religion, sensory and aesthetic appreciation, imagery, imaginary companions, and adventuresomeness. Each of these chapters (chaps. 3–9) begins with some data showing the statistical basis for accepting the involvement's relation to hypnosis and then goes on to specific cases which illuminate the type of involvement and its relationship to hypnosis —including the cases in which the involvement appears to be present although hypnotic susceptibility is low. Chapter 10 is devoted to some involvements unrelated to hypnosis.

In chapter 11, the specific involvements reported in the earlier chapters are summarized according to their intercorrelations and according to the theory of personality that results from their study.

The involvements are not the whole story of hypnotizability; if they were, correlations with hypnotic susceptibility would be more substantial than they turn out to be. The remaining chapters consider some other matters, related but separable, such as normality versus neuroticism, identification with parents, punishment as a mode of discipline, and some relationships between motivation and hypnotizability.

The final chapter reflects upon the findings and their bearing on theories of hypnosis and on theories of personality.

6. Emotional involvement in story during or after reading

7. Special interest in science fiction, etc.

It turned out, coherent with evidence gradually accumulating from other directions, that it was the rating of *emotional involvement in reading* that led to a correlation with hypnotic susceptibility. It must be kept in mind that all of these ratings were made prior to the subject's experience of hypnosis. The relationship between the rated emotional involvement in reading and the later-tested hypnotic susceptibility is shown in table 7, yielding a chi-square significant at the .05 level.

TABLE 7

*Susceptibility to Hypnosis as Related to Rated Involvement in Reading, 1963–64*

| Involvement | Susceptibility (SHSS-C) | | | |
| --- | --- | --- | --- | --- |
| | Low (0–3) | Medium (4–7) | High (8–12) | Total |
| High (6–7) | 2 | 6 | 5 | 13 |
| Medium (4–5) | 8 | 8 | 13 | 29 |
| Low (1–3) | 18 | 16 | 6 | 40 |
| Total | 28 | 30 | 24 | 82* |

Significance test: $\chi^2 = 9.61$, $df = 4$, $p = .05$.
*One case not ascertained.

We thus have sufficient statistical support to give greater cogency to the relationships that were becoming evident through individual case studies.

## The Involved Reader

The kinds of reading which provide fertile soil for the highly involved experience are those in which human beings engage in mental and physical activities and the reader participates in this action through some sort of fantasy, with appropriate emotion. The participation may or may not be an identification with the characters; he need not become the hero or heroine, but he must at least empathize with them. The kinds of literature most conducive to these experiences include biography, autobiography, tales of historical events, novels, mysteries, adventure stories, science fiction. The kinds less conducive are impersonal scientific treatises, mathematics, and analytic or discursive tomes with little of human excitement in them. There are borderline types, such as inspirational books, which may in some cases serve very much as fiction does to stir up emotion and to permit one to feel oneself in the role of another.

Can anything more specific be said about the kind of involvement which develops in this type of reading? It is useful to distinguish *character identification* and *empathic identification*. By the first we mean a kind of participation in the action and feeling as though one were indeed one of the characters; by the second we mean a participation in the feeling of the story even though the separation of the self from the character is maintained. From another viewpoint, it is as though an empathic identification is with the emotion that the author has intended to portray even when the subject cannot, in fantasy, be the character. Some readers can shift back and forth between these types of involvement.

The *character-identification* type of involvement is illustrated by the following quotations from two hypnotizable subjects, John and Waldo. In reviewing his involvement in books, John cited his experience with Orwell's *1984*:

"I identify myself with the character in *1984*, with Winston Smith, who was tortured at the end, fearing rats. His head was in a cage and he felt he would have to submit. I *felt* the fear that he felt as it came closer, closer. Walking back from the Union after finishing the book I had a problem relating myself to my present environment, to the stuff around me, for I was so entangled in the story that I had become exhausted." In *Death of a Salesman* he identified with Willy, and said that he had cried at the end. "I identified him with my father and myself, afterward felt the same way." He said that he was sitting somewhere, watching the rain out of the window for quite awhile after finishing the book, not really thinking of anything, but somehow in a depression relating to the story and how what happened might also happen to him.

Waldo says that he identifies strongly with the characters in a story but interrupts occasionally to criticize or evaluate them. "I don't read: I live the character. I *become* that character. I put myself in his place rather than putting him in my place. I became Rufus in *Death in the Family*, Becket in *Murder in the Cathedral*, Ivan in *The Brothers Karamazov*." He sometimes interrupts this intense identification; for example, he stopped to evaluate Rufus's situation in *Death in the Family*, but then "I went ahead and became him again."

The illustrations suffice to show that some subjects feel themselves to be living the lives of the characters in the story. This, however, is not always the case. We turn now to other aspects of reading involvement.

What we have termed *empathic identification* is illustrated by the cases of William, Beverly, and Raymond, all of whom were hypnotizable.

William made it quite clear that he savored the scenes in the book he was reading as though he were there as an observer, not as a character. "It's almost as if I'm two people. One, I'm me, reading the book, physically here and aware of my present environment; but, two, I'm another me who is sitting next to the first me, aware of the environment of the book, feeling the warmth, smelling the dry air." William here is describing the coexistence of the observing and participating egos. William said he was a slow reader when he got involved because he didn't want to miss anything in the book. He wanted to get the whole book, the whole idea of the surroundings around the characters, a visual impression of the landscape and a sensory picture, for example, of the desert or whatever he was reading about, what everything *felt* like.

Beverly shows clearly how an involved reader can follow the author without identifying with the characters. For example, *L'Assommoir* is a French novel which depicts the downfall and decline of a family. "It would be difficult to identify with the washerwoman or with her daughter, who becomes a prostitute, or with the father, who degenerates and neglects the family. Few people who read it liked it, but I enjoyed it because it portrayed a literary philosophy and had a fascinating character study which the author was making." She described *Lord of the Flies* similarly. "I felt sympathy for Piggy and felt an impatience toward Ralph, the leader of the group. I was quite involved and concerned over the fact that the children were running wild. Once you get the author's point of view it's frightening, how on this island a microcosm of people, left to their own devices, become animals and all this is a reflection of the war that is going on in the rest of the world." She went on to say: "In reading, you suspend yourself, your background, you don't have a personality of your own. You're not using your judgments of right and wrong and standards of value; you're dealing with the author on his home ground. I become more involved with the author than with the characters."

Raymond put it this way: "I don't tend to imagine myself as a character but I tend to *be there* myself, watching what's going on. I guess it's passive participation. When I'm reading a book on Spain, I'm detached from the main character yet involved in what happens." He pointed out that he was outside the characters, although related very closely to them: "I'm aware of what they're feeling and thinking, but it's happening to someone else."

It is thus possible to be deeply involved in two ways: to belong more to those who identify with the characters themselves (character identification with feeling) or to belong to those who feel with the characters, but remain outside them (empathic identification).

The intelligent human subject always resists classification into any narrowly conceived "type." Thus the distinction between the character-identifier and the empathic-identifier is one worth making, but not all involved readers fit into these classifications: some occasionally belong to the one class, occasionally to the other, or to both at once.

Paul for example says, "It takes a book with an outstanding character to make me feel I'm the hero. I can picture the situation, all the descriptive material in detail. I want a complete image of what the author is trying to describe, what he wants me to see as he is seeing it, and that's what I'm trying to do." He gave as an illustration Hemingway's *The Sun Also Rises,* which is a story about a reporter, written through the reporter's eyes. "I felt I was there, and looking out through the character's eyes." "I'll feel that I'm missing things if I hurry too much." Note how he identifies both with the character, and empathically, with the author's portrayal of the whole setting.

Or Virginia. She describes her reaction in *Lord of the Flies.* Toward the end when Ralph was being chased by the rest of the boys and they met a naval officer, she was suddenly aware that she had been the height of a young boy, that she had been running with the boys, and that "all of a sudden, when the young naval officer appeared, I felt I grew a couple of feet." While here her character identification stands out, her whole experience is not readily put into this framework. "I don't know if I identify. When I finish a book I feel I've lived through something. Do I identify with *all* the characters rather than with one? Am I also experiencing the different insights the author talks about?"

## The Development of Reading Involvement

We are dealing in our sample only with successful students, successful enough, that is, to meet the stringent entrance requirements of Stanford University and to survive in its competitive atmosphere. Why, then, in our sample, are we able to find such differences in reading involvement? During the last year of ratings, interviews with eighty-two students turned up only 16 percent in our highest categories (ratings of six or seven), with 35 percent rated at four or five and the rest (49 percent) below that.

The first point is, of course, that we are not equating reading involvement with competent reading skill. It is possible to be a good reader (that is, one who reads rapidly, concentrates on what he is reading, is critically thoughtful about his reading, and is able to recall what he has read) without classifying as an involved reader. Because good reading as just defined is important in a university setting, there are a great many more good readers than those we have classified as involved readers. The involved reader brings a degree of self-transfiguration and emotional participation in what he reads that goes beyond cognitive or rational understanding of the words that he reads. What, then, accounts for this difference?

Later on, we shall be interested in relating reading involvement to hypnosis, but for the present we are still examining reading involvement itself. Our interviews give us some strong hints about ways in which this involvement comes about.

1. *Reading involvement commonly develops early in life, before the onset of adolescence.* We find two different threads running through the history of this early development: first, an identification with parents who read; second, a way of meeting loneliness in childhood.

Parents who themselves are often absorbed in reading commonly read to their young children, not out of parental duty, but out of love for the reading itself, and their enthusiasm may well be contagious. Much of the literature on identification is so preoccupied with sex-typing (the boy becoming like his father, the girl like her mother) that little attention has been given to those many forms of contagious enthusiasm which are not sex-typed, hence can be transmitted by a parent of either sex to a child of either sex. As long as there are no sex taboos operating, a child can copy either parent in reading, in love of music, in sports. Our cases show that the love of reading may come from either parent. The important thing is that the parent has a joy in reading which gets communicated to the child in a way that carries the child along without imposing a difficult task upon him. With this kind of parent the child is more apt to love reading rather than to see reading as an area of work.

It is a different story with the lonely child who turns to reading to fill an emptiness in life. Yet such a child may live vividly in reading through identification with the characters or through the emotional participation with them, so that an involvement similar to that engendered by parental example may result.

Of the eight subjects already mentioned in this chapter, seven came from backgrounds where one or both parents loved reading and probably had communicated love of reading to the children. The one exception among the eight was a boy from a farm family with two sisters who formed a duo which excluded him. There were no close neighbors. He said that in reading he found companionship and a glimpse of the larger world. In this instance neither parent read much, but the father warmly supported the subject's reading interests and ambitions.

2. *There may be a critical period for development of involvement.* If this early development is indeed characteristic, we might raise the question whether or not there is a critical period for the development of involvement. The notion of a critical period is described in William James's discussion of circumstances in which you must "strike while the iron is hot" or miss the opportunity for fulfilling some natural propensity (1890); it is currently studied in connection with imprinting at the appropriate time in naturalistic studies of birds or in the training of guide dogs for the blind. Critical periods of development have been suggested in the work of Piaget and of psychoanalytic writers. Erikson's (1963, 1968) levels of psychosocial development imply mastery of interpersonal problems appropriate to the unfolding stages of development; perhaps the development of involvements could be fitted into his theory of epigenetic development. Might it be that unless a child becomes absorbed and involved in reading early he may never be able to do so? We have found very few readers capable of deep involvement who did not begin reading prior to adolescence. We shall return to a discussion of this theme in connection with religious interests, where we find the latecomer to religion different from the one who has grown up in a faith.

One exception to the rule that late development is not found is the case in which the involvement in reading is grafted upon some other involvement, begun earlier but with similar emotional connotations. In the jargon of psychology, the new involvement has "generalized" from the other, earlier acquired one.

Twenty-year-old Leslie, who was hypnotizable, told us, "Until three years ago I never read a book unless I was forced to. I didn't enjoy it. Since then I've read avidly. (Do you become involved?) I project myself into it somehow and identify with the characters if their situation is similar to mine." From the time Leslie was a small child, he had watched TV to such an extent that his parents had had to set a three-hour-a-day time limit on this activity. TV and movie going were equated. He felt that both afforded him an opportunity to put his own environment aside, pick up another environment on the screen, sit back and enjoy it. He described his experience as both involved and observing in a critical way from time to time. Leslie had shifted to reading when he elected to take more literature in high school as a prerequisite for college entrance. While we can cite no definite evidence to prove the relationship of late-appearing involvement in reading to the earlier involved movie watching, there is a genuine possibility that this occurred. A pathway for involvement in an imaginative field was nurtured and kept open throughout the years.

Only since Robert's senior year in high school, two years before, had he begun to read a considerable amount and to become emotionally involved. Currently reading *Mark Twain in San Francisco*, he felt as though he might have written the book, he was so much identified with its point of view. Now he finds it difficult to put books down, and he is not apt to hear friends and family when they call him. This late development is interesting. Were there other, related, earlier involvements? He had been engrossed at a high level of involvement in movies for many years. He participated: "I do not assume the character, but I am taking part in the action. . . . I'll be there and I can feel the monster coming at me; people all around me are trapped in the cave. I'm not one of them but I'm trapped *with* them and I can feel the fright they feel. . . . I'm following more the mood that the author portrays. I go from scene to scene experiencing the emotional outbursts."

Another problem of interest, both in itself and in relation to the corresponding development of hypnotic susceptibility, is the kind of later experience that on the one hand keeps reading involvement alive and, on the other hand, fails to sustain it or succeeds in destroying it. The sustaining experience appears to be that of continuity of experience and possibly continuity of identification with the parent who may have been the model for the experience in the first place. Thus a shift in identification from a literary mother to a literal-minded scientific father may destroy the earlier involvement. A case illustrating this point is given in chapter 13 on developmental considerations and parental influence.

A shift in motivation need not be related to any very evident shift in identification; yet if the shift is away from the free play of fantasy to realism, or to a striving competitiveness, the possibility of full involvement may be lost. We have subjects who have tried to capture the old excitement once felt in reading science fiction, only to be disappointed.

Parker represents one of those whose early fantasies, stirred up by his interest in science fiction, had given way to an intellectual, analytical approach to reading. Even though he tried, he could no longer recapture his earlier enjoyment. On the basis of his earlier involvement we would expect him to be hypnotizable, but having lost the capacity for involvement his hypnotic ability might also have diminished. In our hypnotic susceptibility tests he scored low—two on the 12-point scale of SHSS-C.

As a child he thought of his bed as a space ship, or he planned trips into space as he was walking to school. He could lose himself for a couple of days after reading an exciting science fiction story. All this was still present in the sixth and seventh grades.

A shift in his reading interests started in high school, when he began, owing to the prodding of his parents and teachers, to feel that certain courses would have to be done well. He knew that he had to have a scientific perspective, that no magic sweep of the hand would bring admission to medical school. He said the biggest part of the change came during his freshman year in college when he really settled down to work.

The analytic attitude that he had developed carried over into hypnosis. He concentrated on the process, and wondered what the hypnotist was trying to do and what he was trying to accomplish. His initial introduction was via a taped voice; the moment the voice stopped, his interest stopped. He did not concentrate on having the experience; his mind was watching all the time.

Recently Parker had tried to become immersed in science fiction and space trips, just for fun, but after a few minutes he was back with the realities of the present moment. He expressed regret because he recalled the degree to which the old fantasies had once produced relaxed enjoyment.

Thus with development of reality orientation, Parker lost the magic of childhood and thereby lost a certain dissociative quality which had been present. It has been interesting to note in a number of similar cases that if such a capacity has been absent for any length of time it cannot be recaptured. Also, the subject is not hypnotizable. This observation may have an important bearing on the gradual lessening of the incidence of hypnotizability as individuals grow up. Many more children are hypnotizable than are adults. Once reality-testing processes have taken hold, they may predominate over areas of imagination and feeling.

One other aspect of this case is worth noting, namely, Parker's tremendous concentration when reading scientific material. In part, does it represent a transformation or relocation of the earlier involvement in science fiction? In a number of young people who turned from science fiction to science we have been struck by their concentration and we have wondered if the earlier involvement in science fiction had played a part in this.

Many of the same considerations that apply to reading may be found in other areas of involvement, as we shall see later on. It appears that some subjects suffer a real loss when these richly rewarding experiences are rendered impossible as they grow up, while others manage to retain them alongside of satisfactory reality orientation. There may be some suggestions for education that arise from these considerations, but we move on now with the picture of involvement as a background for hypnosis.

## Some Characteristics of Involved Readers

Before turning to the relation between reading involvement and hypnosis we shall summarize the characteristics of the involved reader. We may note six characteristics:

1. He is greatly influenced by the power of words. The author of a book uses words to manipulate the reader's ideas and emotions; the involved reader is following this influence. It is important to note that the stirring-up of the reader's imagination is guided by the author; the exercise of fantasy is "stimulus-bound" and not "impulse-bound" as in the spontaneous fantasy of the autistic or self-centered person.

2. He is actively receptive and open, not merely passive. This is hard to put into words, but the involved reader savors the text, moves slowly to get its full richness, throws himself into the action. These are not the passive readers who use a book to put themselves to sleep at night.

3. He intensely cherishes the experience of the moment. Much of civilized life is built around planning toward remote goals, postponing gratification until later. The pleasure of the involved reader is not of this postponed kind, but it is present and immediate, even though he is reading of an event actually remote in time. He is there now and is moved by the events as they are happening. Even though there are flashbacks or glimpses of the future, he lives through the events as they occur.

4. He engages in vivid imagery. For many involved readers the imagery has a hallucinatory quality; that is, the imagery is almost like perception. Often it is carried visually, but others feel the texture and the heat, smell the flowers, taste the dry dust.

5. He suspends critical (reality-testing) processes. The author is temporarily his guide to experience, and the author's values are his own. He may reflect upon the author's words, but this is a

temporary departure from his involvement. Too many such departures, of course, change the character of the involvement.

6. He can distinguish between the reading experience and the normal routines of his life. What this means is that the reading experience is essentially limited to the time of reading. There may be a time of transition before he feels restored to the realities around him, but this is ordinarily short, and soon he goes about his business without being preoccupied with thoughts of the book he was reading. Once he picks up the book again he can become deeply absorbed in it. This temporary departure from the world of reality corresponds somewhat to the concept of Ernst Kris (1952), "regression in the service of the ego," a temporary departure to a life of impulse and fantasy for refreshment or enlightenment, with ready return to normal reality.

It takes little reflection upon the nature of hypnosis to see that these six statements could also be made about the hypnotically susceptible subject. This gives plausibility to the argument of this chapter that the experience of reading involvement may set the stage for, or provide a readiness for, the experience of hypnosis.

## The Connection between Involved Reading and Hypnosis

We began with some remarks of Julie, who had spontaneously detected the relationship between reading and hypnosis. A number of other subjects also recognized this relationship. We asked the question, "Are there some experiences in everyday life in which you would become absorbed to about the same extent, or watchful to the same extent, as in hypnosis?" Replies to this question in interviews following successful hypnosis led to such comments as these:

Winifred: "When I'm reading literature. There I'm watching for the reponses of the characters the way I looked for my own in hypnosis, and I'd be tied up in an aesthetic emotion the same way."

Barbara: "When I'm reading fiction or looking at a movie and really interested. I put myself in the story and can relate it to myself."

Martin: "I can become involved while reading and occasionally while listening to a very dramatic lecturer."

Lillian: "Yes, perhaps in reading a book or even listening in class."

As pointed out by both Martin and Lillian, the power of words is common to hypnosis, reading, and lecturing.

The purpose of this chapter is by now clearer. Thus far we

have tried to show that there is something definable called *reading involvement,* which differs from merely efficient reading, and now we are suggesting that this involvement is in some ways mirrored in the involvement of the hypnotically susceptible subject when he is hypnotized. We discovered the relationship, first of all, from the subjects who spontaneously called our attention to it in the interview. While there were many statements such as those just quoted, a few student subjects were unusually perceptive about it.

Sarah was one of these, and some of her comments are worth reporting in greater detail. She has combined a major in American literature with one in psychology and thus has both the literary background and the psychological sophistication to put her experience into words. She began her reading through the influence of her mother—an origin that we have mentioned is common among those who readily become involved. According to her report her mother likes to read very much, and what she reads is "everything" —historical novels, biographies, novels. "She read to me a lot when I was two, three, four—the children's classics: *Heidi, Little Women.* I learned to read between three and five, the little picture books. She used to tell me stories of her childhood, but these are not too vivid to me now. By now we've read the same books, and when she read them she seemed to have identified with the same people I had."

Sarah finds that reading is an important way of knowing people, seeing many aspects, seeing beyond the people in the books to the authors, to the culture they are representing. She likes to read books by authors like Nabokov, Conrad, and Faulkner.

"I like to read the preface, for it sets a tone, then I thumb through the book. —Finally I start reading. —If it's a new author, I read two to three pages slowly, then I pick up speed (if the author's good) and am not aware of turning pages or of things around me. When I'm reading Faulkner, everything fades except what he's saying—I start living with a book—I'm more identified with Faulkner in the emotion and expression and totalness. I come out to meet him. It's as though nothing else is important. The room has faded—you separate from everything else. It's just the book.

"My father was interested in hypnosis when I was quite small. He learned it from a doctor friend. He tried to hypnotize me, when I was six or seven, but not very successfully, and he has not tried it since. I shied away from hypnosis because I didn't like the idea of Daddy doing it. I didn't want Daddy giving me posthypnotic suggestions to do the dishes.

"I volunteered for hypnosis here for the money—I need

money. The first time I was hypnotized in a group of four, with the suggestions coming over a tape recorder. Although I was nervous, I proved hypnotizable. Then I was chosen to return for an individual session, and I was very relaxed and went into the state quickly. The hypnotist used the method of having me look at my hand and then have it go up to my face, by which time I was hypnotized. I didn't notice the hypnotist as a person—it was the voice that did the hypnotizing. [It may be noted that her hypnotic susceptibility is very high; in the upper 5 percent of the subjects in our study.]

"Once on a later occasion when a graduate student hypnotized me there was a little spark between us, and this interfered with the hypnosis. The more you know the person, the more it interferes—this is true of knowing the author of a book as well."

What hypnosis is like and how it relates to reading is not easy for a sensitive girl like Sarah to put into words, although she was quite willing to talk about her feelings. In reading, she tends to hold in abeyance all critical comment until she has finished, and this she also does in hypnosis. Afterward she reconstructs and then criticizes. During the novel she is too involved in following the author. When asked how she made the leap from the more rational fantasies provoked by books to the occasionally irrational "magic" of hypnosis, she denied that there was really much difference.

"Hypnosis is a different form of reality testing. You explore the possibilities inherent in something that doesn't really exist. You know what cold is by comparing it with hot. In hypnosis you are comparing an accepted irrational nonreality as real. Nothing's really wrong because some part of you is always aware that it's hypnosis though you don't verbalize it at all, not even to yourself. It's like dreaming when you know you're dreaming. When you first go to sleep you lose your feet, you lose your hands, though you know they're there. Even though I'm doing just what the experimenter asks me to, that's secondary; my own recollection and activity are more important."

This complex participation of the hypnotic subject in his own performance, even though it follows very literally the suggestions by the hypnotist, is one of the puzzling aspects of hypnosis, including as it does this continued limited awareness of the observing ego that what is perceived as real is in some sense not real.

A valuable parallel arose in connection with a somewhat extreme demonstration in which analgesia was produced through the posthypnotic suggestion that Sarah would awake from hypnosis to find that she had no hands, but that this would not bother her. When then her absent (invisible) hands were shocked with quite a strong electric shock, she reported that she felt nothing, although there had been no specific analgesia suggestions. This later reminded her of a book in which a hand had been lost, and it is this parallel to which attention is now being called.

"Dr. H. told me that I didn't have any hands. He had a little shocking machine that kept floating around in the air. I was very interested in the fact that I didn't have any hands and I really felt I didn't. He told me it would be funny, and I thought it amusing to see Dr. H. poking around in the air. My silly-looking long sleeves with only circles at the end where the hands would be. Only those ridiculous ruffles were there."

When asked why she was not troubled, she replied, "Somewhere else I absolutely know I have hands. I know they're not cut off. I'm exploring the sensation of not having them. There's no anxiety. He said they would appear gradually at the count of five. He asked me how they came back and I didn't know. I had quit doing what I was doing that was keeping me from seeing them, but whatever it was I was doing was inside me, and I couldn't observe what I quit doing when my hands were again there. It's as though they were there all the time but I hadn't noticed them—they didn't suddenly appear as though they had come from nowhere, and they didn't appear gradually as though there were a film being developed." The difficulty of describing just what has happened is extreme; the analgesia was doubtless genuine, for under hypnosis Sarah can tolerate keeping her hand in circulating ice water for several minutes, remaining fully relaxed without feeling the pain, although insusceptible subjects find this quite impossible.

When asked if there were any bridge between an experience of this sort and what she felt in reading, she gave the following account:

"In reading a novel, some misfortune happens. In one book I read, a hand was cut off—Howard Pease's book about a young man, Jewish-American, a talented musician, captured by Nazis, sent to a concentration camp; he has an arm injury which results in a hand amputation. The most powerful part was the last two to three chapters where he comes back to his friends. In one scene, he sits in front of the piano, plays crashing chords with his one hand, expresses his feelings of tragedy. Then he finds himself through composing music. The reader identifies with this young hero, goes with him through the experience of losing his hand. You *feel* how it is for him to lose a hand. Now you're able to feel with him and sympathize with him—even though you know you have both hands and aren't likely to lose a hand. I could feel the physical pain—I felt horrified—it makes a great difference to me, yet I know I am still whole."

Although she felt that she had shown to her own satisfaction that what she did in reading and what she did in hypnosis were essentially alike to her, there still seemed to be some lack of clarity, and the interviewer pushed her to talk further, using, if she wished, her experience with hands in both settings. She added, "You can take an attitude, establish a new viewpoint. You can feel something that isn't there (like hallucinated heat), or you can lose something that is there (like your hand). You visualize what the author says— that's taking something on; you may visualize something gone, too, as when Dr. H. told me my hands were gone. It's not really losing anything; it's taking on an outlook. With the novelist, it's not so personal; he leaves it up to you; among several characters you choose which one to identify with. With the hypnotist it *is* personal, it has to be you."

While we have these direct reports from subjects who sense a relationship between hypnosis and reading in the normal course of laboratory hypnosis, once in a while something rather unusual happened that in its serendipitous way also brought out the similarity.

Harold had a long history of involvement in reading. Both parents still read extensively, and the mother, in particular, becomes immersed in what she reads; she "devours" novels and is currently reading the fifty-four books of Western Literature. As Harold reads he builds up vivid pictures, and he does not like to see movies of these books because they destroy the pictures he has built up. He tends to follow the author's ideas closely. He feels much as the author intended him to feel. For example, if the author painted a disagreeable character, Harold disliked that character intensely. If the disagreeable character was punished by the hero, Harold was happy. He makes no analysis as he reads, although he sometimes analyzes afterward. He clearly belongs in our group of involved readers.

The incident in his case which served to bring reading into relation to hypnosis occurred spontaneously within his first hypnotic session. Suddenly, in the midst of hypnosis, Harold felt as though he were very small. "It seemed that the chair was a monstrous one and I was a small person sitting in the middle of it. Everything was far away from me." This was not in response to suggested age regression, after which such experiences are more frequent, but happened with no specific suggestion of a size change.

When anything unusual of this kind happened to our subjects, we made it the occasion for further inquiry. Asked about any experience outside hypnosis of which this reminded him, he had no trouble recalling one—from his reading experience:

"It reminds me of when I concentrate very hard in reading and suddenly the page will look far away. The lettering seems concrete, not flat on the paper. The page seems far way—maybe ten feet. I think it's because I suddenly stop being engrossed in reading and look at the page." It is at this moment that the book appears to him to be small and far away.

While just what happened in hypnosis is not clear, the point is that something very like what happens to him in reading also happens to him in hypnosis. Further probing showed that the first recalled experience of this kind was in the hospital after a tonsillectomy at age five. On that occasion the scene on TV had suddenly become very distant, although it remained vivid, sharp, and clear. The experience after that had been repeated only in reading, but now it turned up in hypnosis.

Another somewhat unusual experience served also to relate reading and hypnosis. This was reported by Maude, who was also clearly a member of our reading-involved group and highly susceptible to hypnosis.

Her father had taught her to read before she went to school. First they read books together, and then her parents recommended to her children's books and classics like those of Dickens. They would ask Maude how she had enjoyed the book, perhaps discuss an interesting character. Maude said she became very involved in the characters. "I read fiction and get very involved in thinking what another person is like and what he is doing . . . not in adventure stories, for they don't appeal to me."

Maude is one of the relatively few subjects who reported altered states for a few hours after they left the hypnotic session.

"I found hypnosis a state of complete peacefulness and relaxation. Very enjoyable. I didn't care about the little tensions and worries about me. The first day I felt tired afterward but not exhausted. After the second day, I felt very distant from people. I couldn't settle down to do my work. . . . I just sat. People told me I didn't realize what they were saying. . . . This state lasted a couple of hours. I felt lethargic the rest of the day."

Because of this atypical reaction to the laboratory sessions, she was asked whether she had ever had a similar experience outside hypnosis.

"Yes, after reading. I might be alone and spend the whole day reading; then when people came back I didn't feel I was in the family. I was probably still with the book."

This was placed back during the years when she was growing up. Asked whether there had been anything like this more recently, she replied:

"Last summer . . . I was reading *To Kill a Mockingbird.* It was unusual for me to be alone for a whole day, but I was and I read it straight through. I couldn't tear myself away . . . afterward it took a while before I felt I was back in the family."

Again this rather unusual and unplanned experience following hypnosis indicated a kind of involvement in the hypnosis that bore, for her, some kind of parallel with her involvement in reading.

Both the direct reports and the inferences from some of these unusual experiences have supported the hypothesis that reading involvement and hypnotic involvement have something in common and that, because the reading involvement comes early, it may well provide a background that makes the hypnotic experience both possible and congenial.

### Reading Absorption and Involvement
### Not Leading to Hypnotizability

The relationship between hypnotic susceptibility and reading involvement based on interview data is positive, but the correlation is too low to serve the purposes of practical prediction. The difficulties along the road to firmer prediction are many, and we now wish to turn to some of the cases that demonstrate the difficulties. As has been stated repeatedly, there are good readers who are not what we have called involved readers. The distinction is not readily stated in operational terms that make it easy for the reporting subject to characterize himself well, or for the interviewer to probe appropriately. In much of our interviewing we were not yet sufficiently aware of what we were looking for to do the proper searching; were we to start over, we would be on firmer ground, in part through being alert to the kind of subject about to be described. These are subjects who clearly get absorbed in some way in reading but who fall short of the kind of involvement we have been talking about. While the variation from case to case is great, we may distinguish several kinds of absorption without involvement. Most common are those whose reading is almost purely intellectual; although attention is concentrated, a sense of personal immersion is lacking. This is often the case with scientific reading (*not* science fiction), but it may be found among those who like to read novels also. Another form is a kind of addiction to reading in which the reading produces a kind of escape but the content is evanescent.

In the case of Parker, already mentioned in this chapter, an earlier involvement changed with a shift in identification; the scientific reading became purely intellectual, without involvement, and it was not surprising that he was not hypnotizable.

Georgia knows herself quite well and did not expect to be hypnotizable. In advance of hypnosis she reported, "I never go off in wild daydreams. I probably would not get too involved in hypnosis because I don't get 'lost' in things easily." Her report on her own reading bore out these early conjectures; she lacked the kinds of early experience that produce involvement, and even though she read widely her interests were chiefly intellectual.

"I don't remember ever being read to. They helped *me* to read for myself and write little stories with special blocks my father made for me long before kindergarten. All through school I never read what I was supposed to be reading; I was permitted to go into the library and pick my own. I read mystery stories in elementary school—*Bobbsey Twins, Nancy Drew* books—but I have never, then or now, become involved in characters or in a story. My scientific, practical side keeps them as stories for me." Georgia was one of those least responsive to hypnotic suggestions.

Richard likes to read novels, does not specialize in science reading, gets quite absorbed, but does not meet our picture of involvement. He illustrates, however, the kind of case which, while understandable, could easily be mistaken for involvement. He reads "quite a bit," mostly novels. If he has a good book and has time he becomes so absorbed that he cannot hear himself being called. While he is close to involvement through this concentration of attention, there is a kind of detachment that distinguishes him from the truly involved. He has a deep interest in the plot, likes to predict how it will end, and is a little aloof from what is going on. He does not identify with the characters and never takes part in the action himself. He might feel sympathy for a character, but he is not deeply empathic. Sometimes he theorizes about the book, but he never continues the story after he stops reading or ever feels that he is in it. For example, in a story about two doors (one door concealing a lion, the other a girl), he tried to pick up the clues to help decide in theory who was behind which door, but he was not moved by the dilemma. It comes as no surprise that he was not a responsive hypnotic subject, although a careless interpretation of his close attention while reading might lead to the false impression that he was one of the involved readers.

Ruth's reading addiction is a special situation not often met, but it is informative about the meaning of involvement. This subject scored near the bottom of the group in hypnotizability (a score of two on one day and one on another day). Yet in the interview in advance of hypnosis she was rated at the seven level in absorption in reading. Does this mean that reading absorption is not a predictor of hypnotic susceptibility? Actually, it means that some additional differentiations in regard to kinds of reading needed to be made.

Ruth learned to read early, and she read every available minute. By the age of eight she was reading the *Nancy Drew* books; she read while she was supposed to be napping at boarding school, and with a flashlight after lights had to be turned out. This tendency continued, and in her late teens, while spending summer vacations at a lake with her parents, she would go to parties until 1 A.M. or 2 A.M., then read from 2 A.M. to 7 A.M. before being ready to sleep. If she had an interesting book she would continue to read that; if not, she rummaged through the family library to find another one. Her first year at the university was a fiasco because she would read for days at a time, neglecting classes.

Despite this constant reading, it was difficult to get the subject to describe what reading meant to her. On being pressed for an answer she said: "It's an interest. I must definitely be interested. It is not exactly pleasure." She denied that she could use such terms as "satisfaction" or "gratification" as applicable to her reading. She simply wanted more and more of it; this is evidence of its addictive quality.

"I never imagined myself as one of the characters. I just located the central characters and read very quickly. I don't read discerningly; I read quickly. I couldn't talk about a book with anyone, for I can't recall it that well."

There is no character involvement. "The closest I've ever come is to *try* to imagine what it would be like to be someone else." There is no savoring of the experience while it is going on, no deep feeling, and no residue after it is finished. Her reading has a voracious quality in the sense that she devours a book instead of enjoying it.

These cases, then, of absorption without involvement, and of reading addiction, are distinguishable from involvement and hence are not true exceptions to the correspondence between involvement and hypnotic susceptibility.

Were everything as clear as in these cases the task of prediction would be difficult, but straightforward, provided the proper precautions were taken to probe deeply into the nature of the reading experience. It would lead to a false sense of our progress thus far, however, if we did not report a few cases where the reading involvement meets our specifications but the subject is resistant to hypnosis. This is in part a problem in probability: because *most* involved readers are susceptible, there is a positive correlation between reading and hypnotic susceptibility; however, because of difficult decisions about some cases, and a few genuine exceptions to the rule, the correlations are low. We found four subjects giving evidence of deep involvement in reading, but with low hypnotic susceptibility scores. Two of the four subjects will serve as illustrations.

Alan began reading cowboy and historical novels to himself as early as the second and third grades. Around twelve he became interested in other kinds of fiction. Now he reads a great deal during vacations, several books each month. He becomes identified with the central character, as with Michelangelo in *The Agony and the Ecstasy*. He really lives with the character and his problems. He ignores everything but the book; he does not hear the radio and does not respond when called. There is nothing in this account to conflict with his classification as an involved reader.

Why, then, is he not hypnotizable? Here we are on more difficult ground; it appears that some features of his background have counteracted the influence of this reading absorption. The mother is described as a very negative person; he was in conflict with her much of the time when he was growing up, and positive warmth was missing. His father, too, was lacking in warmth; he is described as stubborn and self-willed. It looks as though certain personality problems deeply rooted in the parent-child relationships interact in a manner to reduce hypnotic susceptibility; in this case it may be the degree of negativism in both parents which is now reflected in Alan's attitude toward hypnosis and the hypnotist.

Tom serves as a second illustration. He becomes thoroughly wrapped up in the story he is reading. "During high school I was very interested in science fiction. I never became really involved in the characters, for I'm more excited by situations, the types of life, telepathy. Science fiction appealed to me because of involvement in action and the situation. It's the type of life they're leading, the pressures, values, excitement, thrills." This again is the picture of the involved reader.

What might have inhibited his potential as a hypnotically susceptible subject? In his case other features of the interview indicated that he was a deeply obsessive-compulsive character, constantly questioning himself and others. His image of himself was so negative that he had to assess it continually by how others were responding to him; that is, he felt in danger of being depreciated and he in turn depreciated himself. When other people were around, the interpersonal reaction was paramount; he wanted to be liked, but the situation was always felt as precarious, so that he was really more comfortable when there was nobody around.

It was difficult for the interviewer to obtain a clear picture of Tom's relationship to his parents. There was a minimum of contact with them before the age of ten, and it was during this period that most of his care came from servants. When Tom was ten, the circumstances of the family changed drastically. Everybody had to work. Tom reluctantly helped his father with the gardening. The family had a large library, and both parents as well as Tom read extensively, but there was no discussion of their reading. There were apparently no areas of shared play or fun. We are not suggesting that reading must necessarily be a shared activity in order for it to become a pathway. What we are suggesting is that *some* areas of activity need to be shared in an enthusiastic or zestful way.

Tom, who said he was identified in personality with his mother, described her as never whole-hearted, as usually having reservations. He felt he was also like his father in his tendency to make lists and organize.

The hypothesis to which these four cases lead is that certain personality problems, while consistent with reading involvement, may be inconsistent with hypnotic susceptibility. The interpersonal element in hypnosis, often so minimal as to be bypassed by involved subjects in favor of following impersonally the voice of the hypnotist, for these subjects may become a major deterrent to hypnosis. They can become involved in reading because the relation to the author is not that of one person to another; they cannot become involved in hypnosis, because the mere presence of another person is reacted to with questioning and doubt. The early basic relationships with parents have not been positive enough to allow this minimum degree of interpersonal contact to be taken for granted; the parental ties have been too negative, too ambivalent, or too minimal. Putting it another way, the interpersonal area is so conflictual that a relatively conflict-free area like reading has remained isolated and cannot be used as a model pathway for hypnosis. Isolation is consistent with the predominantly obsessive-compulsive character of these withdrawn people.

These cases point to the more general problem of factors inhibiting or facilitating hypnotic involvement, in addition to the interest areas which will have our primary attention in the first few chapters. Sometimes the inhibiting factors affect particular areas of hypnotic involvement, such as the more motor or the more cognitive items; sometimes we have evidence of disruption within the reading involvement itself, as the immersion is too frequently or too long interrupted by reflective criticism. Excessive independence, extreme anxiety, impatience, may all affect both reading involvement and hypnosis. We shall be better prepared to go further into these matters after completing a discussion of other areas of involvement.

### The Bearing on Theoretical Interpretations of Hypnosis

As we move through the various kinds of involvement, we shall be picking up leads that bear upon hypnotic theory. In other words, the observations arising through the case materials furnish a set of raw materials according to which prevailing theories can be tested and by means of which a firmer theory can be proposed.

The following indications have been proposed by the material of this chapter.

1. The experience of hypnosis resembles in a number of respects experiences of everyday life outside hypnosis. This has been shown statistically by the prediction of hypnosis through various-experience inventories, such as those initiated by Shor (1960). The particular resemblance pointed out in this chapter is that between reading involvement and hypnosis among the highly susceptible.

2. Because the history of these involvements outside of hypnosis is more readily traced than the experience of hypnosis itself, understanding of the origin and development of an involvement such as reading bears upon an understanding of the possible development of hypnotic susceptibility itself. We know through studies of the hypnotic susceptibility of children of different ages that there is an increase in the years between six and ten or twelve, when language and reading are becoming better developed, but there is a progressive gradual decline after those years. This is based on the statistics of groups. It may be that continuation of involvement in adventure or fantasy literature can prevent this decline for some individuals. Increasing intellectualization, as in scientific reading, on the other hand, may contribute to lessened susceptibility in other individuals.

3. The possibility of a critical period which occurs before adolescence in the development of reading involvement suggests that the same may be true for development of hypnotic susceptibility.

4. It is pertinent that reading involvement frequently has its

origins in a warm relationship to a parent who enjoys reading, and this contagious identification or modeling has to do also with hypnotic susceptibility.

A child may read, however, not in identification with parents, but because he is lonely. Lonesome for the companionship of other children, he may find in reading a substitute for experiences with peers or for experiences in the larger world. Where reading occurs separately from parental identification, it can constitute a pathway for hypnosis if the relationship to one of the parents has provided elements of satisfaction and security. In our series, with one exception, such reading was underwritten by parental support.

There are a number of more subtle features that emerge, having to do with the reality-unreality dimension and the problems of dissociation. The reader may be deeply involved in the suffering of those in a book, feeling their pains, yet knowing very well that he (the reader) is whole; something of the same sort happens in hypnosis, where the subject may suffer paralysis, anesthesia, or absent limbs without anxiety because he somehow knows also that there is another reality.

These, then, are some of the hints that have come through a study of reading involvement in relation to hypnosis. We turn now to some other areas of involvement, showing what they have in common but noting also some variations on the common theme. We shall then be better prepared to return to the problem of the interaction of the variables that affect the hypnotic experience, including aspects of personality that may interfere with hypnosis even when some of the involvements are high enough to lead most subjects into hypnosis.

# 4

# The Dramatic Arts

The hypnotized person throws himself wholeheartedly into the role suggested by the hypnotist; the dramatic qualities of what he does have contributed to the popularity of hypnotic demonstrations as a form of entertainment. The evident relationship between acting and hypnotic performance has indeed led to one of the interpretations of hypnosis, that of *role enactment,* as proposed and elaborated by Sarbin (Sarbin 1950, 1954; Sarbin and Andersen 1967). According to this interpretation, the hypnotizable subject has an ability to enact roles, to commit himself to them, and to become involved in them as though they were genuine; this ability is capitalized upon under the influence of the hypnotist. It must be stated at once that the interpretation does not imply that the behavior is sham behavior, in which the subject is simulating or "putting on an act" in order to please the hypnotist. If this were all that was involved, more people could be hypnotized; the role-enactment interpretation recognizes that there are individual differences in hypnotic susceptibility, apart from the willingness to cooperate. Hence, even though one accepts a role-enactment interpretation, there remain the interesting problems of explaining how the ability to become involved in a role comes about. Our interview program gave us a number of observations bearing on these problems.

## Formal Acting

We shall mean by formal acting the participation in a dramatic production in which the person takes a definite role or part, usually defined by the author of the play, and interpreted under the guidance of a director. The word "usually" has been added because there are closely related forms of spontaneous acting upon a stage which have most of the characteristics of formal acting but may lack both a script and a director.

The literature on acting makes the relationship to hypnosis plausible, at least in some forms of the theory. There is an old discussion, going back many years, concerning the extent to which the actor experiences the emotions he displays (see James 1890, vol. 2, p. 464). In more recent years this has led to two major theories of acting, known as *technical* acting and *method* acting. The name associated with method acting is of course Constantin Stanislavski (1863–1938)—a Russian actor, director, and producer; one of the founders of the Moscow Art Theater—whose books have been widely translated (e.g., Stanislavski 1963). Method acting is most closely related to hypnosis, for the stress is on deep involvement in the part:

> When an actor is completely absorbed by some profoundly moving objective, so that he throws his whole being passionately into its execution, he reaches a state that we call inspiration. In it almost everything he does is subconscious and he has no conscious realization of how he accomplishes his purpose. [Stanislavski 1963, p. 114]

Those who train actors for method acting instruct their actors in hypnoticlike performances, such as imagining, say, a spider in its web so vividly as to hallucinate it. The other interpretation, emphasizing technique, requires the actor to remain outside the part, being completely aware of everything that is being done for dramatic effect. Thus the actor knows that he faces partly toward the audience rather than toward the person to whom he is talking on stage; he knows exactly the position in which to hold his arms, where to stand on the stage, and so on. Any spontaneity is studied, and it would interfere with the perfection of acting to become lost in identification with the role. There must, of course, be some mixture of these attitudes in actual performance; otherwise an actor could not make the necessary changes between scenes. A time limitation on the role involvement, however, is not necessarily an argument against involvement, for this is exactly what we find in hypnosis. The differences in actors, like the differences in hypnosis, may depend upon the actor and not only upon his training.

An experiment of Sarbin and Lim (1963) bears upon the relationship between skill in role-taking and hypnosis. Having tested the hypnotic susceptibility of twenty volunteer subjects through ordinary hypnotic performances, they then had the subjects tested in brief roles by members of the Dramatic Art Department and rated for their histrionic abilities. A correlation of .52, $p = .05$ was reported between the ratings of dramatic ability and susceptibility to hypnosis. It should be noted that, as in all such comparisons, there were some discrepant cases of high hypnotic susceptibles who were rated low in role-taking ability. Sometimes these discrepant cases are the most helpful, and we shall have occasion to report on some of them.

Another comparison which supports the resemblance between role taking and hypnosis lies in the correlation between items in experience inventories of the type developed by Shor (1960), Ås (1963), and Lee-Teng (1965) and hypnotic susceptibility.* In all of these studies, items characterized as role taking or role involvement in daily life outside hypnosis show up as positively related to hypnosis. These include such items as feeling very different in different social settings where role demands are different, and exaggerating incidents in the telling so that they become more dramatic but seem to have happened that way even for the teller. Madsen and London (1966) rated the role-playing dramatic ability of children by means of two tests, one on dramatic acting and the other on ability to simulate hypnosis, and found that the ability to simulate hypnosis correlated significantly with hypnotic susceptibility ($r = .60$), but that dramatic acting did not ($r = .13$).

These leads from other sources are confirmed in our interview material. For example, among subjects who were rated for involvement in dramatic interests of one kind or another, those who were rated six or seven on a seven-point scale were significantly more hypnotizable than those rated lower ($p = .05$) (see table 8).

TABLE 8

*Susceptibility to Hypnosis as Related to Rated Involvement in Drama, 1962–63, 1963–64*

| Involvement | Susceptibility (SHSS-C) | | |
|---|---|---|---|
| | Low (0–5) | High (6–12) | Total |
| High (6–7) | 7 | 18 | 25 |
| Medium (4–5) | 47 | 45 | 92 |
| Low (1–3) | 41 | 29 | 70 |
| Total | 95 | 92 | 187 |

Significance test: $\chi^2 = 6.90$, $df = 2$, $p = .05$.

* For a published list of items in the experience questionnaire, see Shor (1960).

Because of the possible relationship between dramatic involvement and hypnosis, we had earlier tested a small sample ($n =$ 30) of students participating in drama at Stanford (table 4), and these interviews support the later findings in our more general sample, reported in table 8. It turned out that the thirty drama subjects were not at all homogeneous in their interests or training. The twelve who were undergraduates averaged 7.0 on SHSS-C, about what would be expected from a group of volunteering students; the eighteen graduate students were older (average age twenty-five), so that their somewhat lower scores (mean 5.7) were not unexpected. Although these general averages told us nothing, some of the differences within the groups turned out to be informative. Most of them had taken part in a few plays, but those whose interests were actually in acting were in the minority; others were interested in writing or directing plays, in designing scenes, in choreography, in doing filming or broadcasting. The ten subjects who were most interested in acting scored higher on the hypnotic susceptibility scale (mean 8.7) than the twenty whose interests were in other aspects of the theatrical arts (mean 5.0), but we do not know how well this sample of volunteers represents the universe of drama students. The case material proved of considerable interest, however, and some of the cases follow.

Fortunately the small sample of actors contained extreme illustrations of both technical and method acting, so that we have relatively pure cases to examine for the relationship to hypnosis.

Donna is a technical actress. She thinks about the character, what emotions the character must be feeling, and how best to portray these, but she insists that in no sense does she ever "become" the character. She indicated in the interview that she generally has her own ideas, and these often lead to arguments with the director whose ideas differ from hers. A director who knew her well, hearing that she had signed up for hypnosis, predicted that she would not be hypnotizable; actually she scored one on SHSS-C, near the bottom of the scale. Thus, although successful as an actor, she was not hypnotizable.

Lynne is at the opposite end of the continuum in both acting and hypnosis. Unlike Donna, she becomes deeply involved in character roles, specializing in accents and in pantomine. The director makes suggestions, but she develops the character from within. Her hypnotic score was twelve, at the top of the scale. Her whole background reflects the kinds of involvements that we shall be studying in relation to hypnosis, including the contagion of influence from a father who loves music and a mother whose interests include literature and writing. Lynne feels that she has absorbed all the interests and talents of the family to some degree and has found expression for them through drama.

It is important to note that the relationship between drama and hypnosis is not based on mere play acting, but on an involvement in the role. Hence one can find actors who are hypnotizable and actors who are not. While on the whole the actor group was more hypnotizable than those with nonacting interests, we have to be prepared for the actor who is not hypnotizable.

Hypnosis permits a full participation in the experience because the hypnotist is there as a trusted guide; it is his responsibility to see that the subject is safe. Perhaps the director of a play performs the same function. Some subjects, however, become so deeply involved in a play that they occasionally report being frightened by being "sucked into" the role being played.

Martha is one such subject. Although now she has again become a student of drama, and intends to make some aspect of drama her career, she had dropped out of play acting for ten years after being made anxious by it in high school. "I refused to participate again because of fear of being sucked in." Questioned about this, she went on: "It would take my life—I would lose my identity —I wouldn't know who I was. At that moment I felt like a transplant without roots." During the intervening years she had solved her phase-specific adolescent identity conflict and could again participate in some acting.

The remaining cases, selected from our regular samples, attest to many of the same relationships between hypnosis and acting.

Elizabeth shows how the relationship between acting and hypnosis is described by one subject who is both an experienced actress and highly susceptible to hypnosis (score of ten out of twelve on SHSS-A, and eleven out of twelve on SHSS-C). Since fourth grade Elizabeth has participated in plays. She describes how she threw herself into them in high school. "The director could make us feel those parts so strongly. He influenced my imagination so much. He could make us *feel* the part by telling the situation, how one felt; he would keep saying it and drumming it into us. He never said the lines for you, but he influenced you in so many ways by putting you in the frame of mind and telling you how a person with that part would feel."

When asked for an illustration, she answered, "He had us focus on the idea, then he had us close our eyes. I was to play the part of a wife who had been deserted by her husband; I was to feel alone, discouraged, in despair. With my eyes closed, while he talked, in fifteen minutes he had me so afraid in this dark place that I cried." Asked for further details, she went on, "While my eyes were closed he kept saying the room was moving away, that gradually things were getting dark—the blackness of despair. I wasn't sitting on that chair anymore, I was feeling myself another person."

What about her experience in hypnosis? "I was so relaxed and completely enjoying it that I didn't care to do anything except what he (the hypnotist) told me to do." When asked what the experience of posthypnotic amnesia was like, she added, "I was still so completely relaxed that everything was blank in front of me and I didn't struggle against it. As though I was still too tired to care, and he didn't want me to remember. . . . I *knew* there was something to remember, but when I tried to pick a picture in my mind, all was blank."

Asked about her dream under hypnosis, which was one of the Alice-in-Wonderland types occasionally found (E. R. Hilgard 1965), she said, "It just came. I've never been in that type of cave before, the dripping kind. A cave with stalagmites and stalactites, and it kept getting darker and darker as you went into the cave. I was walking, going inside; it was not as if I was watching myself (Elizabeth) doing it. . . . It was not a scary cave. It was a warm and never-ending cave—yet it was darker and blacker in the distance. I went farther into the cave . . ." She had indicated that she commonly analyzes her experiences so as to be objective toward them. When asked why her objective side did not operate, she replied, "Because I saw no reason to worry about the safety of it. I put complete trust in the hypnotist."

The parallelism between what the drama coach and the hypnotist did for Elizabeth was striking, but this does not of course tell us that it was the training under the director that led to her responsiveness under hypnosis; it is equally possible that an ability, there in the first place, was used in both circumstances. We shall return to the questions raised here as we go along, but first a brief account of another hypnotically susceptible actor.

Henry, a mathematics major, scored at the top of the two hypnotic scales, twelve out of twelve on SHSS-A, and twelve out of twelve on SHSS-C. As in the case of Elizabeth, his participation in plays began very early; for him, as for her, at the age of nine. Taking part in college plays had been his all-consuming interest. What he enjoyed most "is the ability to take on enough of another personality to project it to people, to make them experience the emotions that the author of the play has written down."

When asked how he felt in the midst of a role, he said, "In the beginning, I used to live the part, but you get so emotionally involved it wears you out. You have to hold back a little: if you are completely involved, you don't remember where you are on the stage; you mustn't forget where you are—you have to make sure you're standing in the right place. On the stage you're emotionally involved but you're also standing apart." He liked to play all parts, especially character ones. "I enjoyed Bottom, the buffoon in *Midsummer Night's Dream*; Falstaff appealed to me, for I was obese for a while."

Very often hypnotic subjects recognize that they are deeply involved, yet stand somewhat apart, as Henry does in a play. For him hypnosis meant a fuller involvement, for he said he did not have to be sure that he was standing in the right place, as he did on the stage. "Hypnosis is mainly an ability to relax completely, have very few cares or worries. You aren't responsible; it's a sort of dream state."

The correspondences between formal dramatization and hypnosis are so evident that there is little point in belaboring them. It is worthwhile to remind ourselves, however, of some of the similarities, for they help us to gain insight into the nature of hypnosis:

1. There is a temporary departure from reality orientation, to the creation of an *as if* reality.

2. The actor is not merely passive but actively receptive to the demands of the role; he is involved in it and works at it.

3. The role is created by words—the words of the playwright, the words of the director. This power of words is similar to the power noted in our discussion of reading involvement. Most of the actors we have interviewed are in fact avid readers of literature.

4. The absorption is intense, interest is concentrated and empathic, so that emotions are stirred up.

5. The whole is time-limited. While there may be a temporary carry-over, the actor overcomes his mood so as to participate in the curtain call, and he goes about his business in the hours he is not on the stage. Similarly, the hypnotic subject readily distinguishes between his behavior under hypnosis and the demands of reality-oriented daily life.

While a case can obviously be made for the overlap between the role involvements on the stage and in hypnosis, it is important to come to a deeper understanding and not to rest on self-evident relationships. Even in the case of Henry we sense some difference in the degree of surrender involved, and in other cases we find other differences between being on the stage and being deeply hypnotized.

Julie (whom we have met before in chapter 3) was another who gave up acting for reasons similar to Martha's whose experiences were described earlier. In high school plays she had become confused. "I didn't know who *I* was and who was the *character*." Owing to this identity problem, she gave up acting, and found her absorption thereafter in books and other forms of creative ability. In the case of Martha we interpreted the identity problem in acting as possibly phase-specific to adolescence; however, Julie did not return to acting, even though her adolescence was behind her. To hold to the interpretation, we would assume a prolongation of the conflict; perhaps given more time and maturity, her fear of loss of self in acting will diminish.

These cases suggest that extreme susceptibility may interfere with the actor's role. To a point it is helpful, but beyond that the make-believe of the theater is too difficult to bear without anxiety. What this means for our interpretation of role involvement in hypnosis is that it may in many instances be a deeper role involvement than that on the stage, made acceptable because of the lessened stereotype required in hypnosis and the protection against anxiety given by the hypnotist. We had an illustration of this in Elizabeth's tears when she was frightened of the dark by the drama coach, but her calm in the presence of the dark and drippy cave within hypnosis.

As indicated earlier, there is always something useful in the negative instances. The old notion that the exception proves the rule is taken in its original sense—not that every rule must have its exceptions, but rather that the exceptions put the rule under strain —and if we can account for the exception the rule may become clearer. One of the exceptions to be noted here is the successful actor who is not hypnotizable; the other exception, the highly hypnotizable person who cannot act, is harder to demonstrate because there may have been insufficient opportunity for him to demonstrate competency on the stage.

Adeline, a speech and drama major, has acted successfully in a number of plays, but she is in the lower quartile of hypnotic susceptibility on our scales. Her description of her relation to the director differed markedly from that of our other actors: "Whenever I was in a play, I always rebelled against the director. He always had to make me see *rationally* what he was getting at." She would have a discussion with the director and he would usually end up by saying, "Do it your own way and we'll see how it works out."

She clearly objected to relinquishing control and preferred to hold to herself the directing as well as the acting.

This same resistance to control was evident in hypnosis. "I didn't see any purpose to these inane things he told me would happen. . . . It was difficult for me to stop thinking long enough. He'd say something that would make me think of something else, and then I'd come jumping back." The one experience that really worked for her was suggested anosmia to strong ammonia. She was amazed at that, and it is possible that she is a case in which there is a latent ability for hypnosis which is hidden under her need to maintain rather than share control. The objection to control was noted also in the interview; she resented the interviewer's guiding the topics of the conversation.

Thus we see that Adeline's success as a player is not like that of the others. She does not permit the director to control her any more than the hypnotist. To the extent that her attitudes in drama and hypnosis are parallel she does no violence to our interpretation that there is a basic parallelism in the other cases.

### Dramatic Watching

A member of the audience becomes involved in the drama also; he may be moved to anger or tears and thus empathize with the players; this is doubtless one of the satisfactions of watching a play. Unfortunately the opportunity to witness very much legitimate theater has not been provided in many of the communities from which the students in our interview sample come. But they all have had abundant opportunity to view motion pictures, either in the theater or on television. Hence most of the drama viewing discussed in the interviews has been either motion pictures or TV, but our subjects report various degrees of involvement in them quite as they do in reading.

Laura is an illustration of an involved movie watcher who is also a susceptible subject. Her hypnosis score was eight out of twelve on SHSS-A. It is not surprising that Laura was also an involved reader. These two types of involvement have much in common, because the reader is audience for both the book and the movie and participates through identification and involvement. Laura says, "I loved *Lawrence of Arabia* and saw it twice; also *The Miracle Worker* and *David and Lisa*. I forgot my surroundings and became absorbed in the story. My emotions get stirred up, and I identify with the characters. As a child I identified completely with Dorothy in the *Wizard of Oz*. There was never as much identification in books, but it was similar. I cried over *Black Beauty.* I still enjoy science fiction."

During hypnosis she reported that her eyelids became heavy, she felt very relaxed, and then her arms and legs felt heavy according to the hypnotist's suggestions. "At first I had to pull my thoughts back to what he was saying. Then it got so I was just listening to him without effort."

The close relationship between reading and movie watching is reflected in the early origin of both interests in relation to her mother, who is both an avid reader and movie fan. As to her mother's reading, Laura says, "You name it, she's read it. We read the same novels, like *Gone with the Wind* and *Anthony Adverse.* She'd reread the books I'd bring home."

Anne's hypnosis score was ten out of twelve on SHSS-A, and she, like Laura, tended to become deeply immersed in movies. She remembers becoming absorbed in a movie at age four when she went with her grandmother; they had to leave because she was so frightened. She was so identified with Shirley Temple in *Bluebeard* that when a burning tree crashed behind Shirley with the witch in close pursuit Anne was as frightened as if the tree had fallen behind her. She commented that in a film course she had taken they divided moviegoers into two types. The first, the "film fan," watches dispassionately and critically, observing the skill in photography and noting any flaws, such as a zipper in a nineteenth-century film. The second, the "gaga," identifies with the characters and becomes absorbed in the action instead of the technique. Anne belongs to the "gaga" class.

There was little of the absorbed reading in Anne's background so common in other absorbed viewers. Instead, there was a premium placed in her family on telling a story from the day's activities in an amusing manner. Some elaboration or slight distortion was encouraged; everybody realized that the essential facts were correct. This is a kind of role enactment that we shall discuss presently as *informal dramatization.* Its presence from childhood on may have been for her an alternate to the reading found so commonly among others.

A third example of an involved movie watcher is Mark, who also scored ten out of twelve on SHSS-A. Although he, too, does not claim to be much of a reader, he clearly becomes involved in his movie watching. "You're coming out from the movie and not knowing where you're going. I became so involved in *Ben Hur* that during the intermission I felt compelled to sit down and write for fifteen minutes about the true life of the story. I get carried away by strong, deep, emotional things like *Ben Hur*. Not all movies, of course; never by Westerns."

As in our other examples, we have looked for the negative cases—for the involved movie fans who are not hypnotizable. Two of these are worth characterizing for what they tell us about the difference between those who are and those who are not hypnotizable.

Thomas scored two out of ten on the modified SHSS-C. While he reported that he identified with the characters in movies, he limited this identification to disagreeable characters; unfortunately the interview was not carried on far enough to root out the reason for this idiosyncrasy. "After seeing an unpleasant character in a movie I would become that character, by arrangement with who-ever I was with—a friend who had been along at the movie or my roommate." Asked to explain further, he added, "Take Heath-cliffe. I felt a strong association with him, as if there's really too much of him in me. So I somehow project that part of me toward Heathcliffe." This limited involvement, with its pathological over-tones, distinguishes his movie involvement from that of the others just described.

David is quite different. If there is any single phrase that char-acterizes him it is excitement loving. That is what he wants from a movie: excitement. "If there are three people doing interesting things in a movie, I'm there as a fourth one, but invisible." When he says that he forgets the chair in which he is sitting while he becomes absorbed in the movie, he sounds hypnotizable, but when he goes on to say that most movies are not fast-moving enough to hold his attention, we see the limits placed upon his involvement. He loves jitterbugging and rock-and-roll because he can be so active. If he listens to rock-and-roll when driving a car with the radio turned on, he steps on the accelerator. It was not surprising that he did not like hypnosis, although he had come eager for it. There was no excitement; the induction was slow and his thoughts wandered. It had nothing in common with *his* kind of involvement in movies or in music.

It turns out that much motion-picture involvement is of the same order as involvement in books, and for our student sample the fascinations are similar. The movies of course involve visual stimulation along with words, and as noted earlier some of the readers found this interfering, particularly if they had supplied their own imagery earlier, while reading the book on which the picture was based. Doubtless for many persons, however, the motion picture has replaced much of their reading, and for them it may serve similar purposes.

## Informal Dramatization

Not all acting is confined to the stage, and we have found it convenient to speak of "informal dramatization" to characterize the behavior of those who commonly act before the small audiences provided by family, friends, or even casual listeners. This was mentioned as part of the background of Anne's involvement in movies.

If we generalize a little from what we have seen in a number of informal dramatizers we note the following characteristics in what they do:

1. They pay close attention to what is happening about them, and to what will bear repetition, in the way in which a grandmother listens for clever things that her grandchildren have said in order to recite them to her friends. The emotional aspects of these happenings do not escape them, and they are an important feature of the dramatic reenactment to come later.

2. In the later telling they adopt the mannerisms appropriate to the situation: the gestures, modes of speech, facial expressions. It is not merely a matter of gesticulating, but of genuine gesturing appropriate to the story.

3. The tendency exists to exaggerate and embellish moderately so as to enhance the dramatic value of the incident when it is recreated, somewhat as the historical novel adds to the authentic biography of its hero.

The ability to do these things well is of course a form of role-enactment ability, not unlike that possessed by those who act on the stage, but there are some differences, and these differences may prove to be the most useful indicator of what we have learned from our interviews with the informal dramatists.

This can be made somewhat more concrete by considering how Jerry describes his own dramatic storytelling. This Alaskan boy has no trouble drawing an audience around him. He weaves "tall stories" based on fragments that he has heard from others. For example, there was an Eskimo woman named Bessie. He knew people who had actually seen her and talked with her, but he himself had never met her and had heard only exciting fragmentary accounts of her. Undaunted by this lack of acquaintance, he told of many of his experiences with her, mimicking her slurred and gutteral English, throwing in a few Eskimo words. Some of the stories were pretty wild, but he felt that most of his friends believed him; he added that perhaps his roommates knew that everything he said was not true all of the time.

He liked to retell improbable tales that other people had told him. For example, a friend of his, a student at the University of Alaska, had told about an enormous icicle he built by siphoning water over a thread. The icicle grew and grew until it was sixty feet high and four feet in diameter, and it was multicolored. Jerry would tell the story over and over, although he knew it was not true. Each time he relished it as thoroughly as when he had first heard it, and he thought his friends enjoyed it thoroughly, too.

This dramatic streak had had a long history. "My brother and I would make up these wild things and we would back each other up. We had my parents befuddled."

The relationship between this behavior and hypnosis appears to be somewhat indirect; at least it was not spontaneously recognized by Jerry. "Hypnosis wasn't as I imagined it. I thought it would be like going into a trance and not remembering it afterward. I felt the force pulling my hands together and couldn't do anything to stop it. But I also felt I had control over myself at all times. I was thinking clearly; it was like settling back, being very calm and relaxed. This was true of my body, but my mind was the way it normally is. That is, I was alert, trying to figure out what was going on." He commented on being completely unable to smell the strong ammonia; "A couple of times I thought I was going to 'go' and 'pass out!'" Actually his score of seven out of ten on SHSS, modified form C, was a moderate one, but above the average for the group.

Jerry at first did not see any similarity between his story-telling and hypnosis. The mention of role enactment struck a spark. "Yes. I was in the part of 'the Subject' who was hypnotized. I wanted to be hypnotized. That is similar to your being something else from what you normally are, a wild character."

After completing an interview with Ellen, another moderately hypnotizable subject, the interviewer noted, "I think we can safely say that Ellen is constantly telling a story, the story of her life, which has been composed of daily little stories." As she talked to the interviewer and became more at home in this situation she began to be increasingly dramatic, with eyes flashing and with more appropriate gesturing as she told episodes about herself. She is extremely sensitive to her environment and picks up cues from her companions. She is constantly being influenced by the gestures of others, which she incorporates as her own. She recalls this tendency as early as the second grade. When she came home from school her mother would say, "I can tell which friends you have been with today because you've picked up their mannerisms." She would use the facial expressions her friends were using when the events being retold took place; she still does this. There is a girl in the house where she lives at Stanford who is always saying "What?" and Ellen finds herself saying "What?" with this other girl's facial expression. She has a boy friend who frequently says "Right!" with a forceful manner, and shortly after she has been with him she says "Right!" just as he does. Her own phrase describes her very well: "I slip into a role in which I play myself."

The early origin of this role enactment, and its support by her mother, doubtless bears on its relationship to hypnotizability. She always came home from school and reviewed experiences for her mother, using appropriate gestures and manner of speaking. "Mother lives my life vicariously. She is very absorbed in what I do. We are pals and I tell her everything." In relating a joke to her mother, Ellen would embroider a little so that the dramatic flavor of the original would be retained. Mother acted as a fascinated audience.

The significance of mother-as-audience was indicated in the interview with Mary, another susceptible subject (eight out of ten on the modified SHSS-C). She reviewed everything for her mother, everything that had happened at school that day. She sat on a stool in the kitchen relating the experiences for an hour while her mother got dinner. She made the incidents more dramatic than they were because some everyday occurrences had to be dressed up to have the impact on her mother that the original had had on her. "I'd exaggerate a little to make sure I'd impress her. . . . She was enthralled." Her mother and she have been exceedingly close. She volunteered that she does not think she is tied to her mother's apron strings but simply happens to be the kind of person who wants for herself what mother wants for her.

While Dorothy has acted in plays since the age of seven, in high school and in a summer dramatic group, she is so given to what we have been calling informal dramatization that it seemed more relevant to discuss her here rather than as an illustration of more formal dramatization. She immediately saw role enactment as something common to the exercise of imagination, hypnosis, and what she does in daily life. She has a flair for the dramatic that does not require a formal stage; she has enjoyed dressing up as an adventurous character. "You realize all the time that you're not that person, but I get a kick out of pretending that I am. . . . Hypnosis is like that; if you make yourself believe, when you play a part, you tell yourself you are in the mood for a while; that is, for as long as you don't get tired of the mood. Then you can remind yourself that you created it yourself and move to something else. . . . Sometimes, though, I have created a mood that was awfully hard to get out of. . . . In your imagination, if you let yourself believe, you can have an exhilarating feeling. In hypnosis, it can be stronger because someone else as well as yourself is telling you to believe, and that reinforces it. It's like doing something you're told to do, as well as something you'd like to do. . . . If you let your imagination get overactive, you can say: 'It's because I was hypnotized'; that is, you have a reason for being so imaginative. It makes your imagination freer, because you feel you can't have any control over your imagination. . . . Most people are always enacting roles, although at times it doesn't seem like it. If you believe that the hypnotist is going to tell you to do something, you have to do it; there's no way to escape it."

She further described feeling in hypnosis that she was on the brink of consciousness—smooth, sometimes unattached, outside herself. She recalled that three or four years ago an English teacher who was something of a mystic suggested that if she looked at her hand long enough she could become detached. She did so at home and succeeded practically as well as in hypnosis. She added that when one feels like this, everything runs slowly, smoothly, and gracefully, as though one were flying in the air or swimming under water. These descriptions, removed now from role enactment, give a hint that regardless of the door through which hypnosis is entered the resulting experiences are very much alike for the susceptible subject.

As in many of our subjects, these intense experiences have had something to do with the contagious influence of parents. Dorothy's father as a young man was described as very adventurous. The years of maturity and responsibility, however, had converted him into a solid citizen, and Dorothy's mother had been heard to regret that he was no longer the way he was when she met and married him; this mother had given support all along to Dorothy's dramatization of adventurous events in her life.

These informal dramatists are not the highest among our susceptible group of subjects, and we shall later return to consider some of the things they do not do well. It may be noted, in advance of that discussion, that they are weak in posthypnotic amnesia, which is possibly not unrelated to their storing in memory the details they are later to dramatize in the reconstruction of daily happenings.

There are informal dramatists who are scarcely hypnotizable at all, and we need to find out, if we can, why they are not.

The failure to find high correlations between types of experiences which for some are obviously related to hypnotic susceptibility, and to scores on susceptibility tests, is related to the subtle distinctions that have to be made and to which we are calling attention in the interview data. For example, Fern on first acquaintance seemed the very incarnation of an informal dramatist. She was fluent and emphatic in speech, her face was highly mobile as she talked, and she used her hands constantly as she made her points. Why then was she not hypnotizable? Actually she scored a single point out of twelve on SHSS-A. Close review of what she said and did showed that she was not sensitive, as the others described have been, to what happened in experiences with others. She was impatient and did not like to *let* things happen; she wanted to *make* them happen. Her gestures and facial expression were not mimicry of others but were highly stereotyped ways of expressing herself. When she described her daughter's pleading for treats she used a voice full of feeling, and gestures with her hands, but when she told of a neighbor asking her to baby-sit for her she used the same voice and the same gestures. There was almost no change when she told how her husband had invited her to a concert. This quality, then, we have called gesticulating rather than gesturing; the repertoire is limited and always expressive of the individual telling the story. It is very different from the manner of those who are reconstructing experiences, even though with some exaggerations.

The hypnotizable informal dramatists all showed what might be called an empathic review of events to which they had responded with feeling. The lack of genuine empathy shown by Fern was illustrated also by Florence, who was a very successful role taker, but not hypnotizable.

For Florence informal role playing and playacting began in childhood and continues today. She creates the roles, rather than repeating something that she has empathically experienced. She gave two illustrations. For five days in a row, not long ago, in a group where she was not known, she pretended that she was Spanish, that is, Spanish-born and raised, hence speaking English with an accent. She threw herself into this and had everyone fooled by her first-class performance. Another time, on a long bus ride, she pretended that she was deaf and dumb and carried out the role convincingly. If role playing were all that was involved in hypnosis, she should have scored high.

The fact is that Florence retained all functions of the dramatic production. She was the creator, the director, and the actor of the drama. She chose her own roles, developed the motifs, was constantly improvising. She was not participating in a drama begun and partially developed by someone else.

How did she react to hypnosis? She did not permit someone else to direct the production, to create the roles in which she was expected to fit. Even though she wished to be hypnotized, she said she could not let someone else exert this degree of direction or control. Where the hypnotizable person temporarily accepts the stimuli or suggestions of the hypnotist, this aspect was foreign to Florence. She was unable to participate in someone else's fantasy or drama. She did not permit stimuli from the outside, in the person of the hypnotist, to start the process. From this illustration, we perceive the importance of sensitivity to outside stimuli where hypnotizability is concerned.

### The Bearing on Hypnotic Theory

Some similarities and differences among formal actors, dramatic viewers, and informal dramatists give us added hints about the nature of hypnotic involvement. We wish now to review some of the things we have noted and to add some details from the cases already considered so that we can be somewhat more analytical about the circumstances in which dramatic interests are related to hypnotic susceptibility or are not, and about differences within hypnosis that are associated with the different types of involvement.

We may remind ourselves that many of the things said about reading involvement also apply here; there is a parallel between what goes on outside and inside hypnosis and how reading involvements started in early childhood and continued to the present. They were supported by identification with parents or through parental encouragement.

In general, our material supports the role-enactment theory of Sarbin and the involvement theory of Shor. We have also found particularly illuminating those cases in which successful actors, movie watchers, or informal dramatists are not hypnotizable—cases that lay the basis for a more differentiated theory of hypnosis. We recognize the naturalness of the role theories and move from them to greater specificity about the kinds of roles and kinds of involvements in them.

We have noted that the less susceptible subjects among the formal actors are those who are too autonomous to accept direction from the dramatic coach, and that the nonhypnotizable informal dramatists also belong to this autonomous type which creates roles rather than accepts them. Furthermore, the intensity of role identification in very susceptible subjects sometimes makes them frightened of formal acting, so that they withdraw from it lest they lose their sense of identity. The role involvement in hypnosis can indeed be a deep one. The nonhypnotizable movie viewer is probably the "movie fan" type as distinguished from the "gaga" type. Those who seek excitement and are impatient with the development of characters are also less susceptible. Our susceptible subjects almost always indicated that Westerns held no fascination for them.

We turn now to the informal dramatists. It may be noted that the hypnotically susceptible ones are sensitive to situations and people; they react emotionally to the mood that is created, and they reenact situations with felt emotion, even though they modify the details. The nonhypnotic ones tend to create roles for themselves and lack this empathic reproduction of experience. The long practice of observation and retrieval by the hypnotizable seems to block to some extent the capacity for amnesia. Informal dramatists as a group are not very good at the more advanced visual and auditory hallucinations called for in hypnosis. When asked about this, they generally explain that these are piecemeal sensory experiences that do not involve roles.

# 5

## Religion

Religion can provide experiences of deep involvement and self-transcendence. It would not be surprising, therefore, if some relationship were to be found between religious experience and hypnotic susceptibility. Such a relationship has indeed been noted, and there are religious-experience items in the experience inventories that relate to hypnosis. One experimenter of our acquaintance draws his subjects largely from a Protestant theological seminary, where he finds a high level of response.

While there is a good deal of intellectual interest in religion in a modern secular university, the students who express deep conviction about a personal religion tend to represent a rather small fraction, so that we do not have many cases on which to base some of the generalizations that emerge from our interviews with students. There are interesting signposts, however, which bear on the meaning of religion to the involved student as well as upon his hypnotic susceptibility.

### Varieties of Religious Involvement

The problem of estimating where to place a subject on a scale of religious involvement illustrates the difficulties interviewers face when they attempt a study such as ours in which some kind of prediction is required. Shall we accept belonging to a church and regular attendance as a sign of religious involvement? Shall ethical idealism without a firm belief in God be accepted? For us the problem is essentially an empirical one (rather than a theological one), for we had to find out by careful listening and recording just what

aspects were indeed related to our criterion of hypnotic susceptibility.

Some of the distinctions we made along the way are worth
noting. First, we distinguished between a formal participation (attendance, acceptance of the ritual) and a personal religion, in
which God's presence was felt and his help counted upon. Second,
we distinguished between a religion that was part of one's nurture,
shared with parents and essentially conflict-free, in contrast with a
religion that was accepted later in life as a result of a conversion
experience or in response to some sort of felt need. Third, we had
to note kinds of discrepancy in the history of the individual's religious experience, as, for example, shifting from one faith to another, or differences in the faiths or degree of interest of one or the
other parent. Fourth and finally, for the purpose of this summary
we noted individual features of the appeal of religion—whether the
influence was that of the preacher, religious writing, parochial
schools, the opportunity for self-expression, ascendance-submission relationships, and so on. The range within religious experiences is very great indeed, and it is not surprising that we emerge
from this inquiry with some answers that are tentative and some
questions which remain unanswered.

The problems in making the appropriate distinctions among
types of religious involvement, combined with the small proportion of our sample in which there was any appreciable involvement at all, made it difficult to secure statistical support for the
kinds of relationships which were evident within individual interviews. Even so, the results for both years (1962–63 and 1963–64)
were consistently in the same direction, although not meeting the
.05 level of significance by the chi-square test (table 9). In view of
the very few cases with high involvement in religion, it is not surprising that the statistical relationship is weak.

### The Religiously Nurtured Student

There are in our interviews fourteen students who fit well the description of being religiously nurtured, that is, growing up in a faith
shared with parents and persisting today in firm religious belief;
this includes subjects from the year before the sample given in table
9. These fourteen average 8.5 on SHSS-A, or the equivalent on form
C, well above the mean of 5.8 for the Stanford population from
which they are drawn. Of these, four represent relatively "pure"
cases, in that they show none of the other types of involvement in

TABLE 9

*Susceptibility to Hypnosis as Related to Rated*
*Involvement in Religion*

| Involvement | Susceptibility (SHSS–C) | | | | | | | | |
|---|---|---|---|---|---|---|---|---|---|
| | 1962–63 Sample | | | 1963–64 Sample | | | Both Years | | |
| | Low (0–5) | High (6–12) | Total | Low (0–5) | High (6–12) | Total | Low (0–5) | High (6–12) | Total |
| High (6–7) | 2 | 6 | 8 | 2 | 5 | 7 | 4 | 11 | 15 |
| Medium (4–5) | 20 | 21 | 41 | 13 | 13 | 26 | 33 | 34 | 67 |
| Low (1–3) | 31 | 24 | 55 | 27 | 22 | 49 | 58 | 46 | 104 |
| Total | 53 | 51 | 104 | 42 | 40 | 82 | 95 | 91 | 186* |

Significance test (both years only): $\chi^2 = 4.64$; $df = 2$; $.10 > p > .05$.
* One case in total sample of 187 not ascertained.

reading, drama, sports, and so on, that other susceptible subjects show. What can we learn from these four?

Roger, who scored nine points on a ten-point SHSS-C, is an Episcopalian. He believes in God, and personally prays to him. He was an acolyte in the church and active in youth groups in the church, but he is not interested in dogma or denominationalism: for him religion is a very personal thing. His mother is devout, finds satisfaction in prayer, and is active in the church in which she also was brought up. His father was confirmed after marriage: "Mother would show her belief more, but *inside* he would believe, too."

Theresa is a Roman Catholic who is devout, as she puts it, "in a real and deep meaning." She scores above the mean in hypnotic susceptibility, seven on a ten-point scale. She believes in a Supreme Being, finds that she needs religion to sustain her, and could not and would not let her faith be shaken. Her father is a lifetime Catholic and a devout believer; her mother is Presbyterian, and not particularly active. Theresa identifies more with her father.

Karen, also a Roman Catholic, scored just above the mean of susceptibility with a score of six out of ten. She went to a Catholic school for fourteen years, and religion for her has a deep emotional meaning. Both her mother and her father are devout; religion is a real part of their lives. She says "they live by it." Religion to them is much more than ritual; they read about it and talk about it.

Alene, who scored ten on SHSS-A and six on SHSS-C, is the daughter of an Episcopalian minister. She cannot remember when she did not go to Sunday school, and she feels that religion was such a part of her life that she never questioned it. "I knew there was a God and that he was good. You have to just accept this fact, and to me there was proof of God. Everything in life was explained through faith in religion as I grew up. Everything was pervaded by religion. My father did not use a pious or sentimental, prayer-type approach, but a matter-of-fact faith in daily living which is there all the time."

These four, with nothing else about them to make us expect them to be hypnotizable, appeared to be prepared for a slightly better-than-average hypnotic susceptibility by whatever this life-long religious experience has in common with hypnosis. It must be noted that none of them spontaneously related their hypnotic experience to religion, but this is hardly to be expected in view of the spiritual nature of religion and the secular nature of hypnosis.

The other ten students of this religiously nurtured group scored somewhat higher in hypnotic susceptibility than these, but they also had a variety of other interests which, without religion, might have led them into hypnosis. Still, their religious interests were real, as the following excerpts tell us.

Elizabeth (whom we have already met as a drama participant) has a strong Episcopalian background and says, "God is the only one I put complete trust in. When I pray, I'm under the will of God. I'll do my best wherever I am—things are going to get better. I have complete faith in God." With a little searching, she related her trust in the hypnotist in this way. "By putting faith in the hypnotist, I knew he would direct me in the right way. . . . It's like believing in the supernatural and all-powerful in religion. I believed in the hypnotist as all-knowing and went along with it."

Jim underlines the same idea. His mother is very religious. "Religion increased my respect for authority. God you can look up to, be confident in following. To a lesser degree someone in authority (on earth) you'd be willing to follow. . . . Religious belief increases your readiness to accept things on faith that you might not otherwise accept, just on faith." When asked if there was a relationship to hypnosis, he replied, "There is a general confidence that the hypnotist knows what he's doing. You participate and don't have anything to worry . . . You might not understand something but you can still be sure it's right."

Keith has a family that is strongly Episcopalian. He was an altar boy in the church, sang in the choir for five years, and felt that he was a part of the church. He describes himself as a real believer.

Ben is a very serious boy from a Lutheran family, with both parents active in church. His maternal grandfather was a Lutheran minister. He participated in Sunday school, church, choir, youth group, and a special ecumenical study.

Virginia comes from a family active in the Dutch Reformed church. She believes in the church, derives "refreshment" from it. In high school she was in the Youth for Christ movement; she sang in the church choir for nine years.

Fred comes from a very religious family with whom he went to church every Sunday. He is now "searching" for a clearer understanding because religion is important to him, not because he is in any conflict about religion or with his family.

We have now covered ten of the fourteen cases; the other four give similar accounts, but one of these is of such special interest that his case will be given in somewhat greater detail.

Herbert was one of the most versatile, and among the very highest-scoring, hypnotic subjects to appear in our laboratory; because he was a graduate student in psychology and professionally interested in helping us, he talked freely in interviews over several hours at different times. While some details have of course been altered to preserve his identity, the essential history is as given.

He came from a devout Methodist farm family. The parents always went to church and belonged to church groups. Herbert attended church and Sunday school and belonged to all the activity groups, such as Christian Endeavor. He was headed toward the ministry. "Father was a strong churchman and favored the ministry. I identified with a minister who was a very good friend of the family. He had a son four or five years older than I whom I admired. The minister was pleasant but quiet; his wife was very energetic and organized parties. I identified with the whole family, not just the minister himself." By the age of fifteen Herbert had made up his mind to become a Methodist minister. During the three years from age fifteen to age eighteen he did some local preaching and thoroughly enjoyed it. He now thinks that what appealed to him was holding an audience, which he enjoys to this day: "Holding an audience comes from the days when I was a local preacher. I now prefer acting to preaching because you can be more active and play on people's emotions more, hold the audience better."

While Herbert's childhood experience with religion was genuine, and this early direction toward becoming a clergyman was real, what he tells us about his experience in the pulpit is essentially narcissistic. As a matter of fact, however, he did have a religious feeling in the midst of his own preaching, and he was able to relate the involvement in listening to someone else's sermon, or to his own, to being hypnotized before a group by a visiting senior hypnotist. "Our preacher never had much to say, but his manner was kind and he always said good things—the way it was in Dr. X.'s lecture before the group. The minister had a quiet voice like Dr. X.'s. It was Dr. X.'s manner when he gave that speech which affected me. I didn't care what he said; it was his voice that held me and the audience."

There are a number of complexities in Herbert's developmental history. At the age of eighteen, at the end of his trial at being a preacher, there was a man who visited at his father's farm who had a profound influence upon him. The visitor got him fascinated in spiritualism—for which he felt his religious upbringing had prepared him—and it was this interest that led him into psychology. While Herbert is less religious now than he was as a youth, he believes that his current interest in consciousness-expanding experiences is related to his religious upbringing, and that his dramatic interests go back to his experience as a preacher.

The four relatively pure cases of religious involvement—with no other interests related to hypnotizability that we could have detected—indicate that there is a relationship, but one not strong enough in itself to lead in this small sample to a susceptibility much above the mean. Nurtured religious interest, combined with some of the other involvements, is associated in the rest of this small group (including Herbert, one of our most hypnotizable subjects) with quite high susceptibility.

### The Religious Convert

Perhaps "convert" is too strong a word to describe one who has a self-developed religion, but we may use this expression to distinguish another group of subjects from the religiously nurtured group. These are students who express a strong involvement in religion, developed on their own, without religious upbringing in the home. Our interview sample here is very small indeed, with but four cases, and only two of these "pure cases" in the sense that religion is their only hypnotically related involvement. Let us consider these two first.

Michelle had been converted to the Congregational faith only the year before, after a month of intensive questioning and thought. Though very much involved in religious activities, she questioned the existence of God and of the Prophets. "I will always be testing; I am never whole-hearted." For her, religion represented an attempt to solve such questions as, What am I here for? She says, "I want a purpose; I want to know what I am trying to accomplish."

Her score in hypnosis was three out of twelve on SHSS-*A*, a low score.

The second of these cases, Marsha, had gone to Sunday school as a child. Her parents, however, were lackadaisical about church attendance, going only for an occasional ceremony. Before high school, Marsha was not much involved, but gradually, under the influence of a particular clergyman, she became more interested. She began to go to church regularly, and church became more important in her life. Now she goes to the Methodist church every Sunday, feels "renewed" by the Sunday service, but notes little feeling for religion from one Sunday to the next. She feels a little guilty about this at times but cannot seem to help it. She scored near the bottom of the distribution in hypnotic susceptibility, with but one out of twelve on SHSS-*A*.

From these two subjects we infer that a late-developed interest in religion, often filling some need of the adolescent (as it must have in the days when adolescent conversions were very numerous), does not lead to the intensity of conflict-free involvement that is found in those who have been brought up in religion in identification with parents. Such a statement must stand as an impression, because the evidential value of two cases is slight; however, the two do stand in striking contrast to the religiously nurtured ones.

The other two cases of self-engendered religion are not clear one way or the other because they both have other pathways into hypnosis, outside of the religious one, and both score somewhat above the mean in hypnotic susceptibility.

In Sheila's case religion was developed to meet a disturbed life situation. Her religion may be described as a defensive solution to conflict. She spelled this out for us in her comments that she could not see any connection between religion and hypnosis. "I don't want to put myself into a situation where I need religion. . . . If I got into a situation which was *not my fault,* then I would cling to religion; otherwise I want to have complete control of myself." In denying the connection with hypnosis she is saying that she is coming to hypnosis voluntarily, which makes it different from religion; she is also telling us that religion has a problem-solving meaning for her. On this basis, if we were to generalize from the two preceding cases, we would not expect her to be hypnotizable.

Actually she made a score of three out of twelve on SHSS-*A*, but with confidence she raised her score to six out of twelve on SHSS-*C* on a second try. This does not contradict the lack of importance of religion in this connection, because she had other interests that we would suppose might make her hypnotizable, such as the intense enjoyment of skiing, learned early from her father.

The fourth of these cases, Pat, was raised by agnostic parents. She said, "I go through periods of strong belief in God, when I'm sure he is all-powerful and good; then I go through a period when I'm sure he doesn't exist, he has no power, he doesn't care about the world." In answer to probing, she replied, "Yes, I'm afraid these shifts reflect my own moods. I like to feel that when I've really worked for something, I've gotten what I deserved. And sometimes I don't. . . . Or, if I receive a reward for what I haven't done, a mood of depression starts. I think, 'Why do people who don't do anything get credit? Here are people who have worked hard and I just happened along at the right moment to get the credit.'

"I listen to the preacher. I think about it. In different ways what he says influences me. The idea that Christ was a suffering savior I don't deeply believe, but I believe in the basic ideal of Christian teaching. I apply this. Such an ideal as 'a person shouldn't come first, should be willing to sacrifice himself sometimes.' " Her religious interest developed in high school, and we may speculate that it arose in an effort to meet some of her adolescent problems.

On the basis of religion alone, we would not expect Pat to be hypnotizable. In her case, however, as in Sheila's, there were other paths into hypnosis—reading, drama, music, enjoyment of nature. These involvements were intense enough that her interviewer predicted in advance of testing that she would score around ten on SHSS-A; actually she scored seven on form A and seven on form C, moderately high scores within this sample but not as high as the mean of the religiously nurtured group.

Running through the comments of these four who developed religious interest on their own, we find conflict over religious belief, even though religion is a solace when needed. The naturalness of religion, as it is expressed by those brought up in a comfortable faith, is missing. We shall discuss this again in its possible relationship to hypnosis.

## Some Doubtful Cases

It is not hard to see the strain an interviewer undergoes in deciding whether or not a religious involvement is the kind expected to be associated with hypnosis. Were there enough experience to say that childhood nurturing in religion was essential and late development of religious interest inimical, the task would not be so difficult. The necessary distinctions are never made quite this simply, because other issues of intensity are involved. Three of the more difficult cases help show the problems an interviewer faces.

Take Adeline, for example. In her initial interview she said that religion was very much a part of her private life and of her life shared with her Roman Catholic parents. She believed herself to be a good Catholic, and it was only upon further questioning that she was found to differ from the devout Catholic believer. On any ordinary questionnaire inquiry she would have considered herself a faithful practicing Catholic. After she overcame her resistance to talking somewhat more freely about her personal beliefs, she said, "I am not a follower in religion. I don't follow the tenets of the church. I resist the supreme authority of the church because I have a mind of my own and my ideas are not to be completely suppressed. I question the church; I don't accept or believe in the black or white of church ideas. An intelligent person should be able to take these basic things and interpret them." Adeline says her mother questions the church to some extent but still accepts most of the basic doctrines. Her father was a Methodist who had converted to Catholicism some years earlier so that all members of the family could attend the same church.

We have met Adeline before in our consideration of drama (chap. 4). She was the one who preferred to direct as well as act in plays. We feel that Adeline's faith is not representative of those who are deeply involved in a personal religion. She is independent but would not care to admit this, because she wants also to consider herself a good Catholic.

Or consider the case of John, a lifetime Methodist, whose mother is a dedicated believer but whose father is conventionally religious. John is a competitive athlete—the kind of athlete whose interests do not lead to hypnotizability, as we shall see later. His religious interests are somewhat perfunctory, like his father's. On a superficial basis one might classify him as religiously nurtured, and indeed he would so classify himself. Yet on the basis of intensity of religious involvement he falls short of those whose religious involvement provides a natural bridge to hypnosis. He scored three on the ten-point modified SHSS-C.

Finally, there is Arthur. He is willing to describe himself as religious and brought up in a religious atmosphere. His mother, the daughter of a Methodist minister, is a churchgoer and a believer in God. His father was brought up a Presbyterian but follows his own ethics and does not believe in God. Actually Arthur never did join the church, though he has a "Protestant ideal." He feels a religious dedication to what he thinks of as right: the solidarity of mankind, even though only temporary on earth; the love of fellowman. Only through such ethical feeling does man have dignity. He identified his ethical position with that of Camus. Once the story is unfolded, it is again clear that he does not belong with the dedicated, religiously nurtured group, although it would be easy to miss the differences unless he were questioned in some depth. That he scored low in hypnosis, two out of ten on the first day, one out of ten on the second, does not refute the relationship between devout religious involvement and hypnotizability.

## Conclusions regarding Religion and Hypnosis

Discussion of the three groups of cases (the religiously nurtured, the converts or self-developed in religion, and the cases of doubtful religious commitment) readily excites speculation about the relationship between their involvements and hypnotic susceptibility.

The highest-scoring group in hypnosis consists of those who have a deep sense of religious involvement, with little conflict because religion developed naturally in deeply religious homes, where there were, however, other interests also which were absorbed through a kind of contagion. We do not yet know about these interactions, but if religious belief helps to explain the world that is found to be good in other respects, this doubtless reinforces the religious conviction. Here we have the interplay of identification, of joyful participation, of basic trust, of respect for benevolent authority. With these attitudes engendered in early childhood and continued with institutional and parental support, it is easy to accept the demands of hypnosis, the confidence in trusted authority, the lack of questioning when unfamiliar elements are introduced into prosaic reality.

If our few cases are any guide, those who turn to religion in adolescence to solve their problems do not (at least in this segment of the population) completely erase their doubts, and their religious commitment fluctuates somewhat with their moods. Such religion is not conducive to hypnotizability, but it does not appear to be an impediment, either, if there are other involvements present.

We may describe the similarity of response in religion and in hypnosis in a few words. Religion is an experience in which *the usual reality-testing processes of the ego are temporarily set aside.* This is, of course, the old problem of faith versus rationality, and the truly religious person prides himself on his faith. Part of the act of faith is *active receptivity and responsiveness to a higher authority.* This higher authority is conceived as *powerful and all-knowing, as supernatural.* Ego boundaries can safely be merged with an all-powerful being. One goes along in comfort; one does not compete with God.

These attitudes, at secular level, can make the religious person comfortable with the hypnotist, who asks him to set reality testing aside and to share confidently in his power. Modern permissive hypnosis does not ask for surrender to the hypnotist's will, but for participation in the experiences that he opens up to the subject. The parallels are fairly obvious, but because the sacred is being compared with the secular, the subjects often resist making the comparison.

The importance of a *conflict-free* area of involvement has been stressed as we have proceeded from one area of involvement to another. In this chapter we noted that religious involvement is most likely to be conflict-free if it was engendered in early childhood through participation in religious activities and religious feeling with parents who were themselves deeply religious.

# 6

## Affective Arousal through Sensory Stimulation

Hypnotic induction often includes the suggested alertness to bodily sensations—feelings of numbness or heaviness or lightness—and these are made to appear as pleasant accompaniments of relaxation. Sensory experiences and their distortions are also a familiar part of hypnotic reactions, as in tasting things not present to the senses, hallucinating odors or lights or sounds. It turns out that the person who is hypnotizable often has a rich background of the appreciation of sensory experience, and of having his feelings aroused by them. At the higher levels of appreciation we refer to aesthetic sensitivity, as in the enjoyment of art or music, but the more primitive experiences—enjoying a warm breeze or a cool drink or stroking soft fur—are also related.

Our interviews with subjects who varied in their susceptibility to hypnosis brought out many evidences of affectivity associated with sensory stimulation, and in some cases the reinstatement of these experiences in the absence of stimulation, outside hypnosis. Thus a reader may *feel the heat* of the desert as he reads about it, a physical space traveler may *feel his body suddenly light* as his airplane ascends, a swimmer enjoys the *awareness of floating,* a theatergoer is *gripped by bodily emotion* in the midst of the play.

We may bring into focus the kinds of experiences we are considering by discussing them under three headings: first, affective arousal through a variety of sensory experiences; second, the aesthetic appreciation of nature; and, third, involvement in music. A few cases will clarify what we are talking about, and then the matter can be considered more abstractly or theoretically as it bears upon hypnosis.

76

## Affective Arousal through Various Sensory Experiences

Although in our interviewing we asked questions about aesthetic appreciation of nature, we did not search directly for the satisfactions of experiences of touch, smell, kinesthesis, and coolness and warmth; but these turned up sufficiently in the case material to be deserving of comment.

An illustration will show what we mean. A subject spontaneously mentioned how much he enjoyed experiences of touch and illustrated it by running his hand over the smooth desk top, commenting how pleasurable he found this. He enjoys stroking a fur coat and feeling its softness. While he also enjoys looking at textures of various kinds, it adds to his enjoyment if he can experience them through touch. Highly hypnotizable (score of twelve out of twelve on SHSS-A, and eight out of twelve on SHSS-C), he is able to relate this enjoyment of direct experience to what he is asked to experience within hypnosis.

The savored experiences of direct sensory stimulation take many forms. The following list represents some of the things told us in the interviews.

A soft breeze on the skin
Swift wind when one is speeding
Warm sand under bare feet
Cool grass
Smelling fresh air after a rainstorm
Warmth of the sun on the body
Touching fabrics and textures (e.g., enjoying the softness of fur or the smoothness of finished wood)
Gliding upon or floating through water
Water cool and smooth when swimming
Weightlessness in riding, skiing, or flying

These experiences are somehow so organic that they are readily reexperienced in imagination, and this may well be their relationship to hypnotic experience.

There is great variety in the way in which these sensory experiences are felt and described. Thus one of our subjects felt most engrossed when lifting weights, and his experiences in this activity were the only ones we could discover outside hypnosis that had any of the characteristics of the hypnotic experience. Yet he proved highly hypnotizable. As he described his lifting he recalled the anticipation while in the preparatory stance, then the tremendous exertion felt as a wave through the musculature of his whole body, then the climactic effort as the weighted bar was finally held aloft above his head. All of him was involved in the experience, while at the same time it was felt as something *happening to him*, quite as much as something he was doing.

These statements are similar to those made by another hypnotizable subject, who expressed a joy in many aspects of nature. She recalled that, as a child, "In the mountains I would join in a summer storm, running uphill and watching the storm approach." She spoke nostalgically of the wind. "The wind always blew in Montana. I loved it. I would carry my cello over my head in the wind and pretend it was a sail." This time the subject was joining another manifestation of nature, as though she were a boat that was propelled by an outside source.

The pertinent characteristics of these direct experiencs may be summarized in a few statements:

1. The experiences that are most pleasurable appear to be chiefly gentle and mild. Thus the experience reported is that of soft touch, not of hard pressure or pain; so also it is warmth and coolness that are enjoyed most, not heat or cold.

2. The pleasant affect is a passive, sensuous experience. There is no particular triumph or mastery involved, but rather simple primitive pleasure by way of the senses.

3. Involvement is great, even though the experience is mild and essentially passive. That is, there is a channeling of attention, largely effortless, and concentration upon the experience is high. Subjects surrender themselves to the experience and in some cases are practically enveloped by it.

4. The experiences are essentially nonverbal; words play a minor role or are absent. The structure is so simple that a young child can enjoy the experience. One is reminded, indeed, of the sensorimotor stage described as *preconceptual* by Piaget. Of course the experience can be labeled: "I just saw a beautiful sunset" or "The water was just right for my swim." These labels help to reinstate the experiences in imagination later on, but they are not the essence of the experiences themselves, and they communicate little of the actual flavor of the experience.

## Aesthetic Visual Appreciation of Nature

The sensory experiences just discussed—those of touch, temperature, taste, and smell—are sometimes described as belonging to the lower senses, whereas vision and audition are commonly regarded as belonging to the higher senses. The distinction is based largely on the more complex patterns of sights and sounds and the correspondingly greater richness in the experiences they mediate. One basis for the complexity is the overlay that training can bring—there may be an acquired sophistication in the appreciation of art or music. Of course the distinction between higher and lower is a relative one; there is such a thing as an educated palate as well as an educated ear: there are experts in wine tasting as well as in music appreciation.

For the purposes of our investigation of those involvements which are related to hypnosis we have found it necessary to distinguish between experiences in which the person is immersed and affectively involved and those which he analyzes with the critical detachment of the expert appraiser. It is the involved experience, rather than the rationally critical one, which is related to hypnosis, and it may well be that our inability to know where to draw the line has interfered with our achieving more success in using ratings to select the more and the less hypnotizable.

The visual enjoyment of nature can be a rather untutored kind of experience, on the one hand, or it may become part of an intellectual exercise in interplanetary geography, on the other. For the experience to be related to hypnosis, the aesthetic value of the sunset or the wild flowers or the expanse of multicolored fields far outweighs any desire to categorize the sunset's colors according to the spectral analysis involved, or the flowers according to their botanical names. The individual is actually drinking in the beauty through his eyes, not using it as a background to consider the problems it suggests, nor indeed to use it as a tranquilizer while he works out solutions to personal problems. The experience itself, at that moment, is inherently satisfying.

A case of a highly hypnotizable girl can make clear what we mean.

Sally has an extraordinary appreciation of nature learned in association with her father, who had in turn learned it in association with his father.

"My love of nature was shared with my father as I took long walks with him. He showed a different aspect of his personality when we were in the mountains. Ordinarily he has a tendency to worry and be tense, but outdoors he'd be completely relaxed. He'd set the pace; when we rested he'd point out things." When asked whether the things pointed out were scientific, she replied, "There was no scientific sense to it."

After Susan described the complete relaxation she felt in hypnosis, she was asked what other experiences were like those in hypnosis. (She had proved to be highly hypnotizable.) She responded, "Hypnosis is something like drifting from thought to thought, as when lying down listening to music, or when outside. When I was younger I spent a lot of time in the mountains; I'd walk around, sit by a stream or lake or on a hillside, not thinking of anything in particular, just drifting in my thoughts." When asked whether she recalled definite fantasies at such times, Susan denied them. "No, I think of inconsequential things . . . no outside distractions, no worries, no emotional thoughts. *Mostly just looking—at the clouds and sky, at what you see around you . . .*"

There was a kind of surrender in Susan's reaction to nature—a dissolving of the barrier between her and what lay around her. The magnitude of her response, the depth and the absorption, indicate the degree to which she abdicates conscious direction.

Throughout our interviewing we found problems which required us to make distinctions which did not at first seem necessary. The difficulties are illustrated by some subjects who appeared to be immersed in nature and were rated high in this involvement but turned out not to be hypnotizable. On review we found that they did indeed show some differences from the more highly hypnotizable.

One of these was Michelle, who reported a high love of nature in her interview prior to hypnosis, but she scored only three out of twelve possible points on SHSS-C. In reinterviewing, we found that she differed from the subject just reported in that she used nature for her own purposes rather than losing herself in nature. She may be feeling discouraged; then autumn, when things are dying, "produces a lonely and haunting effect." She is feeling happy; then when she steps out into a bright sunny day there is "an aura of contentment." With a thunderstorm in the air, "I feel something impending." "If I have something on my mind when I take a walk, I keep thinking about it." Nature for her is a kind of drug or tranquilizer to exaggerate her own moods or to provide a setting in which she thinks about her own problems. Thus there is something more autistic about her enjoyment of nature than Sally's. Apparently this approach to nature has less in common with hypnosis than the approach wherein the stimulus comes more from without.

Eugene represents another version of nature loving unrelated to hypnosis; he scored one out of twelve on one test of hypnosis and three out of twelve on a second test. He reported in his advance interview that he loved hiking and nature, and hence he was rated high on this interest. His interest was genuine but turned out to be cognitive—analytical and scientific. "Hiking is tied up with biology—the plants and animals along the way. At the beach I look to see how the seaweed is made, or I poke around the tide pool and find a starfish, remember how I learned about them in high school, how they are related to the jelly fish." Such "thinking" responses to nature's wonders differ from the "drinking in" of nature's beauties. It is cases such as these which pose problems for an interviewer trying to decide where on the spectrum of involvement a particular subject's interests lie.

Despite the difficulties in distinguishing between cases which we see as illustrating a genuine involvement in nature, and those who use nature for intellectual experiences of various kinds, whether scientific or personal, we had some success in showing a correspondence between the rating on aesthetic involvement in nature, obtained prior to hypnosis, and subsequent hypnotizability, with the results as shown in table 10. Of those rated high in

TABLE 10

*Ratings on Aesthetic Involvement in Nature as Related to Hypnotic Susceptibility Scores, 1962–63, 1963–64 (N = 184; Males, 113; Females, 71)*

| Involvement | Susceptibility (SHSS-C) | | Total |
|---|---|---|---|
| | Low (0–5) | High (6–12) | |
| High (5–7) | 37 | 53 | 90 |
| Low (1–4) | 56 | 38 | 94 |
| Total | 93 | 91 | 184* |

Significance test: $\chi^2 = 6.27$; $p = .02$.
*Ratings lacking on three cases in sample.

involvement in nature 53/90, or 60 percent, proved high in hypnotizability, while of those rated low in involvement, 38/94, or 40 percent, proved high in hypnotizability. The differences, while not very great, are in the expected direction and statistically significant at the $p = .02$ level.

It should be emphasized that significant differences of the kind shown in table 10 are not of sufficient magnitude to be very useful in helping to characterize the meaning of hypnosis. The advantage in the effort at quantification is avoiding any distortion that might be introduced through an exclusive preoccupation with case material which, while cogent, is necessarily selected to dramatize one or another hypothesis arising from the material.

## Involvement in Music

Music provides the possibility of involvement similar in some respects to visual aesthetic appreciation, but with aspects distinctly its own. It also has the possibility of cultivated appreciation; one can listen for pure enjoyment or listen as a critic. Absorbed involvement in music can be like the pure involvement in nature, an immoderate absorbed aesthetic experience that need not be put into words.

There are, of course, different kinds of music just as there are different kinds of listeners. Although at first we did not attempt to make any sharp distinctions, it soon appeared possible that the relationship to hypnosis was not the same for those involved in listening to classical music and for those involved in listening to jazz. They had in common an intense absorption and obliviousness to the surroundings, and so in our ratings we placed them together, although we now believe that perhaps some of our failure to come up with statistically significant findings may have been due to our failure to make this distinction. It appears from review of some of the case material that hypnotizability is more related to listening to classical music; while the jazz listener may be "sent" by music and absorbed in it, the tendency to respond in a repetitive motor way to the rhythm rather than to the music—to convert the response to body movement—appears less related to hypnosis than the affective response of the classical listener. This is somewhat surprising, and more careful study should be devoted to the distinction. Our evidence is not conclusive, but the case material is suggestive.

Many of those who love classical music are indeed highly hypnotizable, and their own comments establish the relationship that exists for them.

Kathy spontaneously related her experience in hypnosis (as a highly susceptible subject) both to reading poetry and to listening to music. "It's like music, which does the same thing to me." She particularly enjoyed the classical music of the romantics like Chopin. When she is listening to music, she reports, "I'm not thinking. It's mostly a feeling. I'm going along with the music. It's flowing, really." "I went along with the hypnotist's voice in the same way; I went along and followed it." The musical interests were encouraged by her parents; both are musical and they have a good library of records. Her mother plays the piano and both parents sing.

James also related his experiences as a highly hypnotizable

subject to his involvement in music. Music is important to him; he becomes emotionally involved in choral music and religious works of music. "You're part of the whole group. The chorus is one integrated whole of consciousness. It's an aesthetic experience, and religious music is inspired." He gave illustrations of his particular liking for music such as Vivaldi's *Gloria*. He enjoyed the choral interweaving, "as in an Alleluia." His interest in classical music does not forbid an interest in jazz; he described his musical interest as "omnivorous." The childhood origins are conspicuous; he says there has always been music going on somewhere in the house, generally classical music.

In contrast, two other subjects used a very substantial interest in music to meet special needs. One said, "I listen to music often, but it's mostly to fill in a background when things might be empty." Another: "I often get a release from playing the piano when I'm depressed and tired." Neither was hypnotizable.

We have had the good fortune of having a musical expert, a musician and conductor, as one of our research collaborators (John Lenox). He happens also to be highly hypnotizable and readily relates the hypnotic experience to music listening. When listening to a symphony, he points out, one has almost an "induction" experience in the slow, brief, monotonous introduction, in which attention is captured while other processes are inhibited. Examples are Mozart's Thirty-ninth and Forty-first symphonies, about half of Beethoven's symphonies, of which the Ninth would be a prime example, and many of Haydn's works. The listener sits quietly and tends to inhibit voluntary movement. This is in contrast with the violent motor responsiveness of the jazz listener, or the rhythmic responses to martial music. The responsive mood is created, and as the symphony moves on the listener is "transported." The response does not die immediately when the last note is heard but continues during the silence that follows a really good performance. It is as though a partial dissociation has been created which persists for a time. Something along these lines appears to relate listening to classical music to the experience of hypnosis.

The distinction between listening to classical music and responding to jazz has been highlighted for us by a few cases. David, for example, expressed a high musical interest but was not hypnotizable; he scored one on a twelve-point scale.

David's involvement was in rock-and-roll music. "If I'm listening to rock-and-roll while I'm driving, I have the urge to go faster. I may picture myself on a different road. When I listen to rock-and-roll records on the player, the music brings back memories, and this makes me enjoy the music. I don't really hear the music, for the music is keeping me in the past." Music does not mean much to him until he has something to associate to it; music serves as a booster to recollection. "If I hear a song several times and can sing it myself and can tap my foot to it, then I'll drive faster, but my mind remains right where it is, in the car driving. If I go to a party and they play a record and we are dancing, then when I hear it again I'll put myself back at the party." He found no similarity to hypnosis. The voice of the hypnotist was strange, the room was strange; it was all so incongruous that he felt like laughing. While in many ways his responses to music appear compatible with hypnoticlike experiences, in other respects they are like those of Michelle to nature: he is going about his own business, and the music serves his purposes of review of his own experiences. He has not lost himself in the music in the way in which the music lovers who are hypnotizable lose themselves.

A subject who proved unhypnotizable but who became deeply engrossed in Broadway musicals was asked whether he could think of reasons why this particular type of activity was unrelated to hypnosis. He responded, "Hypnosis is quiescence, inactivity. The Broadway musicals are active—I hum, I tap my foot, I dance; there is a consciousness of activity."

Both of the foregoing subjects refer to dancing. Let us digress briefly to a discussion of dancing as a response to music. High involvement in social dancing appears unrelated to hypnosis. A subject who reported that while dancing she was really carried away was asked why this might not be compatible with hypnotizability (she had wished very much to be hypnotized but scored three). She said, "Instead of putting myself into it, I use the dance for myself. I put *it* into myself. I'm not giving myself up to the movement; it's really that dancing gives me a freedom so that I can move well. I'm an exhibitionist and I like to play to the audience and to the people around me. I'm really too conscious of myself all of the time."

In contrast with involvement in social dancing, we came across a few subjects who, highly trained since childhood in ballet, reported losing themselves in this form of the dance. They were highly hypnotizable. Here is an activity where specific movements have been molded by long training and where an individual in essence throws herself into imaginative roles created by another.

Despite the evidence from case studies, we found it difficult to confirm the relationship between music involvement and hypnosis on the basis of our statistical evidence. This arose in part because relatively few of the subjects were in the high-involvement category, so that a significant chi-square was not obtained. But the difficulties in distinguishing between different kinds of musical interest gave a great deal of trouble to the raters. In the 1962–63 sample, musical interests in playing, listening, and singing were lumped together in a single rating, and the result was a chance relationship to hypnotic susceptibility. In the following year, 1963–64, the questioning was more detailed and included the following four questions:

1. In what way has music been important to you?
2. What kind of music appeals to you?
3. Can you illustrate the degree of involvement that you have felt?
4. Number of years interested?

Despite these more penetrating questions, we were not then sensitive to the differences between listening to classical music and listening to jazz, and our ratings of listening involvement turned out to be unsuccessful as predictors of hypnotic susceptibility (table 11). While the overall results do not meet the usual

TABLE 11

*Ratings on Music Listening Involvement as Related to Hypnotic Susceptibility Scores, 1963–64 (N = 80; Males, 61; Females, 19)*

| Involvement | Susceptibility (SHSS-C) | | |
|---|---|---|---|
| | Low (0–5) | High (6–12) | Total |
| High (5–7) | 9 | 15 | 24 |
| Low (1–4) | 30 | 26 | 56 |
| Total | 39 | 41 | 80 |

Significance test: $\chi^2 = 1.82$; $.10 > p > .20$.

standards of statistical significance (chi-square = 1.82, $.10 > p > .20$), they are in the expected direction, with 15/24, or 63 percent, of the high music-involvement subjects classified as highly hypnotizable, and but 26/56, or 46 percent, of the low music-involvement group so classified on the basis of later hypnotic tests. It is apparent that if there is a consistent relationship between musical involvement and hypnosis, as we suspect there is, a more subtle interviewing technique will have to be derived to establish the relationship quantitatively.

### Gratifications through Sensory Experiences as Related to Hypnosis

The relationship between hypnosis and affective arousal through various direct sensory experiences and experiences of music and visual appreciation of nature has already been illustrated by the cases reported, and some of the cautions about interpretation have been pointed out in connection with certain types of cases and limited statistical support. We are now ready to review where we stand.

The basic point is that those who have had these deeply involved experiences, where affect and sensory stimulation have led to enjoyed and savored responsiveness to stimulation, have these experiences stored in such a manner that they are accessible to redintegration in imagination. It has long been known that souvenirs (that is, redintegrating stimuli) are helpful if they include some of the direct experience of odors or textures of the experience to be recalled. Thus a pressed flower may recall a dance of long ago. Pictures, of course, serve as important reminders.

Many of the tasks in the standard repertoire of hypnotic-susceptibility scales call for the revival of sensory experiences—the taste of sweet or sour, the odor of ammonia or gasoline, the feel of a rod which gets hot to the touch. These are the positive hallucinations. The negative ones require the control of sensory processes through their denial in the presence of adequate stimuli. It is our presumption that those who have had rich sensory experiences have something to call upon as the grounds for their positive hallucinations. The inhibition of sensory experience, as in negative hallucinations, requires a somewhat different interpretation, although, as we shall see, there are ways of relating the two.

To the extent that absorption in an activity has resulted in attention to it, some selective inattention must also be involved. It might be argued, therefore, that a subject who is able through imaginative attention to reinstate vivid experiences from the past must be setting aside other stimuli that claim his attention from the real world about him. That is, positive hallucinations imply some inhibition also. It may be, therefore, that those who can manipulate their attention well can produce both positive and negative hallucinations.

The role of childhood experiences in regard to parental prohibitions may be important. Parents assure the child that the medicine is not bitter, using social pressure to get the child to deny what the parents otherwise consider "bad" and to accept what the parents consider "good." Some distortion of sensory experience is doubtless involved.

The primitive nature of direct sensory gratification is recognized by psychoanalysis within the concept of orality. It is not clear that the experiences called *oral* are indeed all continuous with the early gratification through the mouth, but even if used only as a metaphor for primitive sensorimotor satisfactions the concept has relevance. It is not surprising that our language uses the word *taste* to refer to aesthetic sensitivity. We "feast" ourselves upon beauty as well as upon food. The metaphor suggests that there is a primitive quality about aesthetic satisfaction that goes along with the educated sensitivity of the connoisseur. If some regression is implied in hypnosis, as proposed by Gill and Brenman (1959), it is not surprising that those who have kept alive their primitive impulses associated with orality might be among the more hypnotizable.

# 7

# Imagery, Imagination, and Creativity

As we look at the various kinds of involvement found among the hypnotically susceptible, we cannot but be impressed by the capacity of the hypnotizable person to set aside reality and to live in a world of vivid fantasy. In this chapter we examine somewhat more carefully how imagery, imagination, and hypnosis are related by looking at the development of imagery and imagination in the course of individual experience.

During the height of behaviorism, imagery as a report of subjective experience was neglected or even ostracized from psychological research. Fortunately a number of events have aroused interest in imagery and hallucinations over the past two decades. The appearance of hallucinations with sensory deprivation has been studied in the laboratory; practical problems have arisen through perceptual distortions of jet pilots, astronauts, and radar operators; the psychophysiological study of dreams and interest in the relationship of subjective states to EEG alpha rhythms have also contributed. Reviews of such experiences have been given by Hebb (1960) and Holt (1964) indicating a return to respectability for research on imagery and imagination, a respectability in which hypnotic research shares.

Psychologists differentiate a number of kinds of images. These include the afterimages of actually perceived experiences, as when a colored spot is seen with closed eyes after staring at the sun. These afterimages may be of various kinds, positive or negative, or even a flight of colors. They tend to move with the eyes, though they may trail along behind the eye movement as the eyes move from one fixation spot to another. While such afterimages have considerable interest, they are not of very great importance for our topic. Then there are the memory images. After looking at a picture, for example, you can remember what the picture looked like if you turn away from it; if you have good visual imagery you can actually "see" the picture, though you are able to distinguish between the memory image and the picture actually perceived. The memory image, unlike the afterimage, does not move when the eye is moved or the head is turned; what is imaged has "thinglike" quality and preserves its proper orientation in space; it is not a quality dependent upon the adjustment of the sense organs in relation to it. Intermediate between the afterimage and the memory image is the eidetic image, an image which has essentially perceptual quality. That is, a person with good eidetic imagery may look at a page of text, then close the book but "read" the passage from his vivid image. We now move into two kinds of images of imagination. One is like the memory image in all respects except that it is productive rather than reproductive; you can imagine Caesar riding a motorcycle, or an elephant piloting a helicopter. You picture these happenings in "your mind's eye," but to do so you have to combine materials from your memory in novel ways. Another kind of image of imagination is the hallucination, which is perhaps of the order of the eidetic image except that the hallucinating person typically does not distinguish it from perceived external reality. Hallucinations can readily be produced under hypnosis, so that here we have imagination exercised so strongly that the imagined object temporarily is confused with reality. Hypnotic hallucinations may be either positive or negative. A positive hallucination is something present in the absence of the stimulation which should produce it perceptually, while a negative hallucination is something not perceived even when the stimulation appropriate to its perception is present.

The capacity for hallucinatory experience is normal, in that hallucinatory experiences are usual in dreams. Eidetic images have been said to be more common in early childhood and to fade (at least for some people) in adolescence. It is relevant for us to find out, then, about the normal imagery experiences of those whom we have tried to hypnotize—their natural hallucinations in dreams and what spontaneous exercise of imagination they show outside hypnosis. It is plausible to conjecture that those who have vivid imagery experiences outside hypnosis might be better prepared to meet the demands of the hypnotic situation. It is possible, however, that those who have lost an earlier capacity for imagery might recover it within hypnosis. Hence, we have here an interesting topic to follow up with regard to the developmental aspects of hypnosis and with regard to the role of hypnosis in the utilization of existing abilities.

### Evidence Available on Imagery and Imagination

I shall not attempt to recapitulate the incidental reports of images associated with or aroused by reading, watching plays, and listening to music, for these have been discussed in relation to these various involvements. In reading, for example, we learned how subjects developed images that accompanied an author's descriptions, and that these images were often so strong and specific that they interfered with subsequent enjoyment of a screen version of the same story. Similarly, the recall of a play or movie commonly went on through visual imagery. Thus we are alerted to the topic of imagery by these incidental reports.

We made a special attempt to get at the early influences upon imagery through interviews having to do with stories that children heard early in life, whether these stories were told to them or read to them from books. Some of this material will be described presently.

Additional evidence on imagery is provided by efforts to assess imagery through a questionnaire which was a shortened version of the Betts Scale (1909). The quantitative results of this scale were followed up by interviews which gave us additional qualitative information.

With these sources of data we are prepared to be somewhat more analytical than we might otherwise be with regard to the role of imagery and imagination in hypnosis.

### Later Retention of Imagery Aroused by Stories Listened to in Childhood

It has been our supposition that some kinds of affiliative events early in childhood may have to do with hypnotizability later; this is part of our developmental-interactive theory. Some of our earliest interviews led us to search into childhood story listening as a possible background. Two cases will serve to show the plausibility of this idea.

Jane was unusual in that she came from an American Indian family. Students with her background are very rare at Stanford. Her grandfather was a shaman of the tribe and knew its folklore well; her grandmother and her own father also told her the stories of her tribe. The stories are transmitted generation after generation, and Jane's eyes shone as she recounted some of them. Here is one of the tales she had heard so often.

A man was on the peak of a high rock, so precariously perched that he could not move at all without risking a fall. A bird flying overhead saw his plight, and after they talked it over together the bird went to fetch aid. The bird, finding a squirrel, enlisted its help. The squirrel buried a nut near the base of the rock that held the man prisoner. A tree began to grow from the nut, and the squirrel, by running up and down the tree, encouraged it to grow faster, so that it soon reached the man, who escaped his rock by climbing down the tree. The squirrel, perceiving that the man would still need help, gave him a bow and arrow, assuring him that if ever he found himself in serious trouble and shot the arrow, his troubles would be ended. The man then went home to his wife, who was a witch. She wanted to wash his hair for him in the creek, they went there together, and he permitted her to begin. The man came to realize, however, that as she washed she began casting a spell over him. He quickly shot the arrow into the air; it arched through the air, curved groundward, hit and killed the witch, and freed him from the spell.

Jane recounted, "I can see myself standing there by the river while the witch was washing his hair. I can feel a breeze, because it is late in the day. Then I feel it's cold because it's twilight." She felt the atmosphere at the time, she said, because her storytellers felt the story so deeply themselves that they created the setting for her as a child to feel as they did. Yes, she could hear their voices even now.

Jane proved to be highly hypnotizable, and it was thought at the time that perhaps her ability to have visual and auditory hallucinations under hypnosis might be related to the persistence in imagery of these highly imaginative stories listened to and experienced with full imagery in her earliest years.

Another case was provided by Colleen. Colleen had quite a different cultural background, but she was told how her great-grandmother in Ireland had actually seen a leprechaun: the teller was her grandmother, who told her many other Irish tales. Colleen recalls climbing into her grandmother's lap to hear these oft-repeated tales; she was a frequent visitor at her grandmother's. At the age of six or seven she remembers arguing with girls at school when they didn't believe that her great-grandmother had actually seen a leprechaun. Her grandmother believed the story to be literally true, and so did Colleen. The leprechauns were kind.

When a little girl in Ireland had no good shoes to wear to communion, she remained crying in the woods. A leprechaun heard her. That night he stole her shoes, and her situation was more desperate than ever. Of course the leprechaun later returned the shoes, repaired and shined and appropriate for church. This particular leprechaun had been a cobbler. Colleen loved these stories; when in the third grade she belonged to a storytelling club which she helped to form, and her contribution was to tell these stories to her friends.

Her father was also a storyteller. His favorite tale was a continued one, in which twin whales were the chief characters. He would tell of their adventures, ending each episode at an exciting point that made it hard to wait for the next installment. She remembered these stories while she was in the third, fourth, and fifth grades.

The imagery that gave reality to these early stories has continued. While listening to the stories, Colleen says she pictured everything going on. "Now I *see* everything I read." She can recall vividly scenes from books she read in middle childhood—*The Wizard of Oz,* the *Nancy Drew* books. "I can close my eyes now and see the pictures in color. . . . It's like a movie camera in your mind showing a film for you."

These two cases—both Jane and Colleen—show the stirring-up of imagery in early storytelling, and its preservation, partly through reviewing the same stories, partly through continuing the same kinds of experiences in reading.

Because of reported experiences of this kind, we made an effort to explore more systematically the relationship between early storytelling and later hypnotizability. In one sample of forty-five student subjects we explored the matter in some depth. The results were not statistically convincing, although provocative. We found, for example, ten subjects who had had considerable storytelling in childhood and felt that strong imagery had accompanied these stories. Six of the ten were highly hypnotizable, but four of them not at all. Three subjects who strongly retained the imagery were, like Jane and Colleen, all highly hypnotizable; the nonhypnotizable ones were among the seven who had lost much of their childhood imagery. It would be interesting to know under what circumstances lost childhood imagery can be recovered under hypnosis, and under what circumstances it is not recoverable. Unfortunately, our results do not provide any persuasive evidence.

Because of the difficulty of obtaining sufficient information in the midst of an interview covering a wide range of topics, we abandoned the further study of childhood story listening, but we came away with the feeling that we might be close to something important.

Where we found strong present imagery and high hypnotizability associated with stories heard in early childhood, some common features were usually present. The storyteller had been deeply involved in the tale being told, the tales were often repeated, and the child who listened was completely absorbed: he believed and lived the story. The storyteller subtly communicated his own conviction and spoke with feeling. Usually the stories were about exciting experiences from the childhood of an earlier generation, put into narrative form, or, if they were obviously imaginative stories, they carried an aura of belief.

Elsa, for example, recalled that her grandfather, who was familiar with the customs of different Indian tribes because he had spent much time in Indian communities, used to tell her stories about two Indian children in New Mexico. The stories concerned Juan and Juanita, who rode stolen ponies. The children had lost their mother and father and were going from tribe to tribe to find someone to adopt them and give them a home. These were continued stories, and Elsa heard them every night for years. She lived in the grandparents' home until she was five and lived only a few doors away after that, so that she continued to hear her grandfather's stories at least through the second grade. She sat in his lap and "saw" the scenes he described so vividly. "I can picture the scenes now in great detail—the colors, the clothing worn by Juan and Juanita, the designs on the tepee. I can put them in front of my eyes as though a slide projector is projecting them on the wall." She could not hear her grandfather's voice: "I don't think of the dialogue. I think of the people. I relive what they did. It's deeper than on a storytelling level."

Visual imagery, as in the case of Elsa was most often reported. While there were references to other sensory experiences entering into the imaginative picture, they were much more rare, though odor, temperature, and touch experiences occurred along with experiences of sights and sounds. One subject recalled stories about her grandmother's childhood in pioneer country. "There were coyotes in the tall grass. I could picture them as she talked about them and could feel their hot breath on my neck."

The lack of auditory images may be explained in part by the presence of *actual* sounds (the teller's voice), which meant that imagination did not have to be exercised in that respect, or perhaps by the inhibiting effect of silent reading later on. As one subject put it, "When you remember things you read yourself, you never remember them with a voice."

While we decided to discontinue the detailed interviewing on early story listening, we still felt that some study of persisting imagery would be fruitful. We turn now to the results of these later efforts to relate imagery to hypnosis.

## Sense Images and Hypnosis

By the term *sense images* we refer to the memory images of sensory or perceptual experiences. The classical study was by Galton (1883), who inquired, among other things, about the vividness and clarity with which a person could picture the scene at his breakfast table when he was questioned later in the day. Although Binet and Féré (1887) had proposed that vividness of imagery might be the basis of hypnotic hallucination, and Klüver (1933) suggested that eidetic imagery might be related to subjective visual phenomena produced by hypnotic methods, satisfactory investigations have been few. McBain (1954) found little relationship between imagination and postural sway, or between test scores on imagery and hypnotizability.

The most thorough recent study has been that of Sutcliffe (1965). Using a test of imagery based on earlier work of Betts (1909), he correlated scores on the imagery test with those on two hypnotic susceptibility scales, one the Stanford Scale (form A), and the other a scale he developed in Sydney, Australia. The imagery scale as he used it consisted of thirty-five items, five each for seven sensory modalities: vision, audition, cutaneous sensitivity, kinesthesis, gustation, olfaction, and organic sensitivity. (The Sydney modification of the Betts questionnaire appears in the Appendix.) Each item consisted of a statement of the following kind: "Rate the vividness of your image of the sun as it is sinking below the horizon." Then there was a uniform seven-point rating scale, with number one high ("Perfectly clear and vivid as the actual experience") and seven low ("No image present at all; just knowing you are thinking of the object"). It is possible to obtain a score for each sensory modality by summing the ratings for the five items within each modality, or for imagery in general by summing all the ratings. When these ratings were correlated with scores on hypnotic susceptibility, a moderate, but significant correlation was found for a sample of ninety-five college students at the University of Sydney. The correlation turned out to be significant for the male sample ($N = 53$) taken separately, but not for the female sample taken separately ($N = 42$), although both correlations were in the same direction. We repeated the same procedure with Stanford students añd found a corresponding correlation for the sample as a whole, but with the sexes reversed: the correlation was significant for our female subjects, but marginal for our male subjects. The Sydney and Stanford results are presented in table 12 for compari-

TABLE 12

Correlation between Hypnotic Susceptibility and Total
Imagery on the Sydney Modification of the Betts
Mental Imagery Questionnaire
(University of Sydney and Stanford University)

| Betts Imagery Scale | Correlation with SHSS | | |
|---|---|---|---|
| | Males | Females | Total |
| University of Sydney | .58‡ (N = 53) | .20* (N = 42) | .39‡ (N = 95) |
| Stanford University | .17* (N = 65) | .32† (N = 55) | .26‡ (N = 120) |

Sources: For University of Sydney: Data from Sutcliffe (1965). The hypnotic scores were from Stanfard Hypnotic Susceptibility Scales, form A. For Stanford University: Unpublished data from the Stanford Laboratory of Hypnosis Research. The hypnotic scores were from the Stanford Hypnotic Susceptibility Scales, form C.
* Not significant.    † $p < .05$.    ‡ $p < .01$.

son. The most appropriate interpretation is that there is a confirmed small relationship between imagery reported on the Betts type of scale and scores on hypnotic susceptibility scales.

The general replication of the finding in the two laboratories that imagery and hypnotizability are related is a source of satisfaction. There are also some additional confirmatory details. In both laboratories it was found that the scatterplot was not symmetrical but that there was a nearly vacant corner in the plot which would have represented those cases low in imagery and high in hypnosis. Thus in the prediction from imagery to hypnosis there was this limitation, found both at Sydney and at Stanford: those high in imagery might be either hypnotizable or not, but those very low in imagery were predictably nonhypnotizable. With correlations of such modest size predictability cannot be high; the general picture is shown in table 13, from the Stanford data. The table can be read to show that of those high in imagery 23/45, or 51 percent, are

TABLE 13

*Hypnotizability as Predicted from Scores on the Sydney
Modification of the Betts Imagery Questionnaire*

| Imagery on Betts Scale | Low-to-Moderate Susceptibility (0–7, SHSS-C) | Moderate-to-High Susceptibility (8–12, SHSS-C) | Total |
|---|---|---|---|
| High (Mean per scale, below 4.5) | 22 | 23 | 45 |
| Low (Mean per scale, 4.5 and above) | 54 | 21 | 75 |
| Total | 76 | 44 | 120 |

Note: These data represent the scores yielding an overall correlation of .26 between imagery and hypnosis. See table 12. The Betts scales run from 1 for high imagery to 7 for low imagery. The signs of computed correlations have been reversed in table 12 in order to indicate the positive relationship between imagery and hypnosis.

high in hypnosis, while of those low in imagery only 21/76, or 28 percent, are high. The largest number of cases falls in the cell representing low imagery and low hypnotic susceptibility. If extremely low imagery cases are selected, the picture is even more convincing. For example, of the five subjects lowest in reported imagery *all* are low in hypnotic susceptibility, the highest giving a score of five out of twelve possible on form C. If reported *visual* imagery alone is taken as the basis for looking at the extreme cases, of the twenty-five subjects lowest in visual imagery only two show up among those classified as highly hypnotizable. Of the fifty subjects highest in visual imagery, however, there are but eighteen in the high-hypnosis category, just about the same proportion as in the sample as a whole.

In the comparisons shown in table 14, eight hypnotic items were selected from the total of twelve that were possible. Two of the twelve (hand lowering and hands apart) were too easy to be at all discriminating, and two others (hallucinated voice and negative hallucination of one out of three boxes) were too difficult to be discriminating. The remaining eight were divided into two groups, one requiring the production of an experience through imagination or recall, while the other group required the inhibition

TABLE 14

Reported Imagery as Related to Items of the Hypnotic
Susceptibility Scale, 1966, 1967

(10 highest and 10 Lowest Imagery Reports among
45 Female Subjects)

| | Number of Passing Scores | |
|---|---|---|
| Hypnotic Susceptibility Scale | 10 Highest in Imagery | 10 Lowest in Imagery |
| Production of experience | | |
| 1. Taste hallucination | 7 | 1 |
| 2. Dream | 8 | 1 |
| 3. Age regression | 8 | 0 |
| 4. Mosquito hallucination | 9 | 2 |
| Mean | 8.0 | 1.0 |
| Inhibition of experience or movement | | |
| 1. Arm rigidity | 7 | 3 |
| 2. Arm immobilization | 5 | 4 |
| 3. Anosmia | 3 | 2 |
| 4. Amnesia | 4 | 1 |
| Mean | 4.8 | 2.5 |

of a voluntary motor act, a sensory experience, or memory. The
results are of interest in showing a greater contrast between the
imagery and nonimagery subjects on the productive items. The
highest imagery group found the productive items somewhat easier than the inhibition items (mean of 8.0 out of ten compared
with 4.8 out of ten). The lowest imagery group found passing the
productive items extremely difficult (mean of one out of ten
passing each of these), while the inhibition items were somewhat
easier even for these rather unsusceptible subjects (mean of 2.5
out of ten). Evidently part of the relationship between imagery
and hypnosis rests upon the ability of the person with high imagery
to produce the kinds of cognitive experiences called for within
hypnosis.

The correlations, while reproducible and reaching significance,
are not high, and this deserves some comment. A self-report of
imagery on a scale such as that which Betts devised is not entirely
satisfactory, particularly for the diagnosis of imagery types. We

found in follow-up interviews that many of the reported images assigned to other modalities were carried visually. Thus perceiving the tiredness in your legs as you imagine yourself running up the stairs need not be kinesthetic at all but may be an inference from the visual picture of the effort being expended. It was not surprising, therefore, that the results for visual imagery alone were essentially similar to the results for the whole questionnaire, the differences in significance of the correlations (favoring the test as a whole) being attributable largely to the shortness of the visual scale taken alone (five items only, compared with thirty-five for the scale as a whole).

Two cases may serve to illustrate some of the problems in relating imagery to hypnosis. One of these, Doris, reports high imagery and is highly susceptible; the other, Lucy, reports little imagery but is also susceptible.

When questioned about imagery, Doris told the interviewer; "I have a vivid imagination. I can imagine and visualize." She is a mathematics major and visualizes some of her problems in three dimensions.

Doris's visual imagery when reading is exceptionally high. "I feel as though the characters are real people—I live the story, not as one of them, but as an onlooker present with them, watching what is going on."

Her replies to questions about auditory imagery showed some of the difficulty in diagnosing types of imagery. On the Betts questionnaire she had rated the vividness of imagery associated with the sound of escaping steam and the sound of clapping hands as at the highest level on the scale. Still, she couldn't decide how real the sounds were to her: "They are neither out there nor inside my head: sort of on the border. It's the same feeling you have when you have something on the tip of your tongue, when you know it's there but can't always bring it forth." She did not stress the visual intermediary but felt a certain vagueness about a centrally aroused sound as different from one generated by sound waves from outside. In her case, the auditory imagery seemed to be genuine, and supplementary to the visual imagery.

Lucy represents high hypnotizability on the part of one deficient in imagery. She marked her visual, auditory, tactual, gustatory, and olfactory imagery at the lowest level, acknowledging only some kinesthetic and organic imagery.

While she failed the visual hallucination in hypnosis, thus conforming to her deficient imagery, she passed the regression and dream items, which presumably use some imagery. Of these she said, "In regression I *felt* I was there, but I didn't see myself and the scene wasn't clear. It was hazy, as though it was something you couldn't remember very well. . . . In the dream I saw a big train with a locomotive pulling a lot of people. The people at the station waved goodbye. Then the dream switched to a swamp with cattails and rushes; wild ducks rose up and flew away." While the regression was coherent also with the weakness of visual imagery, the dream seemed to be clearly visual and had in it the imaginary shifts often associated with the dreams of the highly hypnotizable.

Lucy is very nearsighted, a condition which began when she was three or four. She remembers that at that time everything became fuzzy, and this fuzzy vision lasted until she was seven years old, when it was corrected by glasses. It is of interest that some of the imagery in regression, as well as in some in the dream, was described by her as "fuzzy." It may be that this early interference with vision influenced the subsequent development of visual imagery.

More remains to be done in comparing strengths and weakness of imagery at different ages to the kinds of imagery reported within hypnosis. What we have thus far found out is enough to establish a relationship, but only the surface has been scratched.

### Imagination, Creativity, and Hypnosis

In the full use of imagination something novel and unfamiliar emerges; although there are of course residues from the past in the materials out of which the new is fabricated, to review imagination only in terms of its sensory content would be to deny much of its interest. We may make a preliminary distinction between stimulus-incited (or situation-incited) imagination, and impulse-incited imagination. The former arises out of the demands of a puzzling situation that needs to be cleared up, of a problem to be solved. It may actually be quite ordinary and matter-of-fact and yet call for imagination: "What color will be appropriate for the new drapes in my office?" The impulse-incited imagination arises from internal needs rather than external ones and is self-referred: "What can I do to win distinction? to be a unique and worthy person?" This second source of imagination may be expressive of unconscious tendencies to a greater degree than is the case in stimulus-incited imagination, although the work of fantasy is probably never free of unconscious influences.

*Daydreaming.* Some fantasy is more self-centered than other types, so that, within fantasy behavior, we may make the distinction between stimulus-incited imagination and impulse-incited daydreams as the two ends of a continuum. We asked questions about fantasy of 289 of our subjects, and the interviewers then classified their answers as indicating primarily impulse-aroused daydreams, or stimulus-incited imagination arising out of external circumstances. When those high in daydreams in childhood were compared with those low, there were no significant differences found in hypnotic susceptibility scores (table 15); by contrast,

TABLE 15

*Daydreaming in Childhood as Related to Hypnotic Susceptibility, 1962–63, 1963–64*

*(N = 183; Males, 113; Females, 70)*

| Daydreaming | Susceptibility (SHSS-C) | | Total |
| --- | --- | --- | --- |
| | Low (0–5) | High (6–12) | |
| High (5–7) | 26 | 25 | 51 |
| Low (1–4) | 66 | 66 | 132 |
| Total | 92 | 91 | 183* |

Significance test: $\chi^2$ = .01; $p$ not significant.
*Four cases not ascertained.

those high in imagination whose fantasies were stirred up by external events proved to be more hypnotizable than those who lacked such kinds of imaginative experiences in childhood (table 16).

TABLE 16

*Imagination in Childhood as Related to Hypnotic Susceptibility, 1962–63, 1963–64*

*(N = 183; Males, 113; Females, 70)*

| Imagination | Susceptibility (SHSS-C) | | Total |
| --- | --- | --- | --- |
| | Low (0–5) | High (6–12) | |
| High (5–7) | 21 | 37 | 58 |
| Low (1–4) | 71 | 54 | 125 |
| Total | 92 | 91 | 183* |

Significance test: $\chi^2$ = 6.72; $p$ = .01.
*Four cases not ascertained.

The relationship to hypnosis may be similar. In hypnosis it is an outside source (the hypnotist) that sets the stage and invites the fantasy or imagination; the subject does not go woolgathering on his own. The background of such fantasy in ordinary experience then is capitalized upon by the subject as he reacts sensitively and appropriately to the directions given by the hypnotist.

*Creativity.* Imagination that serves novelty in inventive or pleasing ways is often called *creative;* while all imagination is creative, that which is usually called creative is the kind that produces products that are valued, as in art, literature, or music. It was of interest to know whether activities commonly defined as creative were related to hypnotic susceptibility. In reply to the single question, "Have you had a serious interest in creative activities such as painting, writing, designing, and the like?" we found positive answers associated with hypnotizability in the 186 cases for whom answers are available (table 17).

TABLE 17

*Present-day Creativity as related to Hypnotic Susceptibility, 1962–63, 1963–64 (N = 186; Males, 114; Females, 72)*

| Creativity | Susceptibility (SHSS-C) | | |
|---|---|---|---|
| | Low (0–5) | High (6–12) | Total |
| High (5–7) | 13 | 24 | 37 |
| Low (1–4) | 82 | 67 | 149 |
| Total | 95 | 91 | 186* |

Significance test: $\chi^2 = 4.70; p < .05$.
*One case not ascertained.

The low relationships found between hypnotic susceptibility and other variables (in this case, interest in creative activities) may not follow merely from the inadequacies of our measures but may represent some fundamental truths, in the sense that within valued activities there may be aspects favoring and aspects hindering hypnotic susceptibility. Thus creativity involves both external ties and autistic ones, the former probably favoring hypnosis, the latter probably not. A musical composer is usually familiar with, and influenced by, the music that he has studied and heard; in that sense, he is stimulus-influenced. A poet, too, if he is to write in meter, has serious reality constraints upon him, and yet he may be a fully imaginative poet. But there is also the other side: the truly creative musician or poet gives expression to feelings deep within himself as he practices his art. Whether the stimulus aspect or the autistic aspect will dominate may not have a single answer; perhaps some creative persons will favor one and some the other, and these differences may be reflected in differences in hypnotizability.

Certain possibilities are revealed by two creative writers who were studied by us.

The first writer scored two on our hypnosis scale and in the interview showed few involvements of the kind we have come to associate with hypnosis; even his reading interests were lacking prior to his becoming interested in writing after he reached college. In college he began to write stories about people who lived in small towns that were like the small towns in which he grew up. He described different aspects of their lives: their frustrations, their worries, and the ways they tried to solve their problems. In these accounts he was clearly describing his own internal conflicts, and one might say that his stories were stimulated by separation from family and the hometown. His urge to write began relatively late in comparison with that of the next subject.

The second case is that of a woman, above average in hypnotizability, with a somewhat uneven profile of items passed but including the hallucinatory items, the dream, and amnesia. She described hypnosis as "concentration on a single thing which is like the writing process where things can happen that you are not aware of." She also compared it with a light nap in which a person is both asleep and yet able to hear something.

Her creative writing had a long history. She started to keep a diary when she was in the third grade. Her imagination was far too vivid for her to set everything down in the diary, however, for her father might find the manuscript, be shocked, destroy it, and punish her. In grades seven to nine she wrote many stories about prisoners who escaped, and some about foreign legions. As a senior in college she edited the college newspaper. Now she is writing a book based on her own experiences. It is not autobiographical but is responsive to the ideas and feelings she has had in relation to the lives of those around her.

The contrast between her and the preceding subject is that her lifelong involvements, particularly in imagination and reading, were of the kind that would cause us to expect hypnotic susceptibility, which she in fact showed.

Both came to us from an advanced project in creative writing, where their creativity was vouched for by those working in the field, so that we did not have to pass this judgment ourselves. That they should have differed so much in their experiences both outside of hypnosis and within hypnosis shows the caution that is needed in making direct assertions about hypnosis and creativity.

In summary, the distinction between stimulus-incited and autistic, or impulse-incited, imagination appears to be an important one in relation to hypnotic susceptibility, with such evidence as we have pointing to greater hypnotizability on the part of those capable of stimulus incitation. This, if confirmed, is understandable, in view of the nature of the hypnotic process. When the hypnotist tells the subject he has a rabbit in his lap, he expects him to find a rabbit there and not to satisfy his own needs by finding (perhaps) a duckling there. These distinctions are not sharp, however. A creative person, such as a writer or painter or composer, may give expression to impulse through his creative productions while at the same time remaining skilled in using the conventions of his medium as a means of communicating with others. The subtle balance of these processes is such that we find some creative persons hypnotizable, others not.

## Summary and Conclusions on Imagery, Imagination, and Hypnosis

Our study of imagery and imagination has raised more questions than it has answered. The two quantitative results that lend encouragement are (1) the finding, confirming Sutcliffe, that self-reports of imagery correlate significantly with hypnotic susceptibility, and (2) significant relationship between imagination instigated by stimuli outside the person and hypnotic susceptibility, contrasted with a lack of relationship of autistic, or inner-stimulated, imagination to hypnotic susceptibility. The first finding led to an additional observation that the correlation was determined largely by those extremely lacking in imagery, who generally turned out to be nonhypnotizable; those high in imagery were not much more hypnotizable than the general population tested.

These results are of interest in a context that may go beyond the prediction of hypnotic susceptibility. They raise questions about the history of imagery and imagination in the life of the individual, the factors that encourage and discourage imagery as development proceeds, and the relationships between kinds of imagery and creativity. While we found a slight relationship between creative interests and hypnotizability, we failed to find any relationship between high levels of demonstrated creative writing and hypnosis. Creative interests, in themselves, do not indicate that combination of imagination and craftsmanship that leads to works valued by critics, and it is quite possible that some fraction of this combination may be antithetical to hypnotizability. This leaves the matter open; a successful creative artist may or may not be hypnotizable. It would be of interest to know why, although we can only speculate without furnishing conclusive evidence. The mixture we are speaking of appears to be that of outer-instigated and inner-instigated imagination. We are unable to extricate these two in the successful creative artist to permit more resolution of the different degrees of hypnotizability found.

The psychology of imagery and imagination has been so much neglected that we do not find much outside help for our hypnotic investigations. The belief that eidetic images show a developmental trend among school children is not supported by recent evidence (Haber 1969), and the relationship between vividness of night dreams and imagery capacities has not been established. With so many unknowns, it is not surprising that our investigations, fitted in the midst of many other inquiries, leave much to be done.

# 8

## Imaginary Companions
## in Childhood

Although a chapter has already been devoted to imagery and imagination, there is one set of imaginative products so interesting that this chapter is devoted to their discussion. These are the imaginary companions so often reported in childhood but little studied within psychological science.

Almost every adult can recall knowing a child who was at some time or other accompanied by a colorful friend of imaginary origin. Children are more likely to share these childish incarnations with adults than with other children, for it is commonly the absence of other children that creates the need for the imaginary one, although, as we shall see, loneliness in childhood is not the only occasion for the imaginary companion.

Our formulations about imaginary companions are based on data the students of our study gave us. Because childhood memories are notoriously feeble, some of the material came from recollections of parents as reported by the students. Our data vary from vivid memories to these second-hand accounts; imprecise as they are, they offer some interesting leads about the phenomena themselves and about their relationship to the experience of hypnosis.

Of 391 cases asked about imaginary companions in interviews between 1960 and 1964, there were 66 who reported imaginary companions; of these, 40 were girls and 26 boys. The total of 66 represents 17 percent of the sample; thus about 1 out of 6 reported having had an imaginary companion at one time or another. The report of an imaginary companion is not in itself diagnostic of hypnotic ability; the mean hypnotic-susceptibility scores of those reporting imaginary companions did not differ from those not reporting them. But as with other aspects studied, once the data are examined in greater detail some relationships emerge.

### The Nature of Reported Imaginary Companions

While one usually thinks of an imaginary companion as a kind of alter ego, hence another child of about the same age, this is by no means the universal picture. Most imaginary companions are indeed persons, but some are animals; in other cases the imagined object is impersonal but is treated animistically—for example, the telephone itself starts up a conversation. Occasionally the role is provided by a story which the child tells himself, without any real embodiment at all. There is some question about including these cases, but they were spontaneously mentioned by the subjects in discussing imaginary accompaniments in childhood. A few subjects were sure that they had had imaginary companions but could provide no descriptive data at all. The types of companion reported bore some slight relationship to hypnotic susceptibility, as shown in table 18. At least those who could not come up with descriptive

TABLE 18

*Type of Imaginary Companion in Relationship to Hypnotic Susceptibility*

| Type | Number of Cases | Mean Score (SHSS-C) |
|---|---|---|
| Person or persons | 36 | 6.3 |
| Animals | 7 | 7.6 |
| Animistic use of object | 4 | 5.5 |
| Story-produced, without embodiment | 4 | 4.5 |
| Total with descriptive data | 51 | 6.2 |
| Unable to provide descriptive data | 15 | 4.5 |
| Total reported imaginary companions | 66 | 5.8 |

Note: Significance test between mean scores of those with and without descriptive data: $\chi^2 = 4.67$; $p < .05$.

data scored below those who could, a finding coherent with the importance of a preserved imagery for hypnotic susceptibility as described in the preceding chapter. Roughly two-thirds of those who were able to give descriptive information about their claimed imaginary companions (thirty-three out of fifty-one) scored above six on SHSS-C, while only one-third of those with vague information scored this high (five out of fifteen). This difference is statistically significant (chi-square, 4.67; $p < .05$).

Because there will be little more to say about those who mentioned that they had had imaginary companions but could give no definite information, it is worth mentioning our exploratory attempt to account for their lower hypnotic susceptibility scores. The most plausible hypothesis appears to be that they are somewhat lacking in a rich imagination (despite the acknowledgment of a forgotten imaginary companion). Thus out of the fifteen cases reported in the "no descriptive data" category, the three who scored high in hypnotic susceptibility (seven, eight, and twelve on form C) all were rated as high in imagination as any in the group. There were, however, some others rated equally high in imagination who did not prove hypnotizable, so that something else may well be involved.

In the remainder of the discussion, the analyses will be confined to the fifty-one subjects of table 18, for whom there was not only an imaginary companion but some descriptive data by which to characterize it (or them, if more than one). It was very common, in fact, for there to be more than one imaginary companion. Among the fifty-one cases, there were twenty, or about two-fifths, who had multiple imaginary companions. In nearly all cases they remained of a common type, that is, more than one person, more than one animal, more than one object used animistically.

The use of an age-mate as an imaginary companion is familiar, but the other categories listed in table 18 are somewhat less familiar, and it may be worthwhile to mention some of the kinds of imaginary companions reported. Among animals, dogs predominated, for they somehow have come to symbolize the faithful companion. But there were spiders, teddy bears, a rat, and even bears and lions. The animistic use of objects in dramatic play was unexpected. One boy reported, "The sprinklers in the yard were characters to me, and I talked to them. The ones with high jets of water were adults; low jets were children." A girl reported, "I used to make up stories and use flower petals for people: like a fuchsia and a rose. I can visualize them now."

A still more confusing category is that of stories made up, without any imaginary companion present, but reported by the subject as relevant. One girl said: "I imagined fanciful playmates. I made up stories of my own and acted them out. I don't recall any now, but Mother reminds me that I'd sit there and talk with them and they were real to me." A boy thought his experience related to having an imaginary companion: "I could create situations that would require a group of people, when nobody else was around. I'd do something and it seemed as if I had a whole bunch of people with me. Sometimes there were people competing against me, a whole team, guys in green and white uniforms. I can still see these pictures, see the uniforms, and sometimes the faces." It was as though he was conducting an elaborate puppet show without puppets.

The phenomenon of an imaginary companion is associated with the preschool years. For the thirty-four subjects who were able to give reasonable approximations of when their imaginary companions began and how long the companions survived, a summary record is given in figure 1. While the beginnings may be shortly after the age of two, most of the companions make their appearance at ages three, four, or five, so that of the thirty-four subjects, twenty-two had their companions with them at age five. They appear to fall off rather rapidly as the school ages are reached, although a few persist into adolescence, and one persisted into the college years. The companion, although arriving early, may remain for a shorter or longer time: for twenty-four of the thirty-three subjects who reported duration, the imaginary companion persisted for only a year or two; for eight it persisted for three to five years; and for the remaining four cases, for eight to seventeen years. These events are happening early in life; hence, if related to later hypnotic susceptibility, they bear upon a developmental interpretation of hypnosis.

### Functions Served by Imaginary Companions in Relation to Hypnotic Susceptibility

It was possible to determine from the interview data the primary functions that the imaginary companions served in most cases. Our later case studies will illustrate the functions in greater detail, but the types may be characterized briefly. The first is a conscience or superego role—like Jiminy Cricket in the Walt Disney version of *Pinocchio*. This alter ego criticizes (or sometimes dares), but it is concerned with issues of right and wrong, of propriety and impropriety. The conscience-related imaginary companion appears to represent a transitional phase of superego development. It is interesting that the subjects reporting this use of imaginary companions score highest in hypnotic susceptibility (table 19). The largest number of imaginary companions are playmates, with whom the subjects interact. The subjects of this group score only slightly above

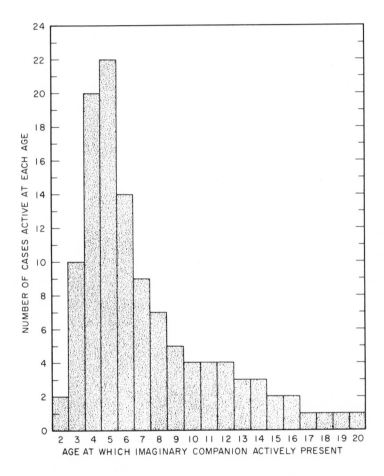

FIGURE 1.   Age at which imaginary companion reported ($N = 34$)

TABLE 19

*Functions Served by Imaginary Companions*

| Function | Persons | Ani-<br>mals | Animistic<br>Objects | Story-<br>Produced | Total | Mean Score<br>(SHSS-C) |
|---|---|---|---|---|---|---|
| Superego-related | 5 | 2 | | | 7 | 8.0 |
| Companionship<br>Playmates | 23 | 5 | 4 | 4 | 36 | 6.5 |
| Companionship<br>Nonplaymates | | | | | | |
|   1. Childhood<br>    sexual object<br>    (husband, boy<br>    friend) | 3 | | | | 3 | |
|   2. Imaginary com-<br>    panion as<br>    audience only | 3 | | | | 3 | 3.5 |
|   3. Companion<br>    shared with<br>    adult | 2 | | | | 2 | |
| Total | 36 | 7 | 4 | 4 | 51 | 6.2 |
| Insufficient recall | | | | | 15 | 4.5 |
| | | | | | 66 | 5.8 |

Note: Significance test between mean hypnotic scores (Kolmogorov-Smirnov test):
    Superego vs. playmates, not significant.
    Superego vs. nonplaymates, $p < .02$.
    Playmates vs. nonplaymates, $p < .01$.

the mean of standardization scores on SHSS-C. There are other companionship roles, however, in which the imaginary companion is not a playmate of the same age with whom the subject plays; instead he is a special object of affection ("husband" or "boy friend"), or serves merely as an audience watching the activities of the subject, or is shared in some sort of continuing "game" with an adult. The eight subjects whose imaginary playmates served these less usual roles proved to be low in hypnotizability. While the numbers are small for convincing statistical tests, the mean differences are not the result of a few extreme cases. Using the Kolmogorov-Smirnov nonparametric test (see Siegel 1956, p. 47), we find the difference between the superego-related and companionship playmates insignificant, but the nonplaymate group scores significantly below both of these.

Another way in which the functions of the imaginary companion can be classified is according to whether the role is a pleasant or an unpleasant one. A pleasant role is one in which the subject is buoyed up and has fun with his playmates; an unpleasant role is one in which the subject appears to be dissatisfied with the companion. Then, of course, there are ambivalent roles—now a pleasant affective contribution, now an unpleasant one. That the roles are predominantly pleasant is not surprising, as shown in table 20, in view of the gratification to be expected from having the imaginary companion.

TABLE 20

*Roles Assigned to Imaginary Companions*

| Role | Persons | Ani-mals | Animistic Objects | Story-produced | Total | Mean Score (SHSS-C) |
|---|---|---|---|---|---|---|
| Pleasant | 28 | 5 | 4 | 3 | 40 | 6.0 |
| Unpleasant | 2 | 0 | 0 | 0 | 2 | 2.0 |
| Ambivalent | 6 | 2 | 0 | 0 | 8 | 8.0 |
| Undetermined | 0 | 0 | 0 | 1 | 1 | 7.0 |
| Total | 36 | 7 | 4 | 4 | 51 | 6.2 |

One is tempted to look for some sort of explanation for the high hypnotic scores in table 20 of those whose imaginary companions serve ambivalent roles. For one thing, this group contains most of the subjects (five of the seven) whose companions were said to be superego-related in table 19. These five leave three others in the ambivalent group, all of whom came from the large group with playmates with whom they interacted (three out of thirty-six). Because the ambivalent group represents five-sevenths of the superego group and but one-twelfth of the interacting playmate group, it is not unreasonable to look for the source of the high hypnotic scores in something related to superego development. There are two aspects of the high-superego situation that may relate it to hypnosis. One is the influence of adults, for it is commonly accepted that a part of conscience arises in connection with dependency reactions toward adults and in response to their authority. This could conceivably be related to responses in hypnosis. The other aspect (reflected in the ambivalence of the imaginary companion) is that a superego reaction commonly arises in a conflictual situation (temptation plus resistance to temptation), and a dissociative reaction, as in hypnosis, may very well be a way out of conflict.

The numerical data presented in tables 18–20 and in figure 1, while more intriguing than conclusive, provide a background against which to examine the case material, to see whether or not developmental strands can be detected that may be related to the later ability to experience hypnosis.

## Superego-related Imaginary Companions

It will be recalled that there were seven cases of superego-related imaginary companions, for five of whom the affective experience appeared to be ambivalent. These five were all highly hypnotizable, and it therefore becomes of interest to see whether or not their case histories can throw any light upon how the imaginary companion may have been a background for later hypnotic susceptibility.

Mabel was one of these. She scored eleven out of twelve on SHSS-C. At the time she was a sophomore, majoring in French.

"I made up an imaginary playmate as a substitute friend. She was a girl friend who was just the way I wanted her. When she was bad, I'd say, 'Don't come back for a week.' I'd make her so realistic that I'd put her in my place and put me in hers. For example, we're drawing and she doesn't want to help me wash windows. I *liked* her to be naughty: I greatly enjoyed it, then I had her punished. She was a more human person than I was. I didn't dare to do anything really mischievous. I was so good. I didn't get into any trouble, but I had two or three friends who did mischievous things and I admired them for their courage." As she reflected on this she tried to get at the meaning of her behavior.

"I guess I relieved my own aggressiveness through my imaginary playmate. I remember once I spilled a bottle of ink on a book of fairy tales. While I was sorry about this and it wasn't *really* bad, I didn't want to think I had ruined my book so I said *she* had wanted to ruin my book because she was jealous of me."

It is characteristic of Mabel's interaction with her imaginary companion that it is a genuine alter ego, with whom she occasionally trades places. She is both herself and the other person. This is a kind of dissociation, sounding very much like what happens in cases of alternating personality, such as the Eve White and

Eve Black case (Thigpen and Cleckley 1957). The capacity for dissociation may well be one link between the experience of the imaginary companion and the experience of multiple personality. A dynamic account would go something like this: the child has very strong impulses, but their gratification is contradicted by a developing, strong superego. The resulting conflict is resolved through projecting the impulse and its gratification upon a split-off portion of the personality (the imaginary companion), while the superego remains in control for the normal personality. This mechanism, in the extreme, may result in a split personality persisting over time. At a simpler level, dissociation may be involved in hypnosis; at least the practice in dissociation may provide a background for the hypnotic experience.

While Mabel's own account of hypnosis is not expressed in just these terms, the sense of detachment from what went on in hypnosis is noteworthy:

"When I woke up and found out some of the things I had done, I enjoyed the utter astonishment. I didn't remember anything at first; it seemed as though I had been dreaming about many things, but I couldn't remember the dreams. Then the hypnotist said I could remember everything. Even though I was still drowsy, the things gradually came back.

"It was as though I had been up late, sleeping deeply, and I needed time to focus again."

Mabel's need for an imaginary companion may have arisen, as she herself hinted, because her own conscience was so strict that she needed some permitted outlet for her wish for nonconformity. We learn from the interview that her mother was the chief disciplinarian; she was strict and was supported in her discipline by her father. Mabel conformed and tried to measure up to standards, although sometimes she was criticized for her faults and occasionally sent to her room. Her mother was the controlling force. "She has a terrific gift for argument. I've never won an argument with her. She usually convinces me, but even if I'm in disagreement, I'll keep it to myself, for she won't give in." The processes by which one person is manipulated by another may take various forms, and it is difficult to determine clearly which of these forms, in a given person, may have been most responsible for hypnotizability. In Mabel's history we find the mother whose powerful words and whose strict code had something to do with the appearance of the imaginary companion; from this manipulation of an imaginative child there later emerges this highly hypnotizable girl.

Another of those whose imaginary companions served a super-ego-related role similar to that of Mabel's companion was Virginia, who scored ten on SHSS-C. Her imaginary companion developed in her preschool years; the companion was a little girl of her own age, serving as a convenient alter ego. Sometimes she blamed this companion for getting her into trouble or for making her hold back from doing something that she should do but did not really want to do and then reprimanding her for it; at other times she referred her problems to this companion, talking things over with her and asking her advice. This splitting-off of the companion as essentially a responsible part of herself is characteristic of others classified in this conscience group. Because conscience develops in relation to responsible adults, we inquired into methods of early discipline. The characteristic method in Virginia's home was by reprimand, with little corporal punishment; there was some praise, but no substantive reward. She felt that these disciplinary practices had turned out well, particularly compared with practices used in the homes of friends. She would use the same with her own children. Here we see, then, an internalization of what the parents have done —first, in her own use of reprimand in dealing with her imaginary companion; second, in her readiness to adopt the parental formula for discipline when she has her own children.

Now, as a college student, Virginia is typical of the highly hypnotizable. She is deeply involved in the church, in the church choir, and in dramatics. Her imaginary companion was not based on any lack of social skills or absence of friends in childhood; she has many close friends and acquaintances now and readily falls into leadership roles.

Only one subject among those whose imaginary companions were judged to be conscience-related proved to be unhypnotizable (score of zero out of a possible twelve). As is often the case, her story helps us, by contrast, to see what is happening in the others.

Jill came to hypnosis as a twenty-one-year-old senior. She reported an imaginary companion who had been very real to her between the ages of four and six.

Jill described Mary, her imaginary companion, as a horrible-looking child who was usually in trouble and often required that adults come to her rescue. Sometimes the Jill-and-Mary team did things that embarrassed the parents in the presence of company. Upon examining accounts of specific episodes which Jill related, it was clear that her companion was frequently a foil by which to gain power over adults or to criticize adults without herself being blamed. In this sense, Jill's imaginary companion conforms to the group of companions to be described presently under "imaginary companions shared with an adult." There was, however, no question about the relation to discipline: Jill was always scolding and punishing Mary in the way in which she herself was scolded and punished.

Jill grew up and entered college as an attractive, responsible girl but saw herself as unhappy. She felt that she could not trust people. She said she had few friends, perhaps because she always found fault with those with whom she was thrown. Thus a certain negative attitude of today toward herself and others was early reflected in the creation of a predominantly negative alter ego.

What is our inference, then, concerning her lack of hypnotizability? First, her imaginary companion, unlike the others described, was consistently unpleasant; second, Mary was chiefly a tool for showing defiance of adults, and the experience was interactive more than it was dissociative. To the interviewer, at least, Jill gave no illustrations of her own interaction with Mary separate from the presence of adults. We have found that punitive discipline often tends to be related to high hypnotizability (see the later discussion, chapter 14) *when it works,* that is, when the child believes that the punishment was deserved or that it turned out all right for her. There is no indication of this reaction to punishment on Jill's part. Finally, distrust of other people is likely to be a poor sign for hypnotizability. As we have had occasion to repeat, no single indicator is likely to prove indicative of hypnosis, unless it is understood in relation to other developmental influences. Thus Jill's conscience-related imaginary companion is no assurance of hypnotic susceptibility, despite the fact that other superficially similar cases proved highly hypnotizable.

### Imaginary Companions Who Were Not Playmates

In table 19 eight subjects with imaginary companions who were not playmates in the ordinary sense were listed, three of whom served as affiliative (or sexual) objects, three as audiences, and two as imaginary companions shared with adults. All of the subjects proved below average in hypnotizability. The following three cases represent these subcategories and are presented in the attempt to account for the low hypnotizability within this group.

*Imaginary companion as a boy friend.* Charlotte scored three out of twelve in hypnotic susceptibility. She was somewhat reluctant to tell of her imaginary companion, because in retrospect she thought herself "a big dope" for having believed in him. This imaginary companion had been a "boy friend" named Charlie, who had for a time become very real to her. She felt now that the fantasy had been a wish fulfillment, evolved as a result of seeing older girl friends in the neighborhood with their boy friends. She said that outside of this episode she had indulged in very little fantasy; her home was very reality-oriented, and her own interests were of a factual, rational nature. Discipline was strict; she had been scolded and spanked until the age of ten.

We may assume that the imaginary companion fulfilled a temporary need, engendered by the social examples of older girls and probably by the forbidding of free discussion in her strict home. This was a passing episode, however; the need passed, and so did the fantasy. There is nothing here of dissociation in which she does not remain herself; on the contrary, she was herself at all times in this little drama. With the rather consistent reality ties and rationality, it is not surprising that she does not become hypnotizable.

Of the attempted hypnosis, she indicated that she had trouble paying attention; she thought of other things, was aware of incidental noises such as the hypnotist's shuffling papers, and wondered how she looked in the chair. When asked about hypnotic-like experiences in everyday life she thought for a while and then indicated that she became absorbed "to some extent" in listening to a symphony but that she had to exercise conscious control in order to achieve that degree of involvement.

*Imaginary companions as responsive audience.* Jacqueline was another of those reporting imaginary companions who proved to be unsusceptible to hypnosis. She scored two out of twelve and showed no posthypnotic amnesia whatever.

She had developed imaginary companions before she could read and continued to have them after she entered grade school. She described herself as a very dramatic child, and she had created her characters primarily as an audience to appreciate her performances. After she went to school, she assigned herself the role of teacher to her companions and put them through long sessions. As she walked to her actual school she often imagined herself out in front, leading an entourage.

We note again that this is not dissociative; she does not trade places with these companions; she is always herself, teaching them or leading them. The purposes they serve have to do with her desire for power and influence. We find this desire to retain control expressed in a curious manner in her description of her relationship to her parents. While she described her mother as gentle, kind, unaggressive, and interested in people, and her father as a counselor who enjoyed lecturing, she said she felt: "I have exerted much greater influence on my parents than they have on me." Rational interests predominated in the home; she liked to approach situations the way her father did, with facts and reasons—the rational way. Except for the imaginary companions, she does not think of herself as having been very imaginative.

While we do not have the full story here, particularly concerning what became of her early dramatization, the failure of the imaginary companions to be related to hypnotizability appears to be accounted for in the fact that there was little that was personally dissociative about the experience.

*The imaginary companion shared with an adult.* One of those who shared an imaginary companion with an adult was Janet, who scored two on a twelve-point scale. There appears to be some consistency in the failure of the cases under discussion to achieve much in the way of hypnotic susceptibility; the question now is whether the lack of dissociation may not be the key, as it appeared to be in the two previous cases. What this means is that the subject remains himself in the games that are played and does not find the companion in any major sense an alter ego or alternating personality.

Janet's companion was an imaginary cowboy named Roger, whom she shared with an uncle. She loved riding and jumping horses, and this cowboy could do the things she liked to do, although it is a little remote to think of him as a genuine alter ego. The way in which the game was played was that she talked to her uncle by talking to Roger, who would then have things to say to the uncle. The uncle's replies to Roger were intended as his replies to Janet. This is somewhat the way in which a ventriloquist uses his dummy, and we may think of Roger as the ventriloquist's dummy. There is some uncertainty in regard to whom we should assign the ventriloquist's role in this case, but we may assume that the uncle, as an adult of wider experience than the child Janet, doubtless did much of the stage managing.

As a young adult, Janet had continued the athletic interests, but without sacrifice of her femininity. She was essentially a realist who liked the feeling of mastery that skill in athletic competition carried with it.

Janet's reaction to hypnosis, despite the low score, was somewhat unusual. Whenever she felt herself drifting into a semiconscious state, her head would start to hurt, and she could relieve this pain by rousing herself. The pain was something like a headache, but she described it as more deep-seated, a quite involuntary reaction. The pain makes it appear that there was something conflictual about the hypnotic experience, that perhaps Janet was drawn toward the experience and yet repelled by it.

If we may take the foregoing three cases as representative of the eight cases for whom the imaginary companions did not serve the usual role of a peer as alter ego, we have a clue about the relationship of hypnosis by way of experienced and practiced dissociation. Not all imaginative supplementation of the environment is dissociative in the personal sense that characterizes hypnotic involvement. In true hypnotic involvement there is a separation between what is perceived as voluntary and what as involuntary, what is the familiar reality and what is a new reality in which the experiencing person participates; the change is in the self as well as in the environment. In these cases there is an imaginative change in the environment (particularly the social environment), but the self is essentially unaltered.

### Sociability and Isolation in the Modal Group with Imaginary Companions

The modal group of imaginary companions is composed of peers who are playmates, mostly of the same age and sex as the person who invents them. We have shown that within this group hypnotic susceptibility tends to average about the same as for those who do not report imaginary companions. This does not mean, of course, that there are not those high in susceptibility to hypnosis, and those low, and perhaps the case material will reveal some differences in the nature of the imaginary companions, and in the purposes served, that will yield some clues.

One contrast to be explored is that between those whose need for a companion is based upon persistent aloneness—genuine loneliness—and those who are highly social and supplement ample companionship with additional imaginary companions to fill in gaps of temporarily absent companions.

The problem of the imaginary companion as a response to social needs can best be studied through a more careful review of the histories of the twenty-eight students (see table 19) who reported active playmate interaction with their human or animal imaginary companions. It turns out that, of these, twenty are in fact quite outgoing and sociable, while only eight tend to be below average in sociability today; what their opportunities for sociability as children may have been is another matter, but at least they are not children who have ended as loners. In keeping with other findings in our study, the more sociable ones averaged slightly higher in mean hypnotic susceptibility than the lonely ones, but within this small group there was considerable variation, and the difference did not prove to have statistical significance. Thus the child who has imaginary playmates may not be a shy or withdrawn one, but instead a social one, who supplements his normal social contacts by adding a playmate when true age-mates are absent.

Two of those classified as highly sociable today, but who used their imaginary companions as playmates when children, are Kara and Anna.

Kara was above average in hypnotizability, with a score of seven out of twelve on form C. She recalled vividly having an imaginary companion at about the age of three. "I had an imaginary dog, Blackie; he was really important to me. I took him everywhere in the car. I pictured him as a small Scotty. I'd talk to him; he'd do tricks for me. I'd say: 'Oh, mother, look! He's climbing up on the window sill, and he's sitting up!' I wanted people to like him." Kara was an only child and doubtless was thrown a good deal with adults, for her parents were warm and outgoing, with many friends. Perhaps her dog friend was welcome among adults at times when children would have been excluded. She described herself as like her father, who was enthusiastic, colorful, humorous, and talkative. Her somewhat dramatic projective behavior, by way of her dog companion, may have been somewhat in his style. She described her hypnotic experience as "a feeling." "I've never felt like that before—a combination of being conscious and at the same time asleep. . . . I thought I would be 'out' but there was a part of me 'knowing.' At the same time I *felt* it so much."

Today Kara is a very active, outgoing person, with both close friends and many acquaintances. There is now little indication of a very active fantasy life.

By contrast with Kara, Anna is a presently sociable student who turns out to be low in hypnotic susceptibility, with a score of three out of twelve on form C. Like Kara, she had nonhuman imaginary playmates, but hers were a family of spiders dwelling under the living room sofa. They were active when she was about four, always playing with her in games. The little family consisted of several spiders with individual names, but she now recalls only the name of Adalaide, the mother spider. This faulty memory for the details of the imaginary companions, it will be recalled, is associated in other cases with lower hypnotic scores (table 18).

Anna's mother had read to her as a small child and told her stories. These interested her, but she had not become deeply absorbed then, and she does not now become deeply absorbed. Her whole family is reality-oriented and not imaginative. She had needed little discipline as a child because she had anticipated demands and performed in advance; she liked the feeling of doing things on her own rather than being asked to do them. This was to some extent reflected in her attitude toward hypnosis, because here she was asked to do things she did not initiate. Still, she had some slight subjective experience of hypnosis. As she said, "I never felt it deeply. I really *wanted* to be hypnotized, and I thought if I concentrated hard enough, I could. Still, I couldn't keep my own mind out of it; I couldn't keep my mind blank. I *did* become relaxed. At one point my hands felt numb, and I thought that I would have to move them to see if they were still there."

Anna's pleasure with spiders did not endure: for some reason, which we did not have time to probe into, she is now fearful of spiders.

Both Alice and Margaret gave more evidence of lonely childhoods, and of less ease in outgoing social relationships today.

Alice was not an only child, but she was an only girl in a family which included two boys younger than she who were very close and virtually excluded her. She was alone in her room a great deal as a little girl and found companionship through an imaginary girl friend. "My brothers had each other. Sometimes we played together, but I mainly communicated with myself." The imaginary companion had the reality of a true person but at the same time was a snow fairy—a combination of supernatural and natural which made a delightful companion with whom to talk and play.

The gratification of her dependency needs had been interrupted through a parental divorce which shifted much of her childhood care to servants. She saw how her brothers had each other, and she found a companion for herself. She had a rich fantasy life in addition to her play with the snow fairy and throughout childhood was deeply involved in the stories she read and the music she listened to. She describes herself as quite introverted up to the college years, though she is now reaching out for friends.

While her score of six in hypnosis is in the middle range, some of the experiences were quite real to her. She described the experience as "like listening to a symphony or watching a sunset or drifting off into sleep. I had a feeling of weightlessness, of floating, of things coming to a point."

Margaret was an only child, and she pointed clearly to her

loneliness as a reason for adopting an imaginary companion or, as it turns out, a whole family! "Yes, there was a whole family, Mrs. McGillicuddy and her eight children. They lived in my grandfather's pea patch. Mrs. McGillicuddy kept losing some of them and I had to help her find them. Sometimes the children came in the house and played with me." When Margaret's own family moved from Colorado to California when she was five or six, she had all of Mrs. McGillicuddy's family move, too.

It would be helpful if we had more details about grandfather's pea patch or early stories for the genesis of the McGillicuddys. All we know is that Margaret's father was off to war and that she and her mother were living with the grandparents. The move to California followed shortly after her father's return from the war. In addition to being an only child, with her father out of the home, her loneliness was accentuated by a number of childhood illnesses. She has gradually outgrown her introversion and now describes herself as friendly with people and generally outgoing.

She turned to reading during her childhood illnesses and could become very involved in the books she read. She also enjoyed movies, and her imagination was stimulated by them. These involvements and imaginative activities may be related to her above-average hypnotic score of eight on form C.

It would be satisfying if the childhood backgrounds of all of the imaginary-companion cases were similar in some striking respect, and their developmental stages predictable, but it does not turn out this way. Perhaps it is just as well, for it alerts us to the complexity of human personality. Earl has something in common with the previous cases which show a period of introversion followed later by outgoing behavior, but he remains distinctly himself. Of the cases reported here he scored highest in hypnosis, eleven out of twelve on SHSS-C.

He was quick to report that he had had an imaginary companion. "Definitely. His name was Joe. I played with him for hours on end. There weren't many others to play with. He was a real companion to me. The family and I sometimes talked about Joe . . . no one was concerned or upset about it . . . I had an active imagination." His experience occurred a little later than those reported by many of our subjects, his companion being most active when Earl was between the ages of six or seven and ten; this may account for the vividness of his recall.

Earl sometimes joined a neighbor to put on plays or skits. After the age of thirteen he had written a number of short stories and poems. He was currently planning a novel. In his extensive reading of fiction he developed strong empathy for the characters. "They come alive and I sometimes lose my objective point of view." He also becomes "fairly wrapped up" in movies and greatly enjoys classical music. He thus shows many characteristics common to the highly hypnotizable.

The story of his sociability is a somewhat uneven one. He did not play with his two brothers, five and eight years younger, because of the age gap and their closeness to each other. Although Earl said he accepted the rules pretty well—firm rules enforced by the successful business-executive father—his infractions did not go unpunished—he was spanked "with a big black belt" until the age of ten. In common with a number of others who received corporal punishment in childhood and ended up hypnotizable (see chap. 14), Earl did not resent the home discipline but felt that it had served its purpose. His mother was warm, had a sense of humor, an interest in the arts, and shared with the father a social interest in people. He felt that he was like his mother in temperament but shared a number of his father's characteristics also, among which he listed difficulty in controlling his temper and a high level of ambition.

Earl describes going through a period of introversion during two years in junior high school. Apparently he withdrew inside himself as he read and wrote, but he did not in fact relinquish all friendships; he limited them to one close friend at a time. This is his own characterization of himself in retrospect; we do not know how he seemed at this time to his parents, teachers, or other observers. In any case this period ended, and he believes himself now to be an essentially outgoing person, with easy familiarity with a wide range of acquaintances. The interviewer described him as a boy who exuded interest and intensity and was able to discuss his family situation with greater ease and with more apt descriptive terms than most of his fellow freshmen.

He was able to give a good description of his hypnotic experience. "It was about the same feeling I once had in a high fever when the room disappeared and my awareness was being pushed in. . . . It was also as though warm water were enveloping most of me and I was going under with pressure on me." Asked by the interviewer what he meant, he said, "I was completely involved except for periods when I would rise out of this and had to push myself down. I was helped by my appreciation of sound or tone. I used to listen to classical records at dusk, in a chair just like the one here, and completely relax. I'd let the music take over and take my consciousness wherever it wanted to go. It was the same thing here, allowing the voice to take over."

Thus Earl combines many of the trends which we have found associated with high hypnotizability: a rich background of involvement in fiction and music, depth of feeling, the ability to dramatize, adequate gratification of dependency needs, strict childhood discipline with a high level of successful punishment, excellent communication, and a high degree of imagination.

The late arrival of his imaginary companion may be related to his closeness with his mother until the age of five and a half, when the next child was born. It was at this time, coincidentally with his going to school, that a new one-to-one relationship, with his imaginary friend Joe, replaced the earlier one. In the early stages of adolescence he again reverted to a one-to-one relationship in the period he described as introverted. Hence there appears to be some continuity of gratification through a one-to-one relationship at times of strain, but it is no longer the basis of his social relationships because he has achieved greater comfort and confidence.

## Concluding Remarks on Imaginary Companions

While the presence of an imaginary companion is no guarantee that the child is going to grow up hypnotically susceptible, it appears that there are important dynamic relationships between what happens in the creation of the imaginary companion and what happens in hypnosis. Our study may make a contribution to the understanding of imaginary companions, apart from this relationship to hypnotic susceptibility. There have been relatively few studies of imaginary companions in recent years. The interested reader is referred to the following: Hurlock and Burstein (1932); Jersild, Markey, and Jersild (1933); Svendsen (1934); Harriman (1937); Bender and Vogel (1941); Ames and Learned (1946); Wingfield (1948); Sperling (1954). Because none of them relates to hypnosis, they are not discussed in this chapter, though they offer many leads to an understanding of the phenomena.

The imaginary companion was reported in about one out of six cases in our university sample, so that this is by no means a rare phenomenon. Of these, about two-fifths had more than one imaginary playmate. It came as something of a surprise to us to find how many of these playmates were animals or even inanimate objects, instead of peers. The higher levels of hypnotic susceptibility were associated with those whose playmates served genuine companionship, and particularly among those in which the alter ego was conscience-related. While some of the playmates arose from lonely childhoods, it appears that in many cases the playmate merely filled in while natural playmates were absent, for example, when the child was doing things alone or with adults.

From a theoretical point of view, interest resides in the relationship of the playmate to dissociative processes, whereby (possibly through projection) one aspect of self-awareness is separated from another aspect. There is a kind of transition here between the imaginary companion as alter ego and multiple personality, in which the person *becomes* (on some occasions) the imaginary companion. Such a transition is represented by Joan's case.

Joan at the time of her interview was a nineteen-year-old sophomore majoring in creative writing. She was the youngest of three children, with a ten-year gap separating her from her next-older sibling. Thus she was essentially an only child.

She reported that her imaginary playmate was a brother, something quite unusual in our sample, because nearly always the companion was of the same sex. "He was a twin brother named John. We did lots of things. When friends of Mother and Daddy came, they'd ask, 'Where's John?' Sometimes I'd run upstairs and jump into jeans and come down, sure they wouldn't know the difference. I was then about eight years old. I just *wished* I was a boy, and it was my way of being that way. I liked baseball and was a tomboy. Then some girls moved into the neighborhood and I began to play with them. . . . Father said he had had an imaginary companion as a child and that they tried to outwit each other."

It may be noted that the twin was named John, a masculine form of her own name Joan. This evident wish-fulfillment was dramatized by her occasionally *becoming* John, when she was sure that others "wouldn't know the difference."

From her accounts of her parents, we detect some reason for her divided male-female identity. Her mother was rather quiet, but effective in caring for the needs of the family, while fully participating in their social life. Her father was more colorful, with an outgoing sense of humor, intense imagination, a sense for the dramatic, a liking for family life and group activities. Joan, as a young college student, seemed to combine the masculine and the feminine. In appearance she was somewhat boyish, with upright posture and closely cut hair. Her voice was high-pitched and feminine. She knew that she was like both parents, but temperamentally rather like her father because of their dramatic reaction to crises.

Thus as a young woman approaching adulthood she carried some of John with her.

Her hypnotic score was seven, just a little above the average, but she felt that she might have gone deeper and did indeed do so on some later occasions. She said, "I sometimes respond slowly to things. . . . When he told me that my arm was no longer heavy it continued to feel heavy." She said the experience was not uncanny at all. "It was completely relaxing, letting someone else direct your thoughts to different areas."

The interesting aspect of Joan's case was that she sometimes took over the personality of her imaginary companion. In this sense, we might think of the situation as transitional to the creation of a multiple personality. In the cases of multiple personality with which I am familiar, the secondary personalities are of the same sex as the dominant personalities. Hence Joan's occasional assumption of the role of John is not a transition to a multiple personality. Such a transition is better represented by an imaginary companion of the same sex who represents an alter ego.

An interesting, and quite independent, support for the interpretation that an imaginary companion may be a transition to multiple personality has recently come to attention through a case of multiple personality studied within hypnotherapy (case courtesy of Bernauer Newton). The pertinent features here are that a child of five and a half with very strong conscious reactions to a difficult home situation began blaming any transgressions (such as breaking a dish while helping in the kitchen) upon the imaginary companion she had created, an alter ego full of impulse gratification and not troubled by conscience. This imaginary companion soon became a second personality, and the alternation through many years has features (including amnesic relations between the personalities) very similar to those of the classical cases reported by Prince (1906), Franz (1933), Thigpen and Cleckley (1957). It is interesting, also, that the woman who is the subject of this study is highly hypnotizable, a fact that has facilitated her treatment.

We thus find that early imaginary companions may prove to be a fruitful subject of study in the search for various aspects of personality development—reactions to lonesomeness, problems of severe conscience, confused identifications—or may even help to reveal the potentialities of creative imagination. The material appears to have implications that go beyond the field of hypnosis. Within hypnosis it tends to strengthen the interpretation of the hypnotic experience as dissociative.

# 9

## Adventuresomeness

Hypnotic involvement implies the ability to step aside from the humdrum of everyday reality into the life of fantasy. Some people, however, find release from ordinary demands by adventurous activity, such as mountain climbing, airplane flying, or cave exploring. Doubtless some fantasy is involved, but the overt expressions come in movement in real space. The question arises whether or not these "adventurers" are also hypnotizable beyond the less adventurous.

The possibility of a relationship between adventuresomeness and hypnosis was brought to our attention through a group of student subjects who volunteered for hypnosis in response to an advertisement in the college newspaper. On the sign-up day volunteers formed a queue outside the laboratory before the doors opened. Among them we found, on the basis of our interviews, two contrasting types of adventurous students whom we called physical and mental "space travelers." The contrast, as we shall see, is between those who depart from reality by exploring actual space in the mountains, in the air, in caves underground, or under the sea (the physical space travelers), and those who do their explorations while sedentary—taking drugs, sniffing glue, reading science fiction or Eastern philosophy (the mental space travelers).

The original sample of forty-eight interviewed in the year 1960–61 was supplemented by another forty-five volunteers in 1961–62; the total group includes fifty-six male and thirty-seven female subjects. This was an exploratory study, and the interviews were conducted following the hypnosis. The relationship between space interests and hypnosis appeared quite strong, especially

among the men, as shown in table 21. While the results were significantly in the same direction for the women, the significance lay
in the lów scores of those with no space interests, for there were
few space travelers among the women. For the total sample, the
relationship appeared to be well established.

TABLE 21

Hypnotic Susceptibility of Volunteer Subjects Classified
as Mental and Physical Space Travelers, by Sex

| | Male | | Female | | All | | |
|---|---|---|---|---|---|---|---|
| | Low or Moderate Hypnosis (0–8) | High Hypnosis (9–12) | Low or Moderate Hypnosis (0–8) | High Hypnosis (9–12) | Low or Moderate Hypnosis (0–8) | High Hypnosis (9–12) | Total |
| Mental or physical space travelers | 9 | 17 | 2 | 5 | 11 | 22 | 33 |
| No evident space interests | 26 | 4 | 25 | 5 | 51 | 9 | 60 |
| Total | 35 | 21 | 27 | 10 | 62 | 31 | 93 |

Significance tests: Male subjects, $\chi^2 = 14.0$; $p < .001$.
Female subjects, Fisher's exact probability, $p < .01$.
All subjects, $\chi^2 = 25.6$; $p < .001$.

While both physical and mental space travelers have something in common that is related to hypnosis, the interview material
showed the two groups to be in general quite unlike in their personalities. The mental space travelers were sedentary and were
rather like those whom we previously discussed under reading involvement, for example, those fascinated by science fiction. We
shall have less to say about them in this chapter than about the
space travelers who play out their adventures in real space. It
should be noted in passing, however, that we could not find any
significant differences in the hypnotic scores of the two kinds of
space travelers. Of the nineteen physical space travelers among
the ninety-three subjects of table 21, twelve, or 63 percent, were
highly susceptible to hypnosis (scores of nine to twelve), while for
the eleven mental space travelers there were seven, or 64 percent,

who were high. This omits three subjects who showed some characteristics of both; all three of these scored high. The contrast in personality between these groups of subjects who scored alike in hypnotic susceptibility helps us to understand why the correlations between standard personality tests and hypnotic susceptibility might be so low. Partly as a result of these observations we were led eventually to the multiple-path, or alternate-path, theory of hypnotic susceptibility to which this book is so largely addressed.

Because of these findings, we incorporated some questions on space interests in the interviews with our subsequent regular samples, but the results were disappointing; in retrospect, the questioning was not searching enough to distinguish between the more involved space interests of some skiers, for example, and the exercise of an impressive skill on the part of other skiers. Still, the general questions on adventuresomeness to which these interviews had led us continued to yield significant relationships to hypnotic susceptibility.

The positive relationship of adventuresomeness, rated in advance of hypnosis, to subsequent hypnotic susceptibility, within samples collected over two years, is shown in table 22. Thus we

TABLE 22

*Hypnotic Susceptibility as Related to Rated Adventuresomeness, 1962–63, 1963–64*

| Rating in Advance of Hypnosis | Susceptibility (SHSS-C) | | |
| --- | --- | --- | --- |
| | Low (0–6) | High (7–12) | Total |
| High Adventure (5–7) | 36 | 38 | 74 |
| Low Adventure (1–4) | 80 | 33 | 113 |
| Total | 116 | 71 | 187 |

Significance test: $\chi^2 = 9.31$; $p < .01$.

have a substantial replication of the findings with the earlier volunteer sample (table 21), if we interpret the earlier classification as based on what we later rated as adventuresomeness. It can be seen that the significance derives from the low hypnotic scores of the nonadventuresome rather than from the high scores of the adventuresome. While the high-adventuresome group falls about equally into the two hypnotic classes, the low-adventuresome group falls predominantly (80 of 113, or 71 percent) into the lower susceptibility category. The sexes separately show the same tendency, with 45 out of 73, or 63 percent, of the nonadventuresome males in the lower category, and 35 out of 40, or 88 percent, of the nonadventuresome females in this low hypnotizable category.

It should be stressed again that a finding of this kind, while satisfactory for analysis, does not in itself have much predictive value. If expressed as a correlation, the relationship between adventuresomeness and hypnotic susceptibility is but $r = .21$ ($N = 187$); this can account for only a small amount of the variance. Still, the positive relationship, established on a statistical basis, permits us to use insights from our case material with greater confidence.

### Some Individual Adventurers

It will help us see the relationship between adventure and hypnosis if we review the interview material from a few of the subjects who were classified as high in this characteristic.

The case of Sidney is fairly typical of the physical space travelers. Many of them, for whom the space interest is the only one relevant to hypnosis, are not deeply hypnotizable, but they tend to score above the mean in hypnotic susceptibility. For example, he scored eight on form C. He is twenty years old and a junior majoring in psychology. He may go into law. His father is a retired air force aviator, now in a professional field.

He said about his adventurous streak, "I call it adventurous. My parents would say foolhardy." Asked about his skin diving, he said, "It's *free* competition, like an adventure. It's exhilarating." The appeal of motor cycling was the "power," the feeling of the wind "whistling by" and the "freedom which is like flying." He was asked about his mention of flying. "I've always wanted to fly and snow ski but I've had no opportunity. I would like to learn to do stunts in flying. My father was a fine pilot." We shall return later to a discussion of the father's influence on the boy. For the present it suffices to note the kinds of satisfactions Sidney derives from adventures in physical space: "the wind whistling by," "exhilarating," "freedom like flying."

A few quotations from other adventurers in space will help round out the picture of what these subjects are like as a group.
>    a. A mountain climber: "because it's there"
>    b. A skin diver: "wonderful to lie quietly on the bottom of the ocean"
>    c. A cave explorer: "there's a mystery about these deep dark spaces"

d. Snow skiing: "you defy gravity as you jump"
e. Airplane flying: "on the thin edge of danger"

The mental space travelers differ from the physical ones in that they often depart from reality while sitting in a chair. They overlap with those we have studied who became deeply involved in reading, particularly the science fiction readers. Some of them, however, move into the world of fantasy in other ways, through becoming involved in aspects of phenomenology, Asiatic religion, or drugs. We did not have many drug cases; the upsurge of drug interest on college campuses was only beginning when most of our interviews were conducted.

Clifford represents the drug group. He came to hypnosis wanting to be hypnotized because "I had a feeling that it might help me to know myself better." He made a score of ten, missing only some inhibitory items (arm immobilization and verbal inhibition). He was one of the few subjects who talked about his experiences with drugs. "I have experienced hallucinations under drugs; I've taken mescaline several times, and I've gone to ether-sniffing parties." When asked about any similarity between drug experiences and hypnosis, he commented, "Hypnosis is the breaking point between the standard way of perceiving and the way of ether and mescaline."

Clifford has commonly found reality to be unsatisfactory, and he is looking for satisfaction through less usual experiences. He is preoccupied with phenomenology as an approach to science and is deeply interested in philosophy and metaphysics. He is capable of imaginative involvement, and this has had a long history.

As a child he saw the movie *Snow White and the Seven Dwarfs* and was so involved and moved that he had to be taken out in the middle of it. While reading as a child he would become completely absorbed for hours, oblivious to his surroundings.

Rather withdrawn as a child, he described himself as "somewhat introverted, but selectively extraverted." He has more friends now but is not very close to any of them.

In interpreting Clifford's hypnotizability, we find the absorption in reading and the childhood imagination probably as important as his contemporary interest in drugs. Most of our highest-scoring mental space travelers had reading interests along with some drug interests: reading in philosophy and existentialism, parapsychology, science fiction, hypnosis.

Instead of summarizing the various ways in which the mental space travelers find their adventures, we may note what they are seeking.

First, there are those who seek adventure in the highly imaginative world of science fiction. James is a small slender boy with glasses who hardly looked at the interviewer. He was very nervous and restless, so much so that it appeared he could never be quiet long enough to be hypnotized, but he did in fact score eleven on form C.

Much time was spent discussing his science fiction interest, which was very strong. When asked what the appeal of science fiction was for him he said, "I can use my imagination, I can let things go. I can think, What would happen if we sent a manned ship to the other side of the moon and then pretended that the moon was a canvas screen so that we could go on to act two? It's a way that I can escape from the real world. I like every type of science fiction. Somehow I'm going along for the ride when I read it. Its main attraction is the use of imagination. It played a big part in my life." We shall consider later how James says this is related to hypnosis.

Second, among the mental space travelers are those who are interested in releasing inner potential, somewhat as in the interpretation given by enthusiasts of psychedelic drugs. It should be noted that our interviews were conducted before the use of LSD and other psychedelics became wdepread on American university campuses. Doubtless a more recent sampling would have uncovered a larger proportion of interested and experienced subjects.

While, in general, the physical and mental space travelers appear to belong to different populations, the one active and outgoing, the other more sedentary and contemplative, occasionally both characteristics are combined in the same person.

Victor, a nineteen-year-old sophomore majoring in philosophy and mathematics, will probably go into college teaching. He scored eight on form C, above average for the group.

Victor had read science fiction since the age of eleven; he read all the science fiction he could find, and this interest continued through high school and into college. Asked what the appeal of science fiction was for him, he answered, "It is uninhibited. For a while you're completely free . . . to let your logic be swept away. You're free and uninhibited. You don't have to think it through . . . for a while you're illogical." It is mostly the plot rather than the characters which appeal to Victor because, as he put it, "The author thought of the ridiculous, the free . . . it's the sweep of the imagination . . . it feels like you're moving . . . it's thinking about the infinite, to the limits of the imagination." Asked, "Your body?" Victor replied, "No, your mind. Things are opening wider and wider. You feel like you're drawn into it." Victor added, to further clarify this point, "You keep looking down . . . it's like looking into a tube. I'm in the middle . . . it's like a cone—everything around me is receding. It's passing by me on the sides." This type of imagery is often reported in dreams within hypnosis and further attests to the similarity between the experiences of some science fiction readers to what is experienced in hypnotic fantasy.

The mental-space aspect of Victor is not all there is to his life of adventure. He also has physical-space interests, such as skiing and flying. He described skiing thus: "Down the slope you have complete control; you go fast and you can feel the wind go by on all sides; it feels as though you take off." Interviewer: "Take off?" "It feels as though you're jumping loose—the faster you go the more you feel you're coming apart from the ground." This skiing interest began at the age of ten.

His second space interest is airplane flying. "My father was a pilot in the war. But my grandfather is the red-hot of the bunch. When the bi-wing planes were new he used to go barnstorming, do loop-the-loops, go wing walking." Grandfather got his first plane thirty to forty years ago and continued to fly until a year ago. Victor's mother, grandfather, and father spent hours at a time talking about airplanes and flying. His father had flown missions in the South Pacific during World War II, flying low over the jungles in order to spot equipment of the enemy on the ground. It is evident that Victor received parental support for his adventurous interests.

## When Adventure Is Not Related to Hypnosis

We noted (see table 22) that the relationship between adventure and hypnosis is complex, in that only half of those considered to be adventurous were highly hypnotizable, while the low adventuresome were more frequently found to be less hypnotizable. What concerns us here is why some of those classified as high in adventuresomeness are not hypnotizable; unless there is some rationality to this we are left with a random relationship. It may be that some differences in the meaning of adventure, among those with high interest in it, is what is responsible for the different relationship to hypnosis.

Among physical adventurers, the component that appears to militate against hypnotic susceptibility is strong competitive or achievement motivation. (We shall meet this similar inhibitor of hypnotic susceptibility in athletes [chap. 10].) Consider, for example, the case of Ralph. He was rated high in physical adventure (physical space travel) because of his liking for skiing, rock climbing, and racing. He scored two of a possible twelve on form C. A second interview brought out some of the differences between him and the other space travelers. The interviewer began by asking Ralph how it was he had not been able to do more in hypnosis. "I'm high-strung. I always try to figure out what's going on around me. I'm always alert." In reply to a question about the appeal skiing had for him he answered, "My motivation is to improve or perfect something requiring perfection and physical stamina. There is a sense of competition. I have raced. It's also a good way to meet people and impress girls." Although he enjoyed the thrill of speed, accomplishment was the dominant motif, with a special emphasis on impressing girls. Next an inquiry was made about his interest in auto racing. "To perfect driving as an art, you have to be aware of what's going on all the time. It's another striving for perfection for me." Similar emphasis on accomplishment, on perfection, accompanied his comments on rock climbing and skiing: the activities were never enjoyed simply for themselves. Thus, while in many respects classifying as a physical adventurer in his interests, his absorption in these activities differed in quality from the hypnotizable adventurers. Another possible inhibiting factor is acquiring appropriate skills too late in life for the enjoyment to be as spontaneous as if they were acquired early. One of my nonhypnotizable colleagues is a skiing enthusiast, but he took up skiing in his thirties. He reports that he is always aware of the effort required for a satisfactory performance and so cannot lose himself in the enjoyment of the experience.

There are also some presumed mental space travelers who are not hypnotizable, and these exceptions also require careful examination. Elliott, for example, evidenced so much interest in ESP and palmistry that, in the quick assessment of the interview prior to hypnosis, he was rated as a mental space traveler. Upon later questioning, however, it turned out that he was primarily searching for evidence proposed by those who believed in these phenomena in order to refute them and to show that nothing was involved. This is very different from being fascinated by the mystery or having the imagination stirred by the phenomena. Elliott scored two on form C.

Charles, another low-scorer (two points), was rated as a mental space traveler on the basis of much reading in science fiction. Subsequently it was clear that his approach was intellectual and rational: he tried to search out what was really probable from what was entirely improbable in the science fiction and did not lose himself in it. Another science fiction reader finds himself racing through the book to get the essential plot, without the savoring of the scenes that is characteristic of true involvement. Thus these cases show subtle differences from those with the true emotional involvement characteristic of the more hypnotically susceptible.

### Attitudes and Personality Characteristics of the Hypnotically Susceptible Adventurers

The adventurers whom we have described as physical and mental space travelers who have turned out to be above average in their hypnotic susceptibility have a number of characteristics in common which permit a few generalizations.

1. *Enjoyment of the feelings of the moment.* The physical adventurers—for example, in flying and skiing—report *feelings* of excitement and exhilaration, as in the free exercise of power; of *sensation,* as of the wind against the face as they pick up speed. We noted how one subject said that in skiing he had a sense of jumping loose, of coming apart from the ground, of taking off into the air. This is freedom from the usual bounds of everyday experience, from restraints which more or less surround the adult as he leaves childhood.

The same enjoyment of feelings and sensations of the moment marks the individual who has embarked on a mental space flight via science fiction, ESP, or LSD.

2. *Escape from the world of reality.* Although the physical adventurer is moving about the real world, it is by no means the everyday world, and part of the thrill is that it is unusual, that it stirs up wonder, and that the connections with the familiar and the usual are temporarily broken. The world that surrounds the skin diver who lies relaxed at the bottom of the sea is not his ordinary world; neither is there anything ordinary about the environment in which the glider pilot finds himself as he floats on the wind.

Mental space travelers escape from the real world by entering the limitless space of an imaginary world. This can occur through reading science fiction, through a belief in mental telepathy, through experiencing the effects of a drug. Instead of probing and testing the physical limits of space, they have embarked on a more extended journey into mental space.

There are differences, however, between the mental and the physical space travelers. On the whole, the physical space adventurers gave the impression of greater discipline. In order to stay alive they have to distinguish between what is permitted and what is not permitted; while some speak of being reckless, more of them express the need for caution and distinguish between being adventurous and being foolhardy. The mental space traveler has fewer restraints upon his imagination; he draws upon his wide reading to open a limitless space for him and is little impeded by the restraints imposed by the world about him.

3. *A time-limited experience.* The adventures our subjects report are episodic. The airplane pilot or the skier returns to his classes and other responsibilities. The reader of science fiction turns back to the reading of his regular assignments in chemistry or physics and engages in the duties of the critical world of the laboratory. The exhilarating experience is enjoyed, then set aside. Were the experiences not time-limited they would be disruptive instead of integrative; thus we are not talking about the excessive reality distortions of the psychotic, or about the excesses produced by drug addiction.

4. *An active involvement.* A life of imagination is not passive but active. These are true adventurers, whether they seek their experiences in the physical world or in a mental world. The overt activity varies, of course, but the person is an active seeker, not merely a passive receiver. The person has to do a certain amount of work to get the most from the experience, and the subjects report that their adventures are enjoyable, but often hard work.

5. *Childlike enjoyment of excitement and power.* There are many attractive features of childhood that tend to be lost in adult life. Whether or not the recapturing of some of these feelings should be called regressive, the facts are clear. Our adventurers have shown a zest for excitement and new experience continuing from childhood—the kinds of experience that we associate with the wide-eyed wonder of childhood. They also have a sense of triumph over nature, a sense of mastery of the world, of omnipotence and freedom from restraint. The experiences we have described add meaning and zest to their lives.

These five characteristics of the attitudes adventurers take toward their experiences help us to see why there may be some relationship to hypnosis.

## What Adventure and Hypnotic Involvement Have in Common

Why are adventurous people, whether physical or mental space travelers, ready for hypnosis and capable of enjoying the hypnotic experience? Some answers have already been indicated. For the physical space travelers hypnosis holds the promise of sensations similar to those experienced in skiing or flying; these are not very verbal persons, and they do not state this clearly, but they do say that they like to try new things. For the mental space traveler hypnosis is readily seen as a challenge similar to drugs or ESP or science fiction. Thus the characteristics detailed above apply to hypnosis because hypnosis represents to these subjects experiences of the same kind in which they have become involved and which they enjoy.

Three major points of similarity between adventure and hypnosis suggest themselves.

*First, reality-testing processes are altered.* For the mental space travelers the usual reality tests are set aside; they feel free from the constraints of ordinary logic. For the physical space travelers the situation is somewhat different. They have a tie to reality, but they test the limits of reality for the varied experiences it can provide. In either case, the reality-testing ego is not absent but present on a marginal basis, in the wings of the stage, so to speak, ready to object if things get out of hand. Thus the space travelers stop short of being foolhardy, and the mental space travelers, as we find them, do not go to extremes. To be sure, there are dangers in going too far in either case—airplane or parachute deaths, ski injuries, and drug addiction—but these are not typical, and no true extremists found their way into our hypnotic samples. Whether hypnotic involvement itself possesses the possibility of a kind of addiction has been argued. It is possible that a near-psychotic person practicing autohypnosis might suffer a continuous disturbance; such a possibility cannot be ruled out. At the same time, it should not be considered a normal hazard of hypnosis. In our studies of sequelae to hypnosis we found nothing of this kind, though it should be added that our experience did not include extremely disturbed persons. (See Hilgard, Hilgard, and Newman 1961).

*Second, responsiveness to external cues, especially the power of words, is retained.* It is part of the paradox of hypnosis that it is a kind of reality distortion in which one is guided very much by an influence from the environment—chiefly the words of the hypnotist. In relation to our adventurers, the point to be made is that the physical space traveler is responsive to the actual environment in which he finds himself, and he exercises appropriate skills while savoring the experience. The mental adventurer follows the lead of the author of the book he is reading, or perhaps of his associates who have prepared together for their drug experiences. His imagination, while rich, is not exactly free. The hypnotic subject, in turn, responds primarily to the words of the hypnotist, not to his own associations.

There is some opposition here between the adventure-hypnosis experiences and some seemingly related experiences which are, in fact, different. Thus the hallucinations of the schizophrenic and the hallucinations under hypnosis doubtless have some similarities, but a major difference lies in the control of the hypnotic hallucinations by the words of the hypnotist, in contrast with the spontaneous and uncontrolled nature of the schizophrenic hallucinations. Some of the more extreme manifestations under drugs also have this spontaneous and uncontrolled quality. Care has to be exercised not to confuse overlapping experiences with identical experiences. Thus moderate injections of LSD may make the subject susceptible to the suggestions of those about him (Sjoberg and Hollister 1965), in which case the experience overlaps that of hypnosis. Uncontrolled impulses that somehow originate within the person, however, differ from hypnosis-induced impulses. Spontaneous experiences induced by extreme states, whether drug-induced or not, may be called *autogenous,* because they are self-initiated; in any case they are not responsive to the influence of demands from without, particularly verbal suggestions, of the kind which characterize hypnosis.

*Third, processes compatible with childhood can be reexperienced.* Omnipotence, power, freedom from restraint, adventure, excitement, direct sensual experiences—all these characteristics of the space travelers are of a kind identifiable in childhood. They are found both in their adventures and in hypnosis.

Such processes can be experienced directly, as in flying (an excellent description of the love of flying and the fear of it can be found in Bond 1952); or in dissociation, as in reading science fiction. (I have treated science fiction as though it were one entity. This does not do justice to the complexities and fascinating varieties of science fiction, some of which may be more related to hypnosis than others. For an informative and delightful introduction to this field, the reader is referred to Amis 1960.) It is possible to describe what happens as a *regressive movement* toward magical wish-fulfillment and impulse gratification, although in being reversible it is the kind of partial regression described as regression in the service of the ego.

It has proved interesting to us that a number of people who describe themselves as impulsive are not hypnotizable. One might suppose that impulse, being associated with primary process, would fit the regressive aspects of hypnosis. It turns out that there is a control of impulse among the hypnotizable subjects; they are capable of departure from reality and of expression of feeling, but there is a channeling of impulse. We have had some subjects with relatively unchanneled impulse, who proved nonhypnotizable. They performed such acts as suddenly "showing off" by climbing to a third-floor rain gutter, throwing water-filled balloons into windows of a girls' dormitory, setting off firecrackers in unexpected places. These are spur-of-the-moment, highly individualistic operations. In contrast, skiing and flying demand structure and discipline in preparing the equipment, in learning the skills, before the freedom of the experience can be enjoyed. Correspondingly, both science fiction and hypnosis provide guidelines set down by author and hypnotist within which imagination is exercised. Thus there is freedom within constraint, as in the writing of poetry within a fixed meter. To consider that such experiences give free play to fantasy and imagination is to describe them partially and incompletely.

### The Developmental History of Adventuresomeness

We have noted, in passing, that some of our students who were flyers made reference to flying fathers (and even to a flying grandfather). It is part of our developmental hypothesis that the support for such activities, encouraged early in life by the example of involved parents, helps to keep alive the hypnotic potential present in children.

Returning to the case of Sidney, described earlier in this chapter, let us note further what he tells us about his father.

Sidney told some fabulous stories of his father's experiences in flying as an air force officer. He flew missions over Taiwan, Iwo Jima, Guadacanal. He was a pilot-photographer on photographic missions over enemy territory, and he did both the piloting and the photography in a stripped-down fighter plane without either armor or radio so that he could out-distance the Japanese who pursued him. Later, as a flight instructor, he used to demonstrate the "hammerhead stall" to young aspirants. In this project you rise to 10,000 feet as straight up as you can go, then remain suspended with the plane's nose pointed up. This can be done only in a propeller plane, which can remain practically suspended at that altitude. After the suspension you drop tail first for quite a distance before pulling out. On one occasion he came down tail first unable to get the plane back under control, with his passenger, not realizing the danger, shouting "Wonderful, wonderful!" Sidney's father was about to have them both bail out when a fortunate breeze righted the plane at an altitude of 2,000 feet, and they landed safely.

This detail is given in the boy's own words because it shows how he caught the flavor of excitement from his father. His father ceased flying after retiring from the air force and became increasingly cautious over the years. Nevertheless his impact on Sidney came earlier. He and Sidney's mother both label Sidney's present exploits "foolhardy," but the grandmother has chided the father for having forgotten his own youth. Sidney has a motorcycle now; his father recalls how he loved to speed in his Model-T.

Sidney said of his father, "I guess he was similar to me when he was young—the tales he tells of what he did as a boy with a gang of boys taking watermelons—his souped-up car." While Sidney thought he resembled neither parent in temperament, on reflection he added, "I would identify with my father as a young man, I guess; now he's too easy-going. Age brings wisdom; he knows what he's going to do; he recognizes foolhardiness when he sees it. I guess I have to learn for myself."

It will be recalled that Victor is another flyer who grew up in a family of flyers, listening to hour after hour of talk about stunt flying.

The early origins of mental space interests are equally impressive. Donald is like many other readers of science fiction, having started early in grammar school. He read a book every two days or so until recently. He identified with the characters, felt himself to be wandering in outer space. Later he developed engineering interests because he decided that he wanted to know what was *actually* going on. "I'd rather know why than just imagine it." He was above average in hypnotic susceptibility. He attributed his early interest in reading to his mother, who had always been an inveterate reader. As noted earlier (chap. 3), reading interests that lead to involvement commonly start early, either encouraged by the parents or as a way of meeting loneliness. In the case of James, discussed earlier, his position in the family was between a sister three years older and one three years younger, and he had little in common with either. It sounds as though he began to read to fill in a void of loneliness. "I read a heck of a lot, the Hardy Boys, mystery stories, adventure stories, Robert Louis Stevenson, etc. I started to read science fiction in the sixth grade. It played a big part in my life."

## Summary and Conclusions on Adventuresomeness

The adventurers (physical and mental space travelers) proved particularly interesting because of what they had in common and because of the ways in which they differed. They helped to convince us that we would not be able to find any single personality measure that would neatly sort the hypnotizable from the unhypnotizable if people as different as these were in the hypnotizable class. At the same time they did have some characteristics in common: a love of selected new experiences, a capacity to enjoy the experiences of the moment, a willingness to tamper with ordinary reality. As in the other involvements we have studied, we also had to be careful to make some necessary distinctions so as not to overgeneralize about the relationships between these experiences and hypnosis. There were the conspicuous exceptions—nonhypnotizable adventurers—who made us take a second look; there were also those who combined at once both the physical and mental space interests, so that we had to be careful not to overplay the contrasts between the two kinds of interest.

We may best summarize our experience with those who did their adventuring in real physical space as follows: They tend to be more motoric than verbal in their interests and thus turn to the active life for their recreation. They are adventurers but not daredevils; they care for and inspect their equipment; they become skilled in what they have to do. It is more favorable for hypnosis if they acquired their skills early in life, so that they grow up with enthusiasm and enjoyment without an overconcern for perfecting their skill. When thus prepared and trained, they enjoy the freedom and excitement of what they are doing in an immediate manner, full of feeling and sensation. While they naturally take some pride in their mastery, the essence is not competitive excellence, but full enjoyment; not trophies won, or the admiration of onlookers, but the joy of defying gravity, the pleasure of the wind blowing against the face, the excitement of power and speed. If there is too high a value on achievement and accomplishment, this leads to some sort of vigilant "How-am-I-doing?" attitudes that interferes with feeling involvement and appears to be related to lower hypnotic susceptibility scores. In common with other areas of involvement, the history of adventure often begins with sagas in the family—for example, of flying grandfathers, flying mothers and fathers. Hence the childhood enthusiasm has never been lost. Even though adults may wish to become involved in venturesome activities later in life, we suspect that there are many difficulties, partly because the adult has to pay so much attention to the details of the newly acquired skill. Thus, for example, few adults become adept at sailing a boat if they did not learn as children. They may know how to do it, but for them it involves more work and less play than for those who learned early.

The mental space travelers are quite different. The contrast between the two forms of adventure is somewhat reminiscent of the classification which Michael Balint (1959) has made between the *philobat* (who, like the acrobat, loves the freedom of space) and the *acnophil* (who loves the security of contact with objects). Our physical space travelers are rather like his philobats, but the mental adventurers are not good representatives of his acnophils. They do not really make much of their contact with objects as a source of security; they too like to wander around in free space, but it is the free space of fantasy. Although they sit in a chair, and thus maintain contact, it is not the contact with the chair that interests them. Our mental space travelers are much more verbal than our physical ones; it was much easier to get them to express themselves freely in their interviews and to tell us what their experiences were really like. It is not surprising that they were fluent, when it is recalled that they were likely to have been avid readers since childhood. The mental adventurers enjoyed the release from the restraint of ordinary doubting and proof seeking; they liked to set logic aside while giving free play to their imaginations. The Alice-in-Wonderland quality that appeals to them is so close to hypnosis, as reflected in many of the dreams within hypnosis, that it is easy to understand their susceptibility and enjoyment of hypnosis. Their earlier experiences are essentially those of the involved readers who were earlier discussed (chap. 3). There is so much in common between the involved reader and the mental space traveler that the distinction is unimportant, except that the space-traveler category includes some others, such as those who go in for drugs, ESP, and other exotic experiences not reflected solely in their reading.

The differences among the adventurers stimulated us to look for alternative paths into hypnosis, a theme to which we shall return from time to time. There is no single preparatory experience that makes a person an unusually good candidate for hypnosis, but in his background, usually beginning in early life, there has been some kind of deep noncompetitive involvement, whatever form it may have taken.

# 10

## Involvements Unrelated to Hypnotizability: Competitive Sports and Reality Ties Through Science

We have found absorbed interest and intense involvement to be related to hypnotizability, whether that involvement is in reading, drama, music, religion, or adventure. At the same time we have noted that the relationship is not simple, and we have had to examine in each case some exceptional individuals who, at first rated as involved, turned out not to be hypnotizable. Usually there was something about them different from the others: they were too achievement-oriented, too skeptical, too rational, too unable or too unwilling to set reality orientation aside even briefly.

The athletes in our sample have provided an unusual opportunity to study involved but unhypnotizable persons. This is not to say that *all* athletes resist hypnosis, but the distinctions between those who are susceptible and those who are not turn out to be helpful. We may begin by looking at some cases of those who are hypnotizable and some who are not, and then turn to the statistical picture.

### The Hypnotizable and the Nonhypnotizable Athlete

Although we shall show that nonhypnotizable athletes are more frequent in our sample than hypnotizable ones, the first athletes to be briefly introduced will be two who are hypnotizable, in order to illustrate the differences when the nonhypnotizable ones are introduced.

Edward has great interest in skiing, and for six years he has been an enthusiastic tennis player. He scores nine on SHSS-C in hypnosis. What is most striking in his case is his combination of

142

high imagination, reading involvement, and interest in the theater along with the athletic interests. His athletic interests do not appear to reduce his hypnotizability, so far as we can tell; it seems likely that reading and imagination are important influences in sustaining involvements closely related to hypnosis.

The female equivalent of Edward is Virginia, who has always enjoyed sports, having been encouraged early by sailing with the family. Like Edward, she is also high in imagination and in reading, theater, and music interests, and these nonathletic interests serve to support her hypnotic susceptibility.

The kinds of sports enjoyed by these more highly hypnotizable subjects are those participated in largely for personal enjoyment, such as skiing, tennis, and boating. While it is possible to enter into contests, there are satisfactions involved other than the winning of victories over a competing team.

When we turn to the nonhypnotizable athlete we are impressed by the importance of a team that wins in the face of competition.

Take the story of Dave, whose only high involvement was in athletics, rated seven, at the top of the scale. No other area was rated higher than three. He scored two in hypnosis on SHSS-C. (Dave's case has been described before, in J. R. Hilgard 1965, pp. 363–64.)

He played basketball and varsity baseball. After his experience in hypnosis had been reviewed, the interviewer suggested that involvement in athletics seemed to be correlated with less hypnotizability and asked if he could help us understand some of the reasons for this. His immediate response was, "It's a lot more real and takes less imagination."

He went on to elaborate: "You have complete control of yourself in almost all situations. . . . Ever since I was very young, I've played ball. My brothers taught me and I got a lot of training. There's a pressure on you to perform, and you can't let emotion in any way impede your physical abilities or response. In a game, you can't let yourself be bothered by any emotion. You control your physical responses and don't let emotion control you at all."

When the interviewer asked, "You lose yourself in a game; why can't you lose yourself in hypnosis?" Dave answered, "You do lose yourself in the game but the game has an object—to put the ball in the basket. You are completely concentrating on something in the real world."

The subject spoke of his genuine wish to be hypnotized. "I

*wanted* to be hypnotized, but I was doubtful because I've always had control over myself."

Dave's emphasis in discussing sports was not on fun or losing himself, but on skill, control, and competitive effectiveness. These attributes we found repeated over and over again in interviews with football and basketball players.

We have more male athletes than female in our sample, but the considerations that apply to male athletes seem to apply also to the female ones. For example, in Helen we have a nonhypnotizable woman who has considerable involvement in sports.

Helen was rated at six in athletic involvement before hypnosis, with no other interest area rated high. She scored at the bottom of the scale on hypnotic susceptibility. (Helen's case has been described before, in J. R. Hilgard 1965, p. 364.)

"I was extremely interested in being hypnotized. I'm not a skeptic. . . . Hypnosis was too much like what you see in the movies. I tried to do it, but it seemed corny."

She began to talk about her athletic interests. She had been swimming competitively since the age of eight and had won trophies in badminton. "People who are competitive," she said, "are far from being imaginative. You realize what you are fighting. It's the reality of the struggle. Imagination and competition are mutually exclusive. In competing, the whole world around you is more real. My imagination is extremely limited.

"In competitive sports you're taught never to take your opponent for granted. You keep a critical eye on everything. Even though your opponent looks scrawny and not apt to do anything, you don't trust that situation. . . . I can never say die. I've got to win. I've always got to try to beat the person; I never give up. Even if I run myself too hard and get ill, I'll keep on trying to win."

In this emphasis upon reality orientation and competition, at the expense of imagination, we have an important indication of the differences between two kinds of athletes, the ones who are participating largely for personal pleasure and the ones who are fighting a battle to win. These may be classified as alternative forms of enjoyment, but in important ways they differ from each other.

## Individual-Skill Sports versus Highly Competitive Team Sports

The foregoing cases called attention to a difference between athletes who became involved in what they were doing for the intrinsic pleasure of the sport and those who were essentially in a battle to win, usually with one team pitted against another. Of course, such a dichotomy is not sharp: there are skiing, swimming, and boating competitions in the Olympics. Tennis matches are competitive, too. Badminton, which for some is a mild pastime, was a highly competitive sport for Helen. Despite these overlaps, it is possible to make a rough sorting of sports into those which lie at the highly competitive team-sport end of the continuum, and those which lie at the less highly competitive individual-skill-sport end. Although there will be overlap, somewhat different kinds of athletic satisfaction are derived from involved participation in the two classes of sports.

In order to determine whether or not some of the inferences from our case material would be supported statistically, we arranged a code for the classifying of those who expressed a preference for one or the other kinds of sport. The code adopted was as follows:

| Highly Competitive Team Sports | Individual-Skill Sports | |
|---|---|---|
| Baseball | Boating | Skating |
| Basketball | Fishing | Skiing |
| Football | Golf | Swimming |
| Hockey | Hunting | Tennis |
| Volleyball | Racing | Track and Field |
| | Riding | |

It was necessary to have an "other" category for less usual sports (curling, Lacrosse, fencing), but it was usually not too difficult to assign these to the appropriate category. Some subjects proved nonclassifiable, in part because their expressed athletic interests were minor or nonexistent.

When those with athletic interests were assigned to these categories, without reference to their hypnotic-susceptibility scores, a difference in hypnotic susceptibility was found, as shown in table 23. Although there are always a few cases that do not fit the generalization, the differentiation between those who prefer the highly competitive group sports and those who derive their satisfaction from the individual, somewhat less competitive individual-skill sports is clear, with the individual-skill group significantly more highly hypnotizable. The contrast is most in evidence in the large fraction of the competitive-team athletes who are in the low group (28/39, or 72 percent) compared with the corresponding fraction for the individual-skill athletes (13/30, or 43 percent).

These contrasts, supported statistically, confirm the impressions from the study of individuals and suggest that a further effort

TABLE 23

Preference for Type of Sport as Related to Hypnotic
Susceptibility, 1963–64

| Hypnotic Susceptibility (SHSS-C) | Sport Preference | | |
|---|---|---|---|
| | Team | Individual-Skill | Total |
| High (9–12) | 1 | 6 | 7 |
| Medium (5–8) | 10 | 11 | 21 |
| Low (0–4) | 28 | 13 | 41 |
| Total | 39 | 30 | 69 |

Note: Among 83 cases, 14 were nonclassifiable on athletic interest.
Significance test (Fisher's exact probability); $p < .001$.

to look at the interview material may provide additional clues to
the differences.

## The Athlete Involved in Highly Competitive Team Sports

Because the highly competitive team sports provide the bulk of
the nonhypnotizable athletes, it is appropriate to take a further
look at some of the individual interviews from this group. It should
be noted here that our original hypotheses did not make any distinction of this sort; team athletes were thought to be excellent
role players, who were very deeply involved in what they were
doing. If role absorption and role enactment were all that was essential to hypnosis, these athletes should have been excellent
candidates for hypnosis. But there was something about these
roles that was unrelated to hypnotic susceptibility.

Perry received a score of three in hypnosis. His only high involvement rated in advance of hypnosis was in athletics at the
seven level. He had played football for ten years and had said in
the interview preceding hypnosis that the appeal was its aggressive
nature and the need for power. He would become wrapped up in
his desire to win, to hit somebody and to crush him. He had also
played volleyball for ten years and felt that this involved skill and
some relaxation, but that it carried nothing of the excitement and
involvement of football. In addition, Perry mentioned liking to
climb mountains.

In contrasting his absorption in football with absorption in
hypnosis, Perry said, "The emphasis in athletics is to win and develop strength within the self; you have to strive constantly. In

hypnosis, you are taking emphasis off the self, and putting yourself in someone else's hands. You're relaxing instead of striving; when relaxing, my thoughts are wandering and I have no concentration of attention then."

Perry continued a description of the total absorption and concentration on the game which is demanded of the athlete. "You train yourself to be conscious of the movements of every other player; it becomes automatic, it's not conscious thought. Nothing else is in your mind than the game and your environment; at no time do you let down, you're always watching the other players. Your mind is directed toward one goal and that's the goal of winning. You're aware of your body and where it is in space. You develop reflexes so you know exactly where your hand is in space while you watch the ball, whether you're playing baseball, basketball, or football."

Perry said that for a person such as he reality was not confined to athletics, but that this need to be aware of the realities around him went throughout his personality.

Allan scored two in hypnosis. He was rated high in sports, having played baseball for twelve years and wrestled for five years. Allan described the similarity between baseball and hypnosis: "They both take concentration, excluding other thoughts." From this point on, Allan thought that the two were quite different. "In baseball, you always have to be aware of what you're doing with your body; you have to have certain muscles tensed, certain ones relaxed, and after a while all this has become automatic." Allan said that there was a constant necessity to study the other players and to know where to play. "You're always shifting around, depending on your predictions of where the guy is going to hit the ball."

In wrestling, Allan said one had to be even more aware. "It takes balance. You have to know where your body is, where your body is without actually seeing it. It takes an instantaneous reaction. When your opponent makes a move, you have to be ready. It becomes more instinct, that is, you feel him going, you move, you haven't thought about moving. You're watching constantly, watching for muscular contractions that would indicate what he's going to do next. Wrestling takes a lot more mental conditioning than baseball. It's tiring because you have to give 100 percent of your strength for a certain length of time. Even though it's only nine minutes, you are so alert that you have to have the mental battle with yourself to try to sustain your effort. After such an effort, it feels as though even to raise the arm would be too much." Allan added, "In wrestling, you're consciously aware of your own limitations, how much effort you can force yourself to exert. It's a mental battle with your own physical limitations."

When the interviewer asked why, with this kind of a background, Allan was not able to concentrate on his physical body in hypnosis and put the effort into forcing his body to react in a particular way, he said, "It couldn't happen, because if the hypnotist said 'You cannot bend it,' you're always aware that you can bend it. You are so aware of your own body's potential strength that to concentrate on being unaware would be impossible."

### Attitudes Characteristic of the Nonhypnotizable Competitive Team Athlete

From interviews with a number of athletes whose outlook resembled that of the two just recounted, we can make a kind of summary of the way in which they see their participation in sports, and how this conflicts with the kinds of involvement more typical of the hypnotizable subject. Athletes repeatedly speak of becoming "lost" and immersed in a game, concentrating to such an extent that they are unaware of anything outside the game itself. Superficially this appears to be like the concentration within hypnosis, with its exclusion of matters outside the focus. Yet this athletic immersion is not related to hypnosis.

Some of the features that differentiate the athletic involvement from the hypnotic involvement are the following three:

1. *Exact information is required of environmental stimuli in a reality context.* The discriminations made by the athlete must be accurate; information from the environment is evaluated precisely in its relationship to the accomplishment of the task at hand.

2. *The focus is on those aspects of environmental input which lead to decision and control.* In these competitive sports there is an adversary to be overcome, so that the alertness to his moves must be supplemented by a strategy for overcoming them. Bodily responses are keyed to coordination and automaticity in the service of decisive action and exact control. Athletes, long trained to know just what body movements they are making, speak of the difficulty with hypnosis when the hypnotist tells them the body is doing something which they know immediately it is not doing. They have well-learned decision signals connected with the body in space.

3. *The stress is on activity.* Achievement and competition in these sports requires constant activity, vigilance, striving. Mental alertness to precise meanings of incoming stimuli is heightened,

physical automaticity of response is well learned. The competitive athlete is on his toes physically, and on the mark mentally.

These three characteristics are almost exact opposites of what is required in hypnosis, and in their turn they exclude some related attitudes familiar among the highly hypnotizable. Nonhypnotizable competitive athletes display the following three attitudes, which are not characteristic of the hypnotically susceptible:

1. They speak of being unable to range widely in imaginative and feeling responses to the stimuli offered by the hypnotist.

2. They are unable to derive the kind of enjoyment that comes from savoring the present moment. Instead of appreciating the immediate present, their satisfaction tends to derive from the final score, the eventual triumph to which their energies are fully committed.

3. There is little *passive* experience, where they are in the mood of receptivity; competitive athletes are activity-oriented and not easily given to a Buddhalike attitude of relaxed contemplation or meditation.

### The Athlete Involved in Sports Emphasizing Individual Skill

Because our statistical analysis showed us that the hypnotizable athletes were more likely to be found among those whose sports emphasized individual skill, and somewhat less competitive inter-action with others, we may well begin by taking a look at some of those who represent this group.

Leslie is a weight lifter who scored nine on SHSS-C, well up into the highly hypnotizable group. He had been lifting weights for two years at the time of the interview, and in a second interview after hypnosis he related weight lifting and hypnosis. "I certainly know when a weight is too heavy to pick up. When my hand got heavy in hypnosis, it was just as though someone had put a fifty-pound dumbbell into it and it went down. It was recognizably real, though I hadn't put together the feeling with such an idea until I started talking about my weight lifting just now."

Throughout childhood and into the present, Leslie had been very involved in movies and, more recently, in reading. We might summarize our description of Leslie by saying that he fits a fairly typical picture of the kinds of involvements (in his case, movies and fantasy) found in hypnotizable subjects in our sample. His weight lifting was not competitive against others, but only in terms of what he could do, and he enjoyed the feelings in his body as he exerted the effort needed to lift the weight. The objections of our competitive athletes that hypnotic suggestions contradicted reality did not bother him; instead he was able to use his real experience of weight lifting to aid the unreal experience of a suggested heavy arm.

The next subject is Herbert, a discus thrower who had been successful in meets. Here we have competition, but there is no genuine adversary: the main competition is against one's own record. This was his main interest, though he had participated in football and basketball in high school and had been bowling "just for fun" for five years. His score of eight on SHSS-C places him above the average in hypnotic susceptibility within our sample.

Like Leslie, Herbert made use of his real experience to help his hypnosis. "If I try to imagine something, I have to start with something real, like the way the discus feels, and then go on from there. . . . I think that's the way I managed to follow the hypnotist's suggestions." He was not as much like the typical hypnotizable subject as Leslie, because he had little fantasy life. While fully cooperative in the interview, he was not articulate, and his ability to communicate was rated at the low average level.

He was not like the highly competitive athletes involved in team sports; he was successful in his individual skill, and he could enjoy the moment of release of the discus. It was noted above that he did a good deal of bowling "just for fun."

In both of these cases we have a way into hypnosis through a motor experience which calls attention to the athlete's own body. It is of interest that practice in using experiences of weighted arms has been found helpful in increasing susceptibility to hypnosis in the laboratory (Sachs and Anderson 1967).

Chester, who enjoys swimming, is in some ways the clearest example of the hypnotizable individual-skill-sports enthusiast. His score of nine on the SHSS-C puts him in the high group within our sample. Although he has been on swimming teams, his own evaluation of the experience is clearly on the side of enjoyment of the experience rather than enjoyment of the victory. He says firmly, "The competition is not as important as the enjoyment." He went on, "I love to get into the water and pretend I'm a seal. I can move like one in that wavy motion. It's a fluid, effortless, almost frictionless feeling. . . . I like being under water more than being on top. I look around and swim. . . . Everything under water has a different appearance, though I guess it is more the feeling of suspended weightlessness, a feeling of easy, free movement."

With his emphasis upon feeling in his favorite sport, it is not surprising to find that he has an aesthetic interest in nature. "I like to sit on a rock in the middle of a stream and just admire what is around me."

The weightlessness of swimming carried over into an enjoyment of flying. The previous summer he had been a passenger on a large jet when it was catapulted from an aircraft carrier. "It was an amazing, overpowering feeling. You're slammed into the back of the seat. Once you're off, you're free. It's like a roller coaster, except three or four times as strong." He would like to fly a plane himself. "I could see myself as a bird. It would be fun—effortless movement through the air . . . weightlessness, power, freedom, a big view."

While Chester's interests did not incline strongly toward intellectual pursuits, such as reading, he could adopt the role of passive enjoyment, and sociability ranked higher for him than competitiveness. For example, he enjoyed tennis because, while playing, he could carry on a conversation with members of his family or friends —scarcely a stance that makes a tennis champion. We feel that these contrasts between Chester and competitive-team athletes are reflected in their different hypnotic scores.

From table 23 we know that a great many athletes, including those who engage in individual-skill sports, are low in hypnotizability. There is something to be said for looking at some cases of nonhypnotizable athletes within the individual-sport category.

Stuart scored two out of twelve on SHSS-C. He participated in water sports of all kinds, some of them more competitive than others. Thus his skin diving and water surfing were for fun, but water polo was very competitive. On the whole, his attitudes appeared to be more like those characteristic of the individual-skill-sports enthusiasts, and therefore his nonhypnotizability was a little puzzling. He found that body surfing offered the ultimate excitement; he loved fighting the elements or becoming part of them. He enjoyed feeling his muscles work. He loved the thrill of skin diving; the danger was fun. He thrilled to the elements: huge waves, a storm, rushing wind, speed.

The first hint that he might not be hypnotizable came in his remark, as he reported for hypnosis, "I'm kind of interested in hypnosis, but I don't know that I can trust putting myself in the hands of someone else." Such a remark has in other cases proved an unfavorable sign, though not universally; some who made similar remarks proved hypnotizable.

He spoke of his need for "activity." When asked about reading, he responded by saying that other activities had precedence but that when he read he wanted the book to be full of action.

Music could be either soft or blaring (jazz or rock-and-roll); he used it a little as an escape or to provide activity when he needed it, but he felt no deep involvement. He had snow skied for the past year but felt there was not as much exhilaration in it as in surfing.

While Stuart is still an enigmatic case, it is a reasonable inference that the hypnotic role was too passive for him: he liked activity, liked to manage things. Most of the hypnotizable athletes combine an imaginative interest or an appreciative interest with their enjoyment of activity.

Edwin provides another instance of interest in essentially individual-skill sports combined with low hypnotizability. He scored one out of twelve on SHSS-C. He was very enthusiastic about sports, particularly tennis, swimming, and water skiing. Of tennis he said, "I enjoy it, I like hitting the ball. I guess it's escapism." Of swimming: "It's racing; it's competition." Here then, we have a combination of enjoying the experiences for itself ("hitting the ball"), and enjoying the competition ("It's racing").

Edwin felt that he could best describe his personality by saying that he liked to do things. He liked to *do* some work during the week and then "explode" on weekends. (It turned out that he really didn't do much work during the week; the weekends were more accurately described.) He did say that he couldn't concentrate very well on his studies. "Concentrating happens so seldom. On daily assignments I never seem to concentrate. When the heat is on for a term paper or an exam, I can." He admitted he generally slept through classes and paid no attention to course work. At the last minute he could respond to the force of "or else" embodied in examinations or term papers. What he liked on weekends was stunts or pranks, for example, filling water balloons and releasing them over girls sunning on their balconies—screams would fill the air, much to his delight. Or he liked a weekend of drinking.

The interviewer described Edwin as a very self-conscious boy who inserted his personality into each answer. True to his statement that he ignored daily assignments, he was still asleep in the dormitory when the secretary from the laboratory called him to remind him that he was late for his appointment.

He felt that he had a negative streak, and this was very apparent in the way he responded to questions he didn't care for in the interview.

In Edwin's case, we suggest that the interest in tennis and swimming is relatively minor in comparison with the interest in unstructured activities. He speaks little of actual enjoyment of the sports in which he engages, using escapism as a descriptive term for tennis and competition as the essence of swimming.

We may say of Edwin, then, that his athletic involvement is not of the kind found in the more highly hypnotizable individual-sports subjects; while his competitiveness and will to win are not like those of the competitive-team athletes either, there is little that makes for hypnotizability. We have found in other cases that pranksters differ from the truly adventurous; the hypnotizably adventuresome are disciplined in their preparation and in the exercise of their skills. The weight lifters earlier described, and the swimmer, train carefully and patiently in order to enjoy the experience of the activity itself.

We can summarize the discussion of the hypnotizable and nonhypnotizable cases among the individual-skill athletes by noting these qualities of the highly hypnotizable:

1. The highly hypnotizable participant tends to emphasize enjoyment over competition.
2. The interest in activity is usually combined with either intellectual or aesthetic interests of more passive contemplative kinds.
3. The active experience is made use of as a way into hypnosis rather than as an obstacle to hypnosis.

When these characteristics are missing, the individual-skill participant tends to fall among the less hypnotizable.

### Sources of Athletic Interests and Attitudes

It may be a truism to point out that athletic interests, emphasis on achievement, and competitive attitudes are apt to run in families. Reviewing the athletes we have already mentioned:

1. *Dave.* This subject has already been quoted as saying that his older brothers provided the stimulation for his early and continued interest in athletics.

2. *Helen.* Helen said that her parents had not encouraged her going into athletics, but she was quite talented in them, and since the trend in the whole family was to excel she thought that athletics became her area of competency and excellence. Both her mother and father showed this same tendency toward excellence in competition, but in different fields.

3. *Perry.* Perry said that his three older brothers were all very competitive and reality-oriented, as he was. Their father was the same.

## What We Have Learned from Interviews with Athletes

Athletes represented the strongest denial of our hypothesis that the ability to immerse oneself in an activity or interest was predictive of hypnotic susceptibility. To begin with, we counted athletic involvement, along with reading, music, religion, and the rest, as a probable path into hypnosis, but the low hypnotic scores of one athlete after another soon made us realize that other factors were operating. In this chapter we have attempted to show why athletic interest alone tends to be associated with low susceptibility. We had to learn this from our subjects as we talked with them.

The main characteristics of competitive-team athletes which militate against hypnosis are (1) careful and vigilant processing of information from the environment, (2) alert readiness to make decisions on the basis of incoming information and to react promptly, and (3) constant, active striving. These are in some sense the opposites of the hypnotic demands to permit imagination to wander freely, to savor and enjoy the moment with little concern over outcome, to accept passive involvement rather than active goal seeking.

When athletes in relation to hypnosis were reported earlier (J. R. Hilgard 1965, pp. 362–68) the conclusions drawn were similar to those of the present discussion, except that the athletes had not been separated into the two groups of more highly competitive team sports and less highly competitive individual-skill sports. The distinction was noted between those who stressed competition and those who became involved in the activity itself, but this was attributed more to individual personality than to the kind of sport chosen. As is so often the case, the truth lies somewhere between, that is, there is an interaction between the kind of person we are dealing with and the kind of sport chosen, but either kind of person may be found in either kind of sport.

The requirements of alertness, planned responsiveness, and activity apply also to those competitive athletes who score high in hypnosis by virtue of other kinds of interests. (What follows draws heavily on J. R. Hilgard 1965, pp. 365–68.) Why, then, do not these other interests (fantasy, free imagination, and so forth) interfere with athletic prowess? This is an interesting question and shows how careful one has to be about making generalizations. There are, in fact, three answers to be considered:

1. Some competitive athletes are able to dissociate the athletic activity from other kinds of absorbing activities, so that the two

spheres are kept entirely distinct. Hence, the absorption evident in these other activities does not interfere with the reality orientation of the competition.

2. Other competitive athletes find ways of making use of their hypnotic abilities in athletic competition, through the kinds of roles they play. A case of a baseball player will be described presently, but presumably track events (such as long-distance running) would permit the same sort of use of hypnotic ability within the sport itself, even though the sport counts as competitive because there are adversaries to be met.

3. Many of the athletes, particularly the individual-skill athletes, are not primarily competitors at all, so that their interests, as we have shown, pose no special problems with respect to hypnotizability.

The third of these points concerning the problem of athletics and hypnotizability has already been discussed. The first two will now be illustrated by cases.

George is an athlete who keeps his athletics separate from the interests that are most closely associated with his hypnotizability. He scores seven out of twelve on form SHSS. In the interview prior to hypnosis he was rated high in reading, especially science fiction, and also in theater and sports.

He is a doer; he loves activity. This is reflected in his athletic interests. He said it was easy to concentrate on athletics because he was directly involved and there was action. It was not easy for him to sit down and concentrate. Playing golf and participating in athletics were for him a challenge to accomplishment and not viewed as relaxation. In this he sounds like other team athletes.

There is, however, another side to him. This is illustrated in his reading. "I don't read. I *live* the character. I *become* that character; I put myself in his place rather than putting him in my place." Thus he is able to combine in one person the realism of the athlete and the reality distortion of his reading; there is no conflict involved.

The next illustration is of the highest-scoring competitive-team athlete in our sample, who scored twelve on the scale. This subject, Vance, a baseball pitcher, showed us how hypnotic ability could be used in athletic competition. This is not to say that what he did could be used by everyone, or that it would be appropriate to all athletic roles. Not all athletic roles are alike, and the different positions within a team may make different demands upon the players. Thus a baseball shortstop has to be alert and ready for whatever happens, while a pitcher has more control over the timing of what happens. Vance, as a pitcher, was in a favored position to make use of his hypnotic skill.

It turns out that he had had many experiences that might be described as essentially self-hypnotic. When faced with a personal problem he often went into a kind of mental trance as he described it. When he came out he would not remember what he had been thinking about; he knew only that the problem was on the way to a solution. This had been his practice for many years.

When asked whether or not the baseball player had to be alert and on his toes all of the time, he answered, "I am different from other people. Before a ball game, I set myself emotionally in a particular mood through concentration on making my senses more keen and my mind more alert. It's a state of mind that carries me through the ball game. It supports itself, once I set myself." He may spend ten minutes or so creating this mood, not concentrating on anything in particular, but rather on nothingness as in a completely dark room. He is able to relax completely, and this "state of suspended animation" (his expression for it) may take from three to five minutes while he gets everything out of his system, such as the problems of the day. The first step is achieving complete relaxation; the second step is building up emotional tension. This is done without words, but his mind is on baseball. "It's a feeling of complete confidence that I'm going to do well, that I'm going to play to the peak of my ability." When asked about the relation of this to hypnosis he said simply and confidently, "I can assume many roles, depending upon the necessity."

The ease with which Vance could assume roles that helped him to achieve his goals was illustrated by his account of how he mastered conversational Spanish. He reported that he was not doing well in Spanish. To overcome his lack of confidence he imagined that he was a student in Spain carrying on a conversation with a real Spaniard. This was a two-way conversation, in which he was sometimes the Spaniard and sometimes the student. With this kind of preparation he developed a feeling of confidence, and his performance in Spanish improved.

Whether or not his use of a kind of self-hypnosis would serve for athletic positions other than pitcher is an open question; at least for him, hypnosis and athletic prowess did not conflict.

Because intense involvement is so characteristic of hypnosis, and because interests reflecting involvement are correlated with hypnosis, it is easy to make the mistake of thinking that all involvements are related to hypnosis. The same could, of course, be said of the role-enactment theory of hypnosis: there are obviously some role enactments that are very closely related to hypnosis, but it does not follow that role enactment is a sufficient characterization of the hypnotic subject unless more is said about the kind of role. Our study of athletes has helped us to avoid overgeneralizing about involvements, for we have among our competitive-team athletes, deeply involved in their roles, a group who score lowest among identifiable groups with respect to hypnotic susceptibility.

### Reality Ties through Science

Are there other kinds of involvement which, like competitive athletic involvement, are antithetical to hypnotic susceptibility? We have identified two more: a deep commitment to science, and recreation which takes the form of work toward a standard of excellence. Commitment to science requires reality orientation, a critical attitude, and alertness to environmental details (including the unexpected) that the untrained observer is likely to miss. While there is an aesthetic element in science, and a role for fantasy, the day-to-day work of the scientist is exacting and demands precision and devotion to duty. Thus our scientists appear less hypnotizable than the readers of science fiction, who enjoy the excitement of science without its day-to-day discipline. So, too, the person who makes violins as a hobby, or crosses exotic plants, is enjoying himself, but he works at his task with achievement as the goal; the immediate experience requires a great deal of patient effort, and satisfaction comes more in the end result than in the process. While he departs from one aspect of reality (the economic aspect, for he does not ask what his time is worth while engaging in his hobby) he, like the scientist, is tied to reality in what he does and what he observes.

### The Less Hypnotizable Science Student

We have in scientific interest something which, in relation to hypnosis, corresponds to competitive athletics, as is shown in table 24. That is, the scientist, like the athlete, can become very absorbed in what he is doing, but if this is his sole preoccupation he is likely to end up nonhypnotizable. It is evident from the table that in our sample the humanities majors are the most hypnotizable, the social science majors in between, and the natural scientists (biologists, physical scientists, engineers) the least hypnotizable.

While the differences by major are statistically significant, we find, as usual, that there are always some members of each group

TABLE 24

Choice of Major in College as Related to Hypnotic
Susceptibility, 1962–63

| Hypnotic Susceptibility (SHSS-C) | Humanities | Social Science | Biological Sciences Physical Sciences Engineering | Total |
|---|---|---|---|---|
| More hypnotizable (7–12) | 9 | 21 | 10 | 40 |
| Less hypnotizable (0–6) | 5 | 21 | 32 | 58 |
| Total | 14 | 42 | 42 | 98 |

Note: Eight subjects were undecided about their majors.
Significance test: $\chi^2 = 9.53$; $df = 2$; $p < .01$.

at opposite ends of the spectrum, and these contrasts provide interesting cases for us to explore further.

Representative of science students who score low in hypnosis
we may consider Eugene, who scored one out of a possible twelve
on SHSS-C, despite having been rated near the top (six of seven)
on his desire to experience hypnosis. He said he had always wondered what hypnosis was like. He had watched it on TV and
thought he would be "pretty susceptible"; he wanted to go along
and knew that he would not fight it. Despite this interest and
willingness, he was unable to have the experience. (Subjects like
this warn against the assumption that the desire to go along with
the hypnotist is all that is needed to achieve the hypnotic experience.)

At the time of his interview in advance of hypnosis, Eugene
was a sophomore majoring in physics and intending to go on to the
Ph.D. Among his broader interests were a scientific interest in nature (in contrast with an aesthetic interest), and a high interest in
work recreation. These interests require some elucidation, because
they are crucial in describing the difference between the hypnotizable and the nonhypnotizable.

We have already reported on Eugene's scientific interest in
nature (chap. 6), but this bears repeating here. His interest in nature
took the form of hiking and studying the plants and animals along
the way. What he really enjoyed was being outside and getting
exercise; the intellectual and analytical interests in the things he
found had none of the feeling overtones of those whose interest
in nature is aesthetic.

He could become deeply absorbed in building and making things and rated this interest among his very highest. He became so absorbed that he paid little attention to anything else, not hearing when he was called to dinner. This interest had been developed alongside his father, an electrical engineer. "He always had me build along with him and help him fix things." They had built a chemistry laboratory together. They had also built a hi-fi set together, and then he had built one for himself. He did repairs around the house, as his father did.

In work recreation he had a capacity for absorption and close attention, as indeed our competitive athletes have in their sports. This, too, is a kind of role enactment, but it is not a role compatible with hypnosis. "When I'm interested I can forget time and meals. While working on my hi-fi I'd stay up until 2 A.M. and eat only one meal all day."

After Eugene scored one in hypnosis, he was interviewed again to see what he would say about his experience. "I tried to let myself go blank. I always think, always tend to analyze what's going on. I think *why, why*, about everything, 'Why is it happening this way?' It's the reason I enjoy physics—you get an answer. It's the same in biology, which is mainly classifying things: how one insect is related to another. . . . I was trying to overcome my analytic trend as I sat in hypnosis. I was trying to cooperate to the best of my ability, but even in the smell test, while I was trying to put everything out of my mind, I thought, 'What is he trying to prove?' . . . I kept thinking, 'What's going to happen?' . . . I'm sort of experimenting for myself to see if it's really what they say."

He expressed genuine disappointment at not being able to experience hypnosis. "I was eager to know and try it and see how it worked."

We reviewed the history of his interest in repairing, building, and science. "My father started me when I was about eight, with simple things, like repairing the cord on the toaster. By the fifth or sixth grade I worked on a radio kit. At first he'd just send me to get parts, but gradually as I knew more, he'd say, 'You finish this, son.' Eugene felt that his father, who was very successful in his work as an engineer, had never been able to do something for sheer recreation alone; the product must serve some useful purpose. Eugene found himself increasingly this way, too.

In Eugene, then, we see the inhibiting effect upon hypnotizability of the habitually questioning and analytic set of the scientist, in combination with the reality-oriented kind of work recreation in which useful products are being made. There is the capacity for focused attention and deep absorption, but the feeling components and reality distortions characteristic of hypnosis are not present.

### The Hypnotizable Science Student

Even though we make the generalization that science students are, on the whole, not as hypnotizable as humanities students, any one science student may prove to be highly hypnotizable, and it is important to know what characteristics have to be combined with scientific interests for hypnotizability to be enhanced.

Ronald, like Eugene, was a sophomore majoring in physics and planning to go on to the Ph.D. Both were eager to be hypnotized, but whereas Eugene failed, Ronald succeeded, scoring eleven out of twelve on SHSS-C. In his interview before hypnosis he expressed his curiosity about it, how friends had found the experience enjoyable. "I hope to be very hypnotizable, because it should be more interesting that way. I am fairly high-strung, nervous, but I can become very engrossed at times."

Ronald, like Eugene, has an interest in nature, but the interest is very different. For Eugene, it is a scientific interest; for Ronald it is almost purely appreciative. "I enjoy the beauty of the outdoors and nature—I find simplicity there—I like to get off by myself, exploring, so others don't distract me. . . . In exploring mountains I have an almost uncontrollable urge to go ahead, an urge that transcends physical exhaustion. I go until I cannot go. I have this *intense* curiosity. . . . I can see ferns, water, a stream making a sand dune, lichens. My eyes are continuously looking, taking in more details, the continuously varying experience . . ."

He doesn't hunt with firearms. "I hunt only with a camera . . . but I take pictures with my eyes more."

While Ronald, like Eugene, also has a laboratory at home, this is not for him an all-absorbing interest. He enjoys literature and philosophy. Ronald's background in reading is similar to that so frequently found among our more susceptible subjects. As a small boy he had read *Twenty Thousand Leagues under the Sea* and was emotionally swept away by it. He felt that he was present during the suspense of being trapped under an iceberg, with the oxygen running out. "I was an anonymous crew member participating in the crisis. I was an observer, yet there as me, as a crew member, in order to feel the emotion. The crisis was my crisis." He reported also that as he read Jack London's *Gray Dawn* he felt an intense excitement, a "stomach excitement."

We find, then, in Ronald, by contrast with Eugene, an aesthetic interest in nature contrasting with the scientific interest, lack of a deep commitment to work recreation, and many evidences of imaginative absorption familiar among our hypnotizables.

Does this mean that Ronald will be a less able scientist than Eugene? Of course we have no way of predicting for these particular two, but we doubt that there is anything essential in these contrasts so far as a career in science is concerned. (It may be noted, in passing, both that creative scientists tend to have high scores on aesthetic values [Barron 1963; MacKinnon 1965], and that many have somewhat unusual interests in addition to their realistic scientific ones [Jones 1957].) So far as hypnosis is concerned, the situation appears to be much what it is for athletes. It is possible that some individuals have a greater capacity for dissociation than others, so that they can carry out their realistic, critical, and analytic activities with full attention and, when they wish, can change over to the carefree, imaginative, aesthetically receptive persons represented by other aspects of their personalities. The notion of personality unity or integration can be misinterpreted if it does not allow for those who can "shift gears" in this manner.

These brief characterizations of scientists bring their activities into relation to the nonhypnotizability of the athlete. To be hypnotizable it is necessary to be capable of departure from reality to a certain extent, something not permitted the competitive athlete, the day-to-day scientist in his laboratory, or the hobbyist with an excellent product to be made. To be hypnotizable, one has to be somewhat passively receptive and able to allow free play to the imagination; this is not the way to achievement on the playing field, to analysis of data in the laboratory, to construction of violins, or to the breeding of plants. While all the activities are of a kind in which the participants may become deeply involved, involvement in itself is not enough; it must be of a particular kind. The distinction is similar to that made by Freud (1911) between primary-process thinking and secondary-process thinking; the former is the more impulsive, the latter is the more conceptual.

The distinction between the competitive-team athlete and the individual-sport athlete has helped us with the understandings that had to be reached. Both tend to be active persons, but for the competitor the activity sets aside the possibility of hypnosis, while for the one who can enjoy his sport for its immediate satisfactions the experience is more apt to become a bridge to hypnosis.

# 11

## Significance of the Involvements

In the foregoing chapters there has been a primary and repeated emphasis upon the significance of imaginative involvements of various sorts for the understanding of the hypnotically susceptible personality. The involvements have been studied one at a time— reading, drama, creative activities, religion, childhood fantasy, aesthetic interest in nature, and venturesomeness—with little concern for their interactions, although the cases have shown repeatedly that the same person may exhibit at once several of these involvements. The task of this chapter is to study the intercorrelations of the involvements as they bear on the prediction of hypnotizability. We may understand from them, also, some of the problems of personality assessment.

### The Additive Assumption in the Assessment of Personality

Most personality inventories have been constructed on the pattern of intelligence tests, in the hope that the relative successes of intelligence measurement can be repeated for personality. An intelligence test consists of a number of questions of varying degrees of difficulty and covering various topics. The more of these questions a subject can answer correctly, that is, in accordance with truth and fact, the more intelligent he is. This is not the place to go into the problems of intelligence measurement, but the basic assumption is clear: the more right answers the more intelligent. This is the *additive* assumption: you add up the answers to get the score. The assumption is carried over into personality tests, even though there are no "right" answers. Still, the number of questions answered "in the right direction" will account for how a person is classified, say, as an introvert or an extravert. To the extent that answers "in the right direction" (by whatever criterion) are added up to derive a score, the additive assumption is being used. For example, in the various experience inventories used to predict hypnosis, the items which have been found related to hypnosis are "added up" to yield a score predictive of hypnotic susceptibility. Thus the additive assumption is a clear one and is often a useful one.

A more sophisticated form of the additive assumption lies in the use of a multiple-regression equation in which the items entering into the score are added, but with weights assigned in accordance with their intercorrelations, particularly their correlations with a criterion. If two tests correlate positively with a criterion, and little or not at all with each other, they are ideal members of the predictive battery and carry substantial weights; if they correlate higher with each other than with the criterion, one of them may turn out to have a high weight and the other little weight at all. The facts of multiple correlation are more complex than can be stated in a few sentences of this kind. For example, sometimes a variable showing little correlation with the criterion may increase the size of a multiple correlation because it acts as a suppressor variable through its correlation with some other variable. These complexities do not affect the discussion here.

We can easily test the additive assumption with respect to our involvement variables by carrying out their intercorrelations with each other and with hypnotic susceptibility. Then we can derive a simple sum of the involvement ratings and correlate it with hypnosis, following the additive assumptions of the usual personality inventory, or we can carry out the multiple correlation to determine the highest correlation that is possible by properly weighting the tests. The results are given in table 25. It turns out that the sum of the ratings correlates $r = .35$ with hypnotic susceptibility, while the more accurate weighting of a multiple-regression equation raises this very little, to $r = .37$. These correlations, while significant, are not high. Perhaps it should be reiterated that the purpose is analytical, not predictive. The correlations tell us that rated involvements are indicative of hypnotic susceptibility, but they do not make it practical, at present, to select hypnotic subjects on the basis of these rated involvements.

The intercorrelations of the various involvements in table 25 range from .05 to .40. Because they are so low they tell us that the interviewers are not giving much of a "halo effect" in their ratings; that is, because a subject is rated high in drama he is not auto-

TABLE 25

Intercorrelations of Seven Involvement Ratings with Each Other and with Hypnosis
(N = 187)

| | (2) Drama | (3) Creativity | (4) Religion | (5) Childhood Imagination | (6) Sensory Stimulation | (7) Venturesomeness | (8) SHSS-C |
|---|---|---|---|---|---|---|---|
| (1) Reading | 40 | 31 | 05 | 40 | 27 | 22 | 15 |
| (2) Drama | | 31 | 09 | 17 | 09 | 10 | 20 |
| (3) Creativity | | | 05 | 19 | 23 | 10 | 20 |
| (4) Religion | | | | 10 | 12 | 06 | 15 |
| (5) Childhood imagination | | | | | 24 | 11 | 22 |
| (6) Sensory stimulation | | | | | | 34 | 22 |
| (7) Venturesomeness | | | | | | | 21 |
| | | | | | | | |
| (8) Sum of ratings | | | | | | | 35 |
| Multiple correlation, variables (1) through (7), with (8) | | | | | | | 37 |

Note: Decimal points omitted.

matically rated high in creativity through a confusion between the two judgments.

There is an obvious convenience in the additive assumption. By the simple process of adding the involvements, we raise the correlation of .22, the highest of any single involvement, to $r = .35$.

## Alternate-Path Theory versus the Additive Assumption

Regardless of the length of personality inventories, or of various refinements made in them, they have been relatively unsuccessful in achieving high predictive significance against the various criteria that have been tried. This lack of success had led some authors (e.g., Mischel 1968) to abandon the thought of any consistency within personality itself, other than the consistency of very specific habits. It is still possible, however, that there is some fault in the model provided by the additive assumption and that some other logic of personality organization prevails. If, for example, a high score in *one* area of involvement indicates the presence of the kind of background needed to predict hypnosis, it may not matter that other predictors have very low weights for this subject. This one area is not enough to predict susceptibility, however, for another person may have *another* area that serves for him. Were this the situation, it is easy to see how the additive assumption would fail. One person, for example, with a high rating, say a seven, in one area would be as hypnotizable as another with three sevens, or a score of twenty-one; while a third subject who had no high rating might have a  score of ten based on, say, five ratings of two. With this kind of composition of scores resulting from addition, only very low correlations would be expected. The general theory behind this interpretation has been called the *alternate-path* theory, as a substitute for the additive assumption. If the measurements could be made appropriately, hypnosis would be predicted on the basis of the highest score in any one appropriate area, ignoring all the others.

An earlier test of this hypothesis was made from the data of this study through comparing fantasy and adventuresomeness as alternate paths (E. R. Hilgard 1964). It was there pointed out that if one of these determiners was high the other was largely irrelevant. Thus for subjects high in fantasy there was a nonsignificant correlation with adventuresomeness, and for subjects high in adventuresomeness there was a nonsignificant correlation with fantasy. Turning the matter around, however, when fantasy was low there was a significant correlation between adventuresomeness and hypnosis, and when adventure was low there was a significant correlation with fantasy. The data are shown in table 26. These results are coherent with the hypothesis that either high fantasy or high adventure can lead to hypnotic susceptibility, thus conforming to the theory of alternate paths.

TABLE 26

*Adventuresomeness and Childhood Fantasy as Related to Hypnotic Susceptibility*

| | Correlations with SHSS-C | |
|---|---|---|
| | N | r |
| Adventuresomeness vs. hypnotic susceptibility | | |
| Low-fantasy subjects | 67 | .32‡ |
| High-fantasy subjects | 37 | .03* |
| Childhood fantasy vs. hypnotic susceptibility | | |
| Low-adventure subjects | 49 | .34† |
| High-adventure subjects | 55 | .11* |

Source: E. R. Hilgard 1964. With permission, University of Nebraska Press.
* Not significant.    † $p = .05$.    ‡ $p = .01$.

A more direct test of the alternate-path theory is made by studying what happens when a number of involvements have been rated. The alternate-path theory predicts that if a person scores high enough (rated six or seven) in any one area he should be as hypnotizable as if he rated equally high in several areas. Results within a sample of forty-five cases, all interviewed by our most experienced interviewer in the winter of 1964, showed this conjecture to hold. The data are given in table 27. The assumption to be tested was that the high rating in a single area was as predictive as high ratings in more than one area, and this turned out to be the case. The predictive significance was supported by the low hypnotic scores on the part of those who did not achieve a high rating in any area at all.

In this small sample, in which ratings were made by the same person and with great care, the correlation between the hypnotic score and the *sum* of the ratings was $r = .39$, while the correlation with the *highest* rating in any area was $r = .42$. The demonstration was not as satisfactory with ratings made by a number of interviewers over the large sample. Then the correlation with the *sum* of the ratings was $r = .35$, as previously reported (table 25), while the correlation with the highest rating was $r = .26$ ($N = 187$). Thus, as a practical matter, the highest rating does not serve as a substitute for the sum of the ratings, even though the possibility is great that the additive assumption is inadequate and that the alternate-path interpretation may be correct.

TABLE 27

*Ratings in Involvement Areas as Related to Hypnotic Susceptibility*

| | | SHSS-C' | |
| --- | --- | --- | --- |
| Rating | N | Mean | SD |
| A. 6 or 7, one area only | 12 | 5.50 | 2.38 |
| B. 6 or 7, more than one area | 14 | 5.36 | 1.38 |
| C. Under 6, all areas | 19 | 2.76 | 1.86 |
| Total | 45 | 4.30 | 2.30 |

Source: J. R. Hilgard 1965. In E. R. Hilgard, *Hypnotic Susceptibility*, p. 351. © 1965 by Harcourt, Brace & World and reprinted with permission.

Significance tests: Between groups: $F$-ratio $= 10.16$; $df = 2.42$; $p < .001$. Groups A and B vs. group C: $t = 6.25$; $df = 43$; $p < .001$.

The technical difficulties in making an adequate test of the alternate-path theory are very great. In the first place, no one "path" has at present been identified clearly enough to provide an assurance that those who rate high in it will be more than slightly above average in hypnotizability, and so much is left to be accounted for. Second, when single ratings are depended on, any errors made by the interviewer are magnified. That is, a test of the alternate-path theory requires that each scale must be sufficient unto itself. When an interviewer has many other matters to attend to, any single rating may be faulty. Thus an additive score may be expected to be more reliable than a single "highest" score, merely because it is based on more data and therefore some errors may cancel. Hence the fact that the overall correlation of hypnosis with the single highest score falls short of the correlation with added scores is not sufficient to disprove the alternate path theory. In view of the unsatisfactory state of personality measurement, further explorations of the alternate-path approach seem to be desirable. The use of so-called moderator variables follows essentially the logic of the alternate-path theory, at least to the extent that it is a corrective to the simple additive assumption in personality testing. See, for example, Saunders (1956).

### Involvements and the Theory of Transference

The special relationship of the hypnotic subject to the hypnotist, historically referred to as *rapport* between them, bears some resemblance to the special relationship between a patient and psychotherapist which in psychoanalytic terminology is called *transference*.

Gill and Brenman (1959, p. 137) believe that there is a difference between the developing transference in psychotherapy and the transference underlying hypnosis. The hypnotic state, as they observed it, appeared to function like a ready-made structure, with a complex but "frozen" transference. By contrast, the transference that develops in therapy is fluid and shifting; it is specific to the interaction between the patient and the therapist, while the hypnotic transference is nonspecific, depending very little upon who the hypnotist is or what the nature of the therapeutic situation may be. They point out that in the therapeutic situation analysis of the transference can proceed without influencing hypnotizability. Related observations have been made by Kubie and Margolin (1944), who feel that the usual transference of therapy is not a basic ingredient of hypnosis. Although some manifestations of transference occur, they are "not the essence of the process or of the state itself" (Kubie and Margolin 1944, p. 621). Macalpine (1950), noting the speed with which the hypnotic state can be induced in some patients on the first encounter, speaks of a "transference readiness" which might be interpreted as related to the "fixed structure" to which Gill and Brenman refer.

These observations and interpretations that there is something less personal to the hypnotist about the transference manifestations within hypnosis, compared with the specifically personal transferences within the more usual therapy, fit in with our discussion of the involvements as a background preparatory to the hypnotic experience. Thus, as a result of many experiences in the past, the susceptible subject comes to hypnosis with a well-developed and relatively fixed ability to participate in fantasies stimulated through outside sources, often (though not exclusively) verbal. The words of the novels he has read, the voices of the actors he has listened to, as well as the stimulation provided by music or beauty in nature, have aroused appropriate fantasies with feeling because of the repeatedly experienced involvements. If our interpretation is correct, the voice of the hypnotist (*any* hypnotist whom he is willing to trust) will capitalize on this established background of imaginative involvements. This, then, is our interpretation of the "frozen" transference, or the "transference readiness" brought to the initial hypnotic session. The fantasies stirred up may be controlled by the hypnotist's suggestions, as they are controlled by the author or dramatist, or they may arise from the rich imagination of the subject's past, as in the hypnotically suggested dream or age regression. It is not surprising that sometimes, as in the reported dream or in a hypnotic age regression, it is difficult to know whether a past experience is being relived or whether the subject is off on a flight of fantasy.

## Involvements and Hypnotizability

The statistical data and the case reports have given consistent support to the relationship between imaginative involvement and hypnotic susceptibility. While the correlations are low, indicating that more is involved, the spontaneous assertions of the subjects leave little doubt that hypnosis capitalizes on features of past experience that have permitted the free play of imagination, the setting aside of reality, and the immersion in an experience that to the subject is absorbing and satisfying.

The subjects who receive top ratings in any one of these areas of imaginative involvement are almost always in the upper half of the hypnotic scale, but they are by no means consistently at the top of the scale, so that involvements do not tell the whole story. The interactions between other aspects of personality and the imaginative involvements are doubtless subtle. For example, there may be the question of the extent to which the involvement is conflict-laden or conflict-free. Hartmann (1958), agreeing with the classical psychoanalytic interpretation that conflicts are at the root of every neurosis, and that the normal ego grows on conflict, has pointed out that there are also many aspects of growth and development—perception, thought, language, skill—that are outside the region of conflict, in what he calls the "conflict-free ego sphere." A conflict-free area of involvement will perhaps permit richer participation in the hypnotic experience than an area which involves some degree of apprehension or anxiety, which may then inhibit the involvement in hypnosis. Doubtless these are all also a matter of degree, and our knowledges and skills do not yet permit us to make the necessary distinctions.

# 12

# Normality and Hypnotizability

There is still some residue from Charcot's theory that the hypnotizable person is ipso facto a hysterical personality. The impression persists that the neurotic is more hypnotizable than the normal, despite evidence to the contrary beginning with Charcot's nineteenth-century adversary, Bernheim. For example, Gill and Brenman (1959) conclude, largely on the basis of a study by Ehrenreich (1949), that the normal person is more hypnotizable than the neurotic, even though, among neurotics, the hysterical person may be more hypnotizable than the others. While our population of successful university students is an essentially normal one, there are personality characteristics within such a population which can be classified along a normal-neurotic dimension, and it is of some interest to see what our findings show about the relationship between ratings in this area and hypnotizability.

## The Hypnotizability of the Normal-Outgoing Person

We used two ratings, one of a dimension which we called *normal-troubled* (which corresponds roughly to Eysenck's stable-neurotic dimension) and another called *outgoing-withdrawn* (which corresponds roughly to his extravert-introvert dimension) (Eysenck 1961). As rated by our interviewers, these two dimensions correlated $r = .64$, and therefore we have combined them into a single scale of normal-outgoing vs. troubled-withdrawn. In 1962–63, we used three-point scales, and in 1963–64, seven-point scales; combined, these become scales of 2–6 and 2–14, with the high values indicating disturbance. These have been converted to a common

170

five-point scale (1–5), yielding very similar distributions on the two years. The effort to use Eysenck's fourfold classification of stable-extravert, stable-introvert, neurotic-extravert, and neurotic-introvert led to a very uneven number in the various cells, with almost none in the neurotic-extravert class. Hence the two-class division was adopted. An earlier test of the Eysenck categorizations had proved unfruitful (Hilgard and Bentler 1963).

The result of these ratings on our student population was a very skewed distribution, with over half of the cases rated at the extreme of normal-outgoing, and the rest spreading over the scale in decreasing numbers toward the troubled-withdrawn end (figure 2).

In the further treatment of the data, in order to have enough cases to be treated meaningfully from a statistical standpoint, the subjects rated at the extreme of normal-outgoing have been contrasted with all others. To describe the "all others" as "troubled-withdrawn" is something of an exaggeration; still, they had something that made the interviewer rate them as either a little more withdrawn or a little more troubled than the run of students in the sample.

When scores are dichotomized in this way, and the hypnotic susceptibility scores examined, the results come out as shown in table 28. For 1962–63 the normal-outgoing group contains significantly more high hypnotizables than the troubled-withdrawn group; the results are in the same direction in 1963–64, but the contrasts are not sufficient to reach significance. Combining the groups over the two years, we reach a significance of $p = .01$. Noting that our troubled-withdrawn group is not really very "neurotic," we find it interesting that despite the lack of sharp contrasts the normal-outgoing subjects score higher overall than the troubled-withdrawn. The relationship is significant statistically but is not a strong one from a correlational standpoint ($r = .22$) and has little meaning so far as predicting where on the scale of hypnotizability any one subject is likely to fall. It does, however, refute the conception that neurotic traits are more favorable to hypnosis than stable, normal ones.

Global personality descriptions such as *normal* and *neurotic* are not very satisfactory unless we know what kinds of behavior are entering into the judgments. The correlations given in table 29 show what kinds of specific ratings were made of the subjects whose overall personalities were assigned to the normal-outgoing or troubled-withdrawn fraction of the sample. For convenience of interpretation, the positive correlations, indicating agreement with

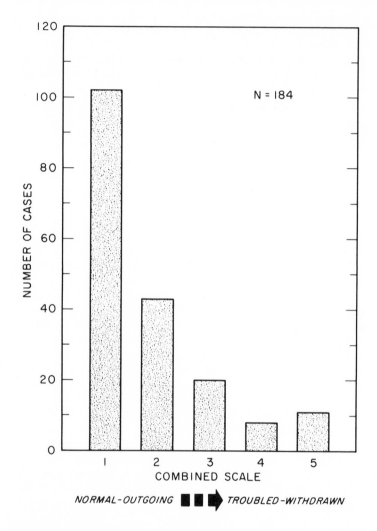

FIGURE 2. Distribution of ratings, normal-outgoing versus troubled-withdrawn.

Ratings for the two years, although obtained on somewhat different scales,
have been combined. Three cases of $N = 187$ were not ascertained.

TABLE 28

*Ratings of Normal-Outgoing Personality vs. Troubled-Withdrawn Personality as Related to Hypnotic Susceptibility*

| Hypnotic Susceptibility (SHSS-C) | 1962–63 | | 1963–64 | | Total | |
|---|---|---|---|---|---|---|
| | Normal-Out-going* | Troubled-Withdrawn | Normal-Outgoing | Troubled-Withdrawn | Normal-Out-going | Troubled-Withdrawn |
| | % | % | % | % | % | % |
| High (7–12) | 48 | 23 | 45 | 31 | 47 | 27 |
| Low (0–6) | 52 | 77 | 55 | 69 | 53 | 73 |
| Total | 100 | 100 | 100 | 100 | 100 | 100 |
| | (N = 58) | (N = 43) | (N = 44) | (N = 39) | (N = 102) | (N = 82) |

Significance tests

| | | | |
|---|---|---|---|
| $\chi^2$ | 6.19 | 1.29 | 7.57 |
| p | .02 | † | .01 |

* Rated 1 on combined scale; ratings of 2–6 classified as troubled-withdrawn (see p. 171). Three cases of the total N of 187 were not ascertained.
† Not significant.

the positive end of the normality scale, are arranged in descending order, with the negative correlations at the bottom of the table. The highest correlations are with the friendship ratings, which doubtless weighed heavily in the judgment of outgoing-withdrawn. Next is the mother-warmth rating, followed by ease of communication in the interview. The negative correlations are with present fantasy (daydreaming), and with caution. Thus fantasy, which tends to be related to the involvements that aid hypnosis, may have worked somewhat against the correlation of normality with hypnotizability. An overall multiple correlation was computed between the listed variables and the normalcy rating, which turned out to be $R = .62$. For the subsamples of male and female subjects the corresponding correlations were, for males .62 ($N = 112$), and for females .71 ($N = 72$).

The correlations in the body of the table are mostly low, but the several high ones are plausible: The number of like-sex friends correlated with the number of opposite sex friends (.61), venturesomeness with ease of communication (.43), mother warmth with like-sex friendships (.29). Venturesomeness, as might be expected, correlated negatively with caution (−.58). We thus get an idea of

TABLE 29

Meaning of Normal-Outgoing Personality as Indicated by Correlations with Other Specific Ratings

| Rating | (2) | (3) | (4) | (5) | (6) | (7) | (8) | (9) | (10) Normal-Outgoing* |
|---|---|---|---|---|---|---|---|---|---|
| (1) Like-sexed friendships | 61 | 29 | 22 | 25 | 16 | 12 | −26 | −20 | 58 |
| (2) Opposite-sexed friendships | | 15 | 26 | 19 | 21 | 14 | −25 | −25 | 44 |
| (3) Mother warmth | | | 20 | 30 | 19 | 11 | −19 | −13 | 33 |
| (4) Ease of communication | | | | 22 | 43 | 07 | 14 | −26 | 24 |
| (5) Father warmth | | | | | 21 | 23 | −26 | −21 | 22 |
| (6) Venturesomeness | | | | | | 09 | −01 | −58 | 18 |
| (7) Reasoning as discipline | | | | | | | −09 | 01 | 09 |
| (8) Present fantasy | | | | | | | | 16 | −16 |
| (9) Caution | | | | | | | | | −19 |
| Multiple correlation of variables (1) through (9) with (10) normal-outgoing | | | | | | | | | R = .62 |

Note: Decimal points omitted.

*The ratings of normal-outgoing vs. troubled-withdrawn have been arranged so that correlations with positive sign are in the direction of normality. N = 184 throughout (three cases of total of 187 not ascertained). Correlations of .14 significant at .05 level; of .19 significant at .01 level; of .24 significant at .001 level.

what the interviewers reacted to when they made a global rating of normality.

Because of the importance assigned to friendship ratings, these deserve some study in their own right; and because hypnosis is a largely verbal interaction, communication is also worth special attention.

## Friendship Patterns

One aspect of a normal-outgoing personality is the ability to make friends and to be at ease with other people. The emphasis upon sexual adjustment within psychoanalysis is justified by the belief that the ability to achieve sexual intimacy in an adult manner is a sign of normal maturing. In our brief interviews we did not go into sexual material, so that friendship patterns are about as close as we got to sex in our more formal questioning, although a good many facts about sex life came out in the freedom of the interview. We could not represent these answers statistically because the topic was not explored with all subjects. We did ask about both like-sexed and opposite-sexed friendships and rated them separately. The rating was based primarily upon the quantity of interactions (many friends) and the quality of the relationships (close friends getting a higher rating than many casual acquaintances).

How these ratings were distributed is shown in table 30, for

TABLE 30

*Distributions of Friendship Ratings*

| Friendship Rating | Male | | Female | |
|---|---|---|---|---|
| | *Like-sexed Friendships* | *Opposite-sexed Friendships* | *Like-sexed Friendships* | *Opposite-sexed Friendships* |
| High (5–7) | 58 | 33 | 36 | 34 |
| Medium (4) | 22 | 28 | 16 | 16 |
| Low (1–3) | 34 | 53 | 20 | 22 |
| Total | 114* | 114* | 72 | 72 |

* Omitting one not ascertained.

like-sexed and opposite-sexed friends for both the male and female subjects. These are quite sociable individuals as a group. Male subjects tend to report relatively few opposite-sex friendships. Perhaps in a university where the men out-number the women by a ratio of three to one the women have a better opportunity for dating than the men, or perhaps dating is less important for the man in college—early in his college years, as most of our subjects were. In any case, these are the ratings available for comparison with hypnotic susceptibility.

In line with the conception that normality is related to hypnotizability, we expected those with higher friendship ratings to turn out to be more hypnotizable. In the ratings of opposite-sex friendships this did not work out; the relationship to hypnosis was not negative but was very close to zero correlation. The results for like-sex friendships were, however, in line with the hypothesis: in the direction of the hypothesis for male subjects, but not significant; significantly in that direction for the female subjects; and significant for the total group (table 31).

TABLE 31

*Rating of Like-sexed Friendships and Hypnotizability*

| Hypnotic Susceptibility | Male* Like-sexed Friends | | Female Like-sexed Friends | | Total* Like-sexed Friends | |
|---|---|---|---|---|---|---|
| | Low (1–4) | Medium-High (5–7) | Low (1–4) | Medium-High (5–7) | Low (1–4) | Medium-High (5–7) |
| | % | % | % | % | % | % |
| High (6–12) | 43 | 53 | 36 | 74 | 40 | 57 |
| Low (0–5) | 57 | 47 | 74 | 36 | 60 | 43 |
| Total | 100 | 100 | 100 | 100 | 100 | 100 |
| | (N = 56) | (N = 58) | (N = 36) | (N = 36) | (N = 92) | (N = 94) |
| $\chi^2$ | 1.28 | | 5.56 | | 5.52 | |
| p | † | | .02 | | .02 | |

* One male subject in sample nonascertainable.
† Not significant.

The failure to find even an interesting trend in opposite-sex friendships is disappointing, although the difficulty probably rests on the assessment of heterosexual friendships. A hurried interview lasting one hour and with many areas to cover is not the place for this particular rating to be made. In other words, not much weight should be given the failure to find a relationship; the positive finding with respect to one friendship pattern (in this case, like-sexed) is important.

## Ease of Communciation

Hypnosis is an interpersonal interaction between hypnotist and subject, and it is reasonable to expect some evidence of the influence of handling of interpersonal relationships outside hypnosis. This has already been demonstrated in the neurotic-normal dimension, on the assumption that the normal-outgoing person is more comfortable in his personal relationships. Friendships provided another indication. A third approach is via ease of communication, as reflected in the interview itself.

Ease of communication in the interview was rated by the interviewer at the end of the interview and was based on the spontaneity shown by the subject in following the lead of the interviewer and on the skill with which words could be used to describe personal experiences. It may be noted, in passing, that hypnosis depends primarily upon words, and one of its most striking features is the profound changes in the subject that may take place as the result of simple verbal suggestions. A rating of verbal fluency was also made, but the interviewers had difficulty in distinguishing between ease of communication and fluency, and the two ratings correlated $r = .94$. Therefore, the fluency rating is not being used here.

The correlation between ease of communication in the interview and hypnosis is $r = .27$. This correlation is better understood, as in the case of neuroticism-normalcy, by noting the distribution of cases. A stratification of cases by three levels of rated ease in communication is given in table 32. While the differences are not dramatic, they are significant ($p = .05$). Of those who rated high in

TABLE 32

*Ease of Communication in Interview as Related to Hypnotizability, 1962–63, 1963–64*
($N = 187$)

| Ease | Susceptibility SHSS-C | | Total |
| --- | --- | --- | --- |
| | Lower Half (0–5) | Upper Half (6–12) | |
| High (6–7) | 24 | 36 | 60 |
| Medium (4–5) | 31 | 33 | 64 |
| Low (1–3) | 40 | 23 | 63 |
| Total | 95 | 92 | 187 |

Significance test: $\chi^2 = 6.98$; $df = 2$; $p = .05$.

communication, 36/60, or 60 percent, scored in the upper half of hypnotic susceptibility, while of those who rated low, 23/63, or 36 percent, scored in the upper half.

Something can usually be learned by studying individual cases which support the generalizations to which the correlational findings lead, and the cases which do not, and thus reduce the size of the correlation. The cases here discussed will include those that represent the expected pattern of high communication and high hypnosis or low communication and low hypnosis. Then there will follow some cases which do not agree with the generality.

*High communication and high hypnosis.* Ursula was one of those rated well up on ease of communication who proved also to be high in hypnotizability. She scored nine on the SHSS-C. The interviewer noted the ease with which she talked, and the accompanying play of humor. It came out that her mother had encouraged a great deal of conversation in the home. "I always found it very easy to talk with her." This easy conversation, along with a number of involvements characteristic of our highly susceptible subject (reading, drama, interesting trips in the company of both parents) may have been responsible for her high scores.

Sue was another who fitted this pattern—high in communication, with a score of ten on SHSS-C. She described herself as outgoing, really liking people, and having a large group of good friends. The interviewer found her pleasant to talk with, helpful, thoughtful. When asked to explain a remark she readily provided pertinent illustrations. For example, when asked about reading she went on spontaneously to give details. "I get very involved in the story. I will feel moved by the book, to the point of crying if someone is hurt." She brought up Steinbeck's *Pearl* and Mitchell's *Gone with the Wind,* naming the characters and telling how she had wanted to help them. There were other background features favoring hypnosis, such as a firm childhood discipline which had included punishment (see chap. 14), and a high present motivation for hypnosis. The point is not that communication ease in itself made her hypnotizable, but that it is a characteristic often found among our highly hypnotizable subjects. Her talking in the interview was spontaneous and free-wheeling, leading to her high rating on ease of communication.

*Low communication and low hypnosis.* A correlation is determined by both the high and low cases. Morgan was one of those who fitted the generality by being both low in his ease of communication and in hypnosis, receiving a rating of two in communication and a score of two in the subsequent SHSS-C. The interviewer noted: "He is painfully quiet. He responded with monosyllables, could give few illustrations. When pressed for elaboration, he often responded, 'I don't know.' "

It was hard to get enough information to serve as the bases for ratings. When asked whether he had had an active imagination as a child, he replied, "I probably did." This is the kind of response that led the interviewer to rate him low in communication.

He described himself as serious, quiet, reserved. Even when he ventured a positive reply, he soon came up with reservations about his answers. This was as true in the interview following hypnosis as in the one in advance. He appeared to have some interest in music, but it could not be interpreted as the kind of involvement of those who become hypnotizable.

Wendy is another subject low in both communication and hypnosis. She was rated three in communication and scored three on SHSS-C. She appeared younger than her eighteen years. She was smiling, pleasant, but somewhat self-conscious and apprehensive about the impression she was making. She was frequently vague and unsure of her responses. She touched the surface of many interests but found commitment to none. It did not surprise us that she proved so little susceptible to hypnosis.

*High communication and low hypnosis.* Now for some cases which reduce the correlation—the exceptions that test the generality.

Linda was rated high in communication, at the six level, but scored two in hypnosis. The interviewer described her as animated, somewhat dramatic, able to talk easily of herself and her background. If most easy communicators are hypnotizable, why wasn't she?

Others have noted, as we have, that marked obsessive-compulsive traits tend to interfere with hypnotizability (e.g., Gill and Brenman 1959, p. 80). Phyllis showed various evidences of such traits. For example, she read the Bible every morning, often without thinking of the words. When questioned she said that it was better that way. Without much show of emotion she went on, "It's a ritual, like keeping your room neat or taking a bath every day."

She had a strong need for autonomy, which she showed as she described how she felt about hypnosis. She said that she had cooperated because she did not want the hypnotist to think she was not cooperative. At the same time, she went on, "But I wouldn't want anyone to have this kind of control over me. I want to put my own facts together. I don't want to be a person with no thoughts or beliefs of my own."

She indicated some involvement in reading and music but differentiated these from hypnosis. "Music and reading do not involve another person. They make me a fuller person. I could identify and really live another life—a whole range of experience—from a book, but in hypnosis he can tell me I'm going to forget and he has that power over me. If I lose myself in reading, *I'm* doing that."

While communication ease is commonly associated with hypnotizability, Linda shows that its presence is not enough to overcome obsessive-compulsive traits and the desire to remain out of the control of another person.

Another high communicator, rated at six, scored two in hypnosis. She seemed totally relaxed and at ease in the interview, occasionally sprawling in her chair or leaning forward to make a point. She talked with enthusiasm about her interests and her family. The interviewer described her as an attractive, colorful, buoyant girl. She spoke with enthusiasm about the conversations at home: "We'd end up sitting at the dinner table discussing things until nine o'clock. We like to discuss and argue in the family." She easily achieved a high rating on ease of communication.

What held back her hypnosis? She was rather analytical and rational in her approaches: following a mathematical interest of her father's she was now majoring in mathematics and hoping to train herself for work with computers. She approached hypnosis with a curiosity about what was going on. In an interview after hypnosis she said, "I was held back by my curiosity to observe what was going on which superseded my wish to feel it. I wish I could have done both . . ." The same attitude was true of the kinds of interests in which she had noted her friends could become deeply involved. Of activities and interests of this kind she said, "I didn't give  myself to the doing. I halfway observed and halfway participated, as I did in hypnosis."

*Low communication and high hypnosis.* The final combination, which explains the generally low correlation between communication and hypnosis, is that of low ease of communication combined with high hypnotizability. Two cases exemplifying this combination will complete our illustrations of the relationship between communication and hypnosis.

Bob was rated at three in communication, below average, but scored above average in hypnosis, with an eight on SHSS-C. The interviewer who talked with him prior to hypnosis reported: "He responded slowly, in a deliberate, serious, and thoughtful manner. He labored to express himself adequately." He said of himself that he had a few friends but really liked being alone, and he derived no pleasure from large groups. Both parents appeared to be somewhat withdrawn from social contacts, and he seemed to have identified with them.

In view of these negative indications, what accounts for his susceptibility to hypnosis? We turn again to the involvements, and we find that he can become deeply immersed in reading. "I become part of the book when I'm reading something I am interested in. This happened in *Crime and Punishment;* I became the character and lived it. . . . My involvement is the same now as it has been all along, or maybe even more because I now have greater understanding." He also shares the disciplinary history of so many of our high-scorers: discipline was stern, primarily by way of corporal punishment, and he was whipped until age thirteen, but only once thereafter. (The relationship between childhood punishment and hypnosis is examined in chap. 14.) Thus we are led to see hypnotic susceptibility as the result of a complex interaction of the experiences that we have found related to it, some positive and some negative. Were we able to weigh them more accurately, we would know how much to subtract from susceptibility when communication is poor, but a case of this kind suggests that we are not quite ready to do this.

Norman is our final case. He rated three in communication but scored nine in hypnotic susceptibility. He had difficulty in talking in both interviews prior to hypnosis. The interviewer commented after the first interview, "He moves and speaks slowly, almost reluctantly, in a low voice. He needed much help in finding words, yet I had no feeling of hostility from him." After a second interview, the same interviewer noted, "The subject made an even more withdrawn impression today. At least his responses this hour were in such a low voice, so labored and exceedingly slow, that the whole interview became painful. Every word about his parents had to be extracted piecemeal, with long pauses, and he could not mention anything at all that might have a negative connotation."

Can we find some path that led him into hypnotic susceptibility? The clue comes from his active interest in certain kinds of sports and from other activities of an *essentially nonverbal kind.* He had enjoyed sailing with his parents since childhood. Swimming was another favorite. He had started skin diving at the age of seven. He had been on the track team in high school—running, shotput, discus, javelin, broad jump. "I still do a little throwing for my own fun." He had been spelunking (cave exploring) from the sixth grade on. He has an aesthetic appreciation of nature. "Nature can be awesome—the solitude is nice. I used to like being alone, sailing —the adventure attached to it appeals to me." He has enjoyed flying and hopes soon to do some sky diving.

Norman felt that he identified with his father, who had been adventurous as a flyer when he was younger and still had a good many active interests. He admired his father for his quiet, rational, and understanding approach. His mother was outgoing and friendly: "Warm, comfortable, less adventurous than Father. It's easier to be emotionally close to her."

Here we have a subject who participated enthusiastically in activities of a kind found associated with hypnosis: the more individual and less competitive sports, the aesthetic interest in nature. The kinds of adventure in which he finds satisfaction involve physical activity, rather than talking; using this pathway into hypnosis, the lack of ease in communication is no hindrance.

These eight cases, running the gamut of the relationship between ease of communication and hypnotizability, help to reinforce what we have learned about alternate paths into hypnosis. Ease of communication is associated in general with high hypnotizability, because it is so commonly manifested by those with enthusiastic involvements, outgoing personalities, and an eagerness for the new experience of hypnosis. This association with hypnotizability, though statistically significant, does not make ease of communication a *requisite* of hypnotizability, as the last two cases show, nor does such ease *assure* high scores in hypnosis, as the earlier cases demonstrated.

### Results of Personality-Inventory Studies

While in this book the data presented are all from the interviews, a program of personality testing was a part of the whole research enterprise, which thus included the three major aspects of (1) objectively scorable personality inventories, (2) interviews, and (3) objectively scorable hypnotic susceptibility. Because the results from the personality inventories have been given in detail elsewhere (E. R. Hilgard 1965), it will serve our purposes here merely to repeat the summary from that account.

Although, in common with the results of other investigators, the use of personality measures resulted mostly in low correlations, there was some yield, summarized as follows:

1. Significant self-predictions of hypnotizability (Melei and Hilgard 1964).
2. Significant correlations between attitudes and hypnotizability for females (Melei and Hilgard 1964).

3. Significant positive correlations between responses on experience inventories and hypnotizability, particularly those reflecting role-involvement, trancelike experiences, and impulsivity (Lee-Teng 1965).

4. Significant negative correlations with the number of motoric interests, particularly with competitive recreational (athletic) interests (Hilgard 1965, using scale of Stein and Craik 1965).

5. Significant positive correlations with the excess of ideational over motoric interests (Hilgard 1965; Stein and Craik 1965).

6. Significant positive correlations with the acquiescence tendency as reflected in the sum-true score in the MMPI (Hilgard, Lauer, and Cuca 1965).

7. A significant correlation (for females) between scores on the rod-and-frame test and hypnotizability, indicating that the field-independent are more hypnotizable. These are the subjects guided more from within. (Roberts 1964.) Results from another sample have yielded a similar significant correlation for male subjects (unpublished data, courtesy of Arlene H. Morgan 1969b.)

The generalized personality description that would result from these findings is very similar to what emerges from the interviews. That is, the hypnotizable person is one who has rich subjective experiences in which he can become deeply involved (experience inventory, field-independence); one who reaches out for new experiences and is thus friendly to hypnosis (favorable attitudes, self-predictions); one who is interested in the life of the mind, rather than being a competitive activist (negative correlations with competitive athletics, positive with ideational interests). These statements do not sound so different from our emphasis, as a result of the interviews, on imaginative involvements, favorable attitudes toward hypnosis, the inhibiting aspects of competitive athletics and achievement motivation.

## Concluding Remarks on Normality and Neuroticism in Relation to Hypnosis

Our data indicate that the normal-outgoing subject is more likely to be hypnotizable than the troubled-withdrawn one. We have not studied any extremely disturbed subjects, but there is no evidence to make us believe that studies of frank neurotics would change the picture. There are both highly hypnotizable subjects and subjects low in hypnotizability in any group of persons sorted along any of the dimensions that we have been able to study, and therefore it is easy to see why a practitioner who is dealing with a particular group of patients might attribute certain of their qualities to their symptoms, even though these same qualities might characterize any normal population.

Hypnosis is a highly verbal interpersonal relationship. It is related both to ease of communication and to a general comfort with people. Examining these characteristics helps to account for the general relationship between being normal and outgoing and being hypnotizable.

The special role of the hypnotist is not well understood. This is due in part to lack of data from sources outside the clinical situation. In clinical cases there is the special relationship of patient to physician or of client to counselor, with the "cry for help" coloring both the communications and other aspects of the interpersonal relationships. It is difficult to distinguish between what belongs to the therapeutic relationship and what is distinctive about the hypnotic relationship. Our study lies outside the special relationship that develops when someone comes for personal help. While this is to some extent limiting, it has the advantage of separating out what is characteristic of hypnosis itself, when the subject comes to experience hypnosis, not to be treated for something that is bothering him.

# 13

## Childhood Development: Identifications and Contagion of Parental Interests

The importance of early childhood as a background for later coping with the environment can scarcely be doubted; the "as the twig is bent" interpretation has not waited for either psychoanalysis or Piaget to call attention to the importance of childhood. It is natural, therefore, to expect that certain early experiences will be important for later hypnotizability.

There are two major possibilities regarding the background for the highly hypnotizable young adult. These may be described as the *producing* of hypnotizability, on the one hand, and the *maintaining* of hypnotizability, on the other, possibilities which are not mutually exclusive. The "producing" theory searches for the kinds of influences exerted by other persons on the child, through processes commonly called *identifications,* which lead to his becoming hypnotizable. The "maintaining" theory considers hypnotizability natural, like the ability to sleep or to dream, and claims that what is important in development is maintaining this ability through *not* learning ways of behaving which interfere with or inhibit it. Thus the one view is essentially that hypnotizability can be learned, the other that nonhypnotizability can be learned. There is no reason to doubt that both developmental conditions can go on simultaneously; that is, some features of development will enhance hypnotizability, while other features will reduce it. The result, for any one individual, is a compromise or integration of these developmental strands.

### Age Changes in Hypnotizabilty

The view that hypnotizability is a natural, and perhaps well-nigh universal, ability is made plausible by two important facts, first, that children are very highly hypnotizable, and, second, that for those who are hypnotizable the induction of hypnosis is easy and prompt when the conditions are right. The effects of age on hypnotizability are by now fairly well established: susceptibility scores rise between the ages of six to nine or ten and then fall off thereafter. Figure 3 shows data from three studies done in other laboratories with substantial numbers of children. Although there are some differences, they all point in the same direction—a peak near nine or ten and a decline thereafter.

Tests used in hypnosis demand response to verbal suggestions and so are of little help before the age of six. It may be that the rise in the early part of the curve is not a true picture of the development of hypnotic susceptibility, but instead an indication of increasing responsiveness to words. More subtle tests would doubtless find hypnotic responsiveness in the early years—perhaps a responsiveness to rocking, or to a mother's lullabies, or to restraint of movement, as by a cradleboard—but we do not have the evidence.

The data of Figure 3 can now be supplemented by a larger body of data over a longer span of years, gathered in the Stanford laboratory (figure 4). The data plotted are from a study in which whole families have been hypnotized on one occasion, although each family member was separately and individually hypnotized. The SHSS-A was used throughout, with only a very moderate amount of change of wording for the younger children (e.g., for the word *relax* we substituted *take it easy*). The same items appear throughout the age range. The typical pattern of figure 3 is repeated, with low scores for those under six, a rise to a high point somewhere between ages six and fifteen, and a progressive decline thereafter. Because these data are from fathers and mothers and children of the same families, there is a control for socioeconomic status. Our university samples (not shown on figure 4) reveal the same trends, that is, a progressive decline within the four years of college. If we sort our college students by age, we find a mean for the seventeen- and eighteen-year-old students of 6.3 ($N = 183$); for the nineteen- and twenty-year-old students, 5.7 ($N = 430$); and for the twenty-one- and twenty-two-year-olds, 5.0 ($N = 59$). These differences with age are statistically significant (unpublished data courtesy of Leslie M. Cooper). The scores from the university sample probably represent a somewhat higher socioeconomic status than the family sample, which may account for the relatively low means compared with the means of the twenty-six- to thirty-five-year-old parents. In addition, the parent sample is a volunteer sample and hence may have the somewhat higher scores characteristic

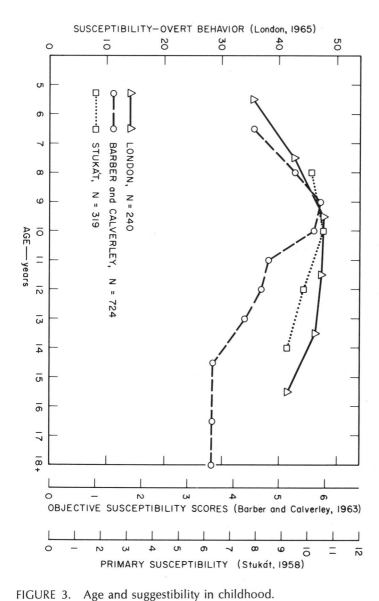

FIGURE 3.   Age and suggestibility in childhood.

Results of three investigations (London, 1965; Stukát, 1958; Barber and Calverley, 1963). From E. R. Hilgard, *Hypnotic Susceptibility,* p. 288. © 1965 by Harcourt, Brace & World and reprinted with permission.

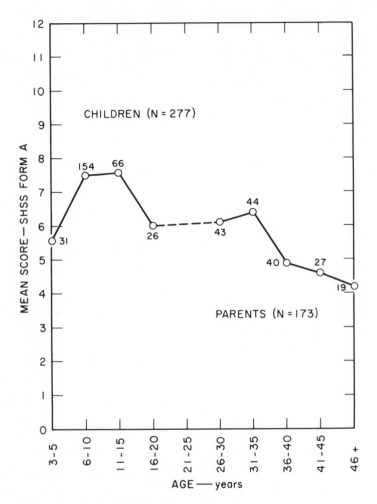

FIGURE 4. Decline of hypnotizability with age.

The children and adults are from an unpublished study under way in the Stanford laboratory (Morgan 1969a), and appear here through the courtesy of Arlene H. Morgan. A few parents were tested at ages 21–25, but they totaled only twelve and are omitted from the figure, which is based on upwards of twenty-five cases at all points except the last, as indicated within the figure.

of such samples (Boucher and E. R. Hilgard 1962). While of course there is no way to pinpoint the decline with age without very careful investigation, one may hazard the guess that the conditions of increasing rational sophistication and the needs for competency and achievement bring with them a decline in wonderment; these changes with age somehow counteract the imaginative involvements so important in hypnosis and substitute for them interactions on a reality level that make hypnosis increasingly difficult.

In this chapter we shall review the influences in early life which determine the reasons why, for some people, the usual decline in hypnotic responsiveness does not occur.

## The Pattern of Identifications with Parents

In the mid-1960s we began to hear much about the generation gap and the desire of youth to separate itself from parental values and "the establishment." It might be supposed that prevailing interpretations of identification of children with parents will be misleading. Two things need to be said. In the first place, our interviewing was done before the alienation between generations became acute among college students, so that our subjects were willing to see and report resemblances between themselves and their parents. In the second place, conflicts between growing youths and their parents are nothing new, and childhood identifications do not require a complacent acceptance of parental values.

Identification with parents is one of the most-studied of psychological aspects of personality development. One reason for this is that we have two clearly contrasting personality types within our culture, the "socialized male" and the "socialized female." Any striking departure in the opposite direction, a sexual inversion, is conspicuous. It is commonly supposed that sex-typing begins early in childhood, based on some kind of modeling of the behavior of the appropriate parent. Studies have shown that this does occur, as early as age three or four. This is not the place to go into the evidence with respect to sex-role identifications, which is well summarized elsewhere (e.g., Kagan 1964; Sears, Rau, and Alpert 1965).

The *non-sex-role* identifications have been more often neglected, although they are also important in personality development. It is evident that parents have individual personalities that are not associated with the role of being a father or a mother, or a man or a woman, and these other aspects of personality have an influence upon the children. The interest in sex (or, better, gender) roles has led to a neglect of these non-sex-roles. To be sure, many discussions can be found to bear upon them. The mixed identifications have been emphasized, for example, by Erikson (1959), who sees the problem the individual has of finally harmonizing the strands into an *identity* that is his own. Slater (1961) has proposed a dualistic theory of identification. He distinguished between what he calls *personal* identification, which is taking as a model the parent as an individual, and *positional* identification, taking as a model the adult role of the person (the adult father or mother, with appropriate roles of authority and power). This dualism bears a resemblance to what we have called non-sex-role identification and sex-role identification. Thus a boy or a girl learns kinds of behavior from each parent, and some of these behaviors are not strongly sex-typed. It is possible for either father or mother to be interested in music, or athletic events, or in the aesthetic appreciation of nature. Even though only *one* parent has such interests, it does not matter very much whether the parent is of the same or the opposite sex of the child who uses the parent as the model, as long as in the area of sex-typing the parent is appropriate and has respect for the other parent as a representative of his (or her) sex. There are many of these non-sex-typed areas, of which reading, enjoying the theater, sense of humor, general sociability, are illustrative. In what follows we shall examine the possibility that hypnotic susceptibility is strongly influenced by modeling of these non-sex-typed aspects of parental figures.

We made the assumption that most of our subjects were appropriately sex-typed, and hence we were more interested in the non-sex-typed identifications. It was important, however, to select some aspect of mature interest (other than sexual behavior) that would reflect appropriate sex-typing. For this we chose work interest or, more generally, identification with the parent's *work ego*, or style of involvement in chosen work. The assumption is that the boy would more generally resemble his father, and the girl her mother, in these attitudes. The other two that we chose, *temperament* and *recreation*, are less sex-typed, and we made no prediction about how they would come out, except that the predominance of sex-typing might carry over into these identifications also. The actual findings are somewhat at variance with expectations, in that cross-sex identification is more common than anticipated.

Our measure of identification is *resemblance* of the child to the parent, as reported by him in the interview. This sometimes took the form of clear recognition ("I'm just like my mother in this"), sometimes put in the words of someone else ("My relatives tell me I have my father's temper"). In any case, the described resemblance seemed to serve as an index of the parent who served as the model for the behavior studied.

The overall results for the male subjects are given in table 33.

TABLE 33
*Identifications of Male Subjects with Parents*

|  | Work | Recreation | Temperament |
|---|---|---|---|
|  | % | % | % |
| Father only | 33 | 44 | 47 |
| Both parents | 27 | 11 | 19 |
| Mother only | 23 | 25 | 30 |
| Neither parent | 13 | 18 | 3 |
| Not ascertained | 4 | 2 | 1 |
| Total ($N = 115$) | 100 | 100 | 100 |

While we expected the male subjects to report that their work habits were essentially like those of their fathers, this was not strikingly the case, with only one-third of the male sample stating that they resembled their fathers in work habits and attitudes; nearly as many (27 percent) said that they were like both parents in this respect, so that 60 percent actually included the father (though not exclusively) in their work identifications. Almost a fourth (23 percent) selected the mother as the model for their work habits and attitudes. When it came to play and temperament, there was a slightly greater tendency to choose one parent, more often the father, but the mother was selected in an appreciable number of cases.

For the female subjects the corresponding figures are in table 34. The results are not so different from the males, so far as work ego is concerned, with slightly more girls identifying with their mothers, a total of 65 percent including their mothers in their work identifications. Again an appreciable number chose the parent of the opposite sex, 26 percent of the girls mentioning their fathers. When it comes to play and temperament, however, the girls a little more often numerically (though not to a statistically significant extent) select their fathers as models. Thus both sexes seem to find more frequently in their fathers models for play and for expression of temperament.

These results, while telling us something about what happens in the homes of highly selected college students, provide an op-

TABLE 34

*Identifications of Female Subjects with Parents*

|  | Work | Recreation | Temperament |
|---|---|---|---|
|  | % | % | % |
| Mother only | 37 | 31 | 29 |
| Both parents | 28 | 25 | 33 |
| Father only | 26 | 33 | 35 |
| Neither parent | 6 | 10 | 3 |
| Not ascertained | 3 | 1 | — |
| Total (*N* = 72) | 100 | 100 | 100 |

portunity to see what relationship, if any, there is between these identification patterns and hypnotizability. For this analysis we shall take a look at each of the kinds of identification separately.

### Identification with Parents in Work Habits and Attitudes

We are on somewhat unclear ground when we consider the meaning of similarity to one or both parents in work habits and attitudes. The work of the world tends to be strongly sex-typed, so that we felt that the work identification might reflect sex-role identification more than recreational interests or temperament. Thus it is fairly common for a son to follow in his father's occupational footsteps, and if the mother is happy in her role as housewife it doubtless improves the chances that her daughter will be. But life is not that stereotyped, and the father may be a poor model because he does not enjoy his work, the mother may be an indifferent housewife, and all other shades of attitude toward work may exist. Furthermore, the father's work is carried on in most instances outside the home, and therefore the young child may have little feel for his father's work, while the mother's is more visible. The many replies within the interview concerning similarity to both parents, to the opposite-sexed parent, and to neither parent show that a simple work identification with the like-sexed parent is not altogether common. We thus test our comparison between parental identification in work without any very clear hypothesis about what the relationship to hypnosis might be. The empirical findings are shown in table 35.

The identification groups have been arranged in the order of descending mean hypnotic scores. This order, from highest to lowest, is similarity to the opposite-sexed parent, similarity to both

TABLE 35

*Identification with Parents in Work Habits and Attitudes as Related to Hypnotizability*

| Parent Identification | Hypnotizability (SHSS-C) | | |
|---|---|---|---|
| | N | Mean | SD |
| Opposite-sexed parent | | | |
| Males resembling mother | 27 | 6.3 | 2.9 |
| Females resembling father | 27 | 6.1 | 3.8 |
| Total | 54 | 6.2 | 3.4 |
| Both parents | | | |
| Males resembling both parents | 31 | 5.6 | 3.3 |
| Females resembling both parents | 20 | 5.0 | 2.9 |
| Total | 51 | 5.4 | 3.1 |
| Like-sexed parent | | | |
| Males resembling father | 37 | 5.0 | 3.2 |
| Females resembling mother | 19 | 5.6 | 3.2 |
| Total | 56 | 5.2 | 3.2 |
| Neither parent | | | |
| Males resembling neither parent | 15 | 4.1 | 2.5 |
| Females resembling neither parent | 4 | 2.7 | 1.5 |
| Total | 19 | 3.8 | 2.4 |

Significance tests: Total, opposite vs. like, $df = 108$; $t = 1.54$; $p$ not significant. Total, opposite vs. neither, $df = 71$; $t = 2.83$; $p = .01$.

parents, similarity to like-sexed parent, and similarity to neither parent. The order for the total sample holds for males, but females show a numerically higher mean for like-sexed parent than for identification with both parents. The variabilities are great, and the only difference that holds up statistically is that between the extremes, that is, between those identified with the opposite-sexed parent and those identified with neither parent ($p = .01$).

It is coherent with our general interpretation that those who are identified with neither parent might prove to be low in hypnotizability, as indeed they are found to be. The somewhat high hypnotizability of those identified with parents of the opposite sex is a serendipitous finding; we shall return to its interpretation later, after we note somewhat stronger evidence for it in the case of temperamental identification.

### Identification with Parents in Recreational Interests

On the assumption that hypnosis is a kind of playful experience, in which there is a departure from reality into a make-believe world, it might be supposed that those who can enter this world most freely are those who can recapture the imaginative experiences of childhood play. If these experiences have been supported by adult models, this could be important in the preservation of such abilities. Again we ought to know something more about the kinds of recreational interests we are talking about. We have defined one kind of recreation as *work recreation,* in which, while the adult finds the hobby satisfying, it is done according to standards of excellence that prevent the child's full participation. Hence the contagion is less likely to be there than in the other kind, which we have called *playful play,* in which what is done is for the joy of the moment, without a high degree of competitiveness or expertness (like bait fishing from a boat with cork and sinker), a kind of recreation which the child can share and enjoy early in life.

Because there are many kinds of playful enjoyment that are not sex-typed, it might very well be that the child somehow chooses to resemble the parent whose recreation is the kind in which he *can* participate, and thus the one most likely to sustain his playful involvement. This would tend to lead to an association with hypnotic susceptibility and the selection of one parent as the model, regardless of the sex of the parent. If the parental recreation is inappropriate, the play models may be siblings or other children, so that we might expect to find somewhat more children who report resemblance to *neither* parent in recreational interest. This is, in fact, the case, as noted in tables 33 and 34. The percentages of both male and female subjects who reported resemblance to neither parent were higher for recreation than for either work or temperament. It might follow also that lack of resemblance to parents in play might not interfere with hypnotizability because of these other models (peers) who are available to sustain the interest. Much of this is conjectural at this stage; the empirical evidence is in table 36.

Comparing the data in table 36 with that in table 35, we note some trends that are alike, and some slightly different, between identification in work and in play. Although the highest means of hypnotizability in both cases are in identification with the opposite-

TABLE 36

*Identification with Parents in Recreational Interests as Related to Hypnotizability*

| Parent Identification | Hypnotizability (SHSS-C) | | |
| --- | --- | --- | --- |
| | N | Mean | SD |
| Opposite-sexed parent | | | |
| Males resembling mother | 29 | 5.9 | 3.7 |
| Females resembling father | 24 | 5.9 | 3.2 |
| Total | 53 | 5.9 | 3.5 |
| Like-sexed parent | | | |
| Males resembling father | 50 | 5.1 | 3.0 |
| Females resembling mother | 22 | 5.9 | 3.1 |
| Total | 72 | 5.4 | 3.0 |
| Neither parent | | | |
| Males resembling neither parent | 21 | 5.2 | 2.6 |
| Females resembling neither parent | 7 | 4.4 | 4.1 |
| Total | 28 | 5.0 | 3.1 |
| Both parents | | | |
| Males resembling both parents | 13 | 4.8 | 2.6 |
| Females resembling both parents | 18 | 4.4 | 3.4 |
| Total | 31 | 4.6 | 3.1 |

Significance test: Opposite vs. both, $df = 82$; $t = 1.71$; $.10 > p > .05$.

sexed parent, the difference does not hold even numerically for female subjects in the case of recreation. Resemblance to *neither* parent in recreation is not associated with as low hypnotic scores as in work identification, in accordance with the prior supposition regarding the influence of peers in sustaining recreational interests. We are dealing with differences that do not meet standards of statistical significance in the data on recreation, which may be due in part to the complexity of distinguishing between work recreation and playful play. The tendency for the mean hypnotic scores of those identified with both parents in recreation to be low may mean that to answer "both" in this case was not much different from answering "neither," in that the recreational interests of neither parent may have been very vivid.

Because of the lack of significant differences among the identification groups in recreational interest, almost the only findings of importance are, first, that the higher rank of those identified with opposite-sexed parents is coherent with the same rank for work habits, and, second, that those identified with neither parent in recreational interests do not score as low as those identified with neither parent in work interests. Even these observations depend upon giving somewhat more weight to numerical differences than the statistical significances justify. However, the general consistency of the results for the sexes separately suggests that there may be some reality to the indicated trends.

### Identification with Parents in Temperament

Temperament, by which is meant the general level and nature of emotional tone and mood, is not strongly sex-typed. A man and a woman can be jovial or sullen; either can be slow to anger or quick "to fly off the handle." Our subjects could often tell us which parent they most closely resembled in temperament, and this seemed to us a particularly useful place to test the importance of non-sex-role identification. It will be recalled (from tables 33 and 34) that 30 percent of the boys and 35 percent of the girls indicated a temperamental identification with the parent of the opposite sex, higher than the opposite-sexed identifications for work and recreation. In temperament, the opposite-sex identification is related to susceptibility to hypnosis (table 37).

For both work and recreational identification the highest hypnotizability was found for those who identified with the opposite-sexed parent, but the differences between those identifying with like-sexed and opposite-sexed parents did not reach statistical significance. In resemblance in temperament, however, the difference does reach satisfactory statistical significance ($p = .01$), again in favor of those identifying with the parent of the opposite sex. There are very few cases who identify with neither parent, but these few score so low in hypnotizability that they lie significantly below those who identify with the opposite parent ($p = .05$).

The influence of parental temperament upon hypnosis is of course attenuated by the kind of temperament shown by the parent whom the subject resembles. This is difficult to untangle, but it is a reasonable hypothesis that if the parent resembled were hypnotizable, the chances would be better that the child (of either sex) would also be hypnotizable. An analysis of the data along these lines was attempted by E. R. Hilgard (1964), who used an estimate of parental

TABLE 37

Identification with Parents in Temperament as
Related to Hypnotizability

| Parent Identification | Hypnotizability (SHSS-C) | | |
|---|---|---|---|
| | N | Mean | SD |
| Opposite-sexed parent | | | |
| Males resembling mother | 35 | 6.1 | 3.3 |
| Females resembling father | 25 | 6.8 | 3.4 |
| Total | 60 | 6.4 | 3.3 |
| Like-sexed parent | | | |
| Males resembling father | 54 | 4.9 | 2.8 |
| Females resembling mother | 21 | 5.3 | 3.2 |
| Total | 75 | 5.0 | 2.9 |
| Both parents | | | |
| Males resembling both parents | 22 | 5.5 | 3.4 |
| Females resembling both parents | 24 | 4.2 | 3.3 |
| Total | 46 | 4.8 | 3.3 |
| Neither parent | | | |
| Males resembling neither parent | 3 | 3.7 | 1.2 |
| Females resembling neither parent | 2 | 2.5 | 2.5 |
| Total | 5 | 3.2 | 1.9 |

Significance tests: Opposite vs. like, $df = 133$, $t = 2.61$, $p = .01$.
Opposite vs. neither, $df = 63$, $t = 2.12$, $p = .05$.

hypnotizability to distinguish those who would be expected to be
hypnotizable from those expected not to be hypnotizable on the
basis of the kind of parent with whom the child identified. The evidence of parental hypnotizability was so indirect, however (derived
from interviews with the son or daughter), that the results, while
supporting the hypothesis, were scarcely definitive.

There is a line of argument, however, which could support
the association of the temperamental resemblance to the opposite-
sexed parent with higher hypnotizability, without requiring any
direct measurement of the parent's hypnotizability. This argument
begins with the assumption that most social pressures favor identification with the like-sexed parent, so that identification with the

parent of the opposite sex is a matter of selection of that parent as a model on the basis of something attractive to the child. If the parent of the opposite sex were more fun, more enthusiastic, more supporting of the child's interests, these qualities might attract the child to model after that parent. It is exactly these traits that we find related to hypnotizability. Thus the child, in choosing an opposite-sexed parent as a model, is quite likely to choose a hypnotizable parent and in so doing tends to become hypnotizable himself. This, then, is one plausible line of argument for the greater hypnotizability of the child identified with the opposite-sexed parent, particularly in an area such as temperament, which is less sex-typed and therefore can be shared with a minimum of conflict.

The supposition that the subject may turn to the opposite parent when there is something inviting about this parent is given moderate but inconclusive support in the correlation between rated parental warmth and hypnosis (table 38). The only significant

TABLE 38

*Parental Warmth and Hypnotic Susceptibility*

| Parental Warmth | Correlation with Hypnotic Susceptibility | | |
|---|---|---|---|
| | Male Subjects (N = 115) | Female Subjects (N = 72) | Total (N = 187) |
| Mother warmth | .24* | −.03 | .11 |
| Father warmth | −.02 | .18 | .06 |

* $p = .05$.

correlation is that between maternal warmth and *male*-subject hypnotizability, but the only other correlation that approaches significance is that between the father's warmth and *female*-subject hypnotizability. The complexity of the relationships of warmth to other factors, such as its relationship to punishment (to be described in the next chapter, especially in table 41) has resulted in no general predictability of hypnotizability from parental warmth.

We have little firm information to go on until studies are completed with actual families, in which parents and children are hypnotized so that their differences in hypnotizability may be determined, and their identification patterns studied concomitantly. Until then, we can merely offer more or less plausible hypotheses.

In addition to the preceding surmise in regard to the choice of a hypnotic model, another can be considered.

This second possibility is based on a concept of dissociation. The argument would be made in two stages. First it is assumed that in this normal population most of the everyday kinds of social behavior will be appropriately sex-typed, and hence based on modeling after the like-sexed parent. So, in reality-oriented social behavior the son is like his father, the daughter like her mother. But in the life of fantasy there may be some unintegrated strands derived from the other parent, who has personal qualities that the child values but does not give full play to. The second stage of the argument would be that in hypnosis there is a departure from reality ties, and a greater freedom for the strands derived from the opposite parent to find expression. If the presence of these strands is important for hypnosis, then some identification with the opposite-sex parent may be important to hypnosis. That the child recognizes some similarity in temperament or attitude to the opposite parent does not mean that all the strands of his personality are fully expressed in ordinary reality-oriented social behavior; in other words, the dissociation theory does not require that the dissociated material should be "unconscious" outside of hypnosis, but that it is not as freely used and enjoyed. The concept of dissociation is a difficult one, but in the extreme, as in cases of multiple personality, we may find evidences of distinct identifications which have never become fully fused. The interpretation is that something like this may be going on in all of us, and especially in those who enjoy the hypnotic experience.

## Parental Contagion of Enthusiasm and Involvement as Features of Development

In each of the chapters concerned with involvements we had the opportunity to note how frequently the child's involvement began in association with a parent who had the kind of enthusiasm that could be shared with a child. Not all enthusiasms turned out to be of this kind: if the parental hobby required the kinds of skill in which a child could not well participate, there was little communication of the enthusiasm. This is one reason that do-it-yourself fathers are sometimes surprised that their sons do not share their enthusiasm for tools. Scientific interest in nature does not communicate as well as aesthetic interest—a genuine love of the out-of-doors, an appreciation of the beauty of the sunset.

All of these observations can fit together: identification with parents, selecting as a model that parent who represents the kind of involvement that the child can share (even if a parent of the opposite sex), a favorable reaction to punishment (see chap. 14), which gives respect for authority and order while not interfering with a life of fantasy.

At this point we do well to examine from this point of view a number of the individual subjects whose involvements were earlier described. While occasionally the relationships to their parents were touched upon, in a number of cases there is more to be said concerning the manner in which involvements develop.

The chapter on reading (chap. 3) serves as an anticipation and summarizes the main ideas in regard to involvement, development in the family, shifts with age, and bearing on the theory of hypnosis. It was there indicated that reading involvement commonly develops early in life, before the onset of adolescence, either in identification with parents or as an offset for loneliness. Sarah, for example, (chap. 3) one of our most hypnotizable subjects, was sure that she had developed her reading through her mother's influence. Her mother was deeply involved in reading herself and had read to Sarah a great deal when she was between the ages of two and four; Sarah herself learned to read between ages three and five.

There is more to be said about Julie, the first subject mentioned in the reading chapter. She developed her interests because of a richly stimulating environment. Her parents read widely and encouraged their children to read and to report on what they had read in family discussions. Julie's mother is imaginative, creative, a mimic, and has dramatic talent. "She can be funny, is perceptive . . . happy . . . interested in the welfare of minority groups." Asked about her mother's warmth, Julie said, "She is very demonstrative. One is never in doubt about her feelings." Her strong points included "openness, compassion, empathy." Janet's flair for reading, for imaginative pursuits, and for dramatic expression were stimulated by her home, particularly this identification with her mother. She feels that in different ways she is identified with both parents. She described her father as even-tempered, understanding, objective, not emotionally bound, quiet, serious, warm, and affectionate. Both parents were responsible for discipline which consisted very much of reasoning, but of some physical punishment (so typical of our highly hypnotizable). "I was spanked—slapped for being impudent and losing my temper."

When Elizabeth was discussed in chapter 4 (drama) and chapter 5 (religion) little was said about her childhood, except to mention that her religion had been nurtured within the family.

Elizabeth's father had artistic talent, which he put to use in his work as a draftsman for an architectural firm. He shared his interests in drawing and in listening to music with his young daughter, and she grew to be temperamentally similar to him, especially in modeling after his sense of humor. Her father encouraged her art by buying materials for her to work with when she was quite young, and he taught her how to use them. She still does occasional oils and pastels. She thinks her art is much like her father's, representing what she notices about her, rather than being an escape through fantasy. Her mother entered the picture, too, both in religion and dramatics. She was a devout Episcopalian, and Elizabeth grew up with a natural and unconflicted religious interest. Both parents encouraged the dramatic interests, by helping her learn her parts and by being present for her performances.

Although the parents tried to be fair in their discipline, telling Elizabeth the rules in advance and distinguishing between right and wrong in terms that she could understand, she was still punished severely for infractions. Her father could become very angry and punitive, so that the severity of her punishment was rated at the top of our punishment scale (rating of seven). In reviewing her present-day attitude toward her discipline, she said that she did not like it at the time, but that it had been effective. She does not plan to be as strict with her children, but will temper her use of punishment with a little more reasoning. It may be noted that high use of punishment does not prevent a close identification with parents, including the one who does the punishing, for Elizabeth has been much influenced by her father.

The fact that the parents were present at her dramatic performances was noted as one of the influences upon Elizabeth's dramatic interests. The support of parents as "audiences" was observed in a number of cases which were described as "informal dramatization," that is, an interest in being dramatic in an interpersonal situation, even without a "theater." Three such cases (Jerry, Ellen, and Mary) were described in chapter 4 (drama). While Jerry tells of having his parents "befuddled" by his stories, they must have given him attention to encourage this behavior by him and by his brother. Ellen, dramatic at all times, came home from school and reported the day's experiences to her mother, who lived her life "vicariously." Mary also had a fine audience in her mother. She sat on her stool in the kitchen and told about the day while her mother prepared the meal; she exaggerated a little to impress her mother. The encouragement by these audiences doubtless reinforced the dramatic involvements of these children.

Henry, mentioned in chapter 4 (drama), scored at the top of the hypnotic-susceptibility scales. His interest in drama derives directly from his mother—a specific illustration of the cross-parent identification that shows up so commonly in our statistics. As noted earlier he began to play in skits at the age of nine. His mother has always been interested in plays, from her high school and college days; she has written plays. In addition to this dramatic interest, Henry has enjoyed reading from the first and second grades. His mother had first read the Wizard of Oz books to him and then helped him to read them. He described himself as "carried away" by science fiction from the seventh grade to the present time. It represented escape into a different realm, into a world of his own where he could set the capabilities and shortcomings. After finishing a book he could daydream on his own. As noted, this reading interest began early, in grade school.

The mother entered the picture somewhat more strongly than his father, a practicing physician who "worked too hard" but managed to find time for his family. The parents participated together in an active social life, golf, and swimming. Henry believes himself to have been more identified with his mother in the past but is gradually moving toward his father, particularly in work habits. The adolescent boy's rediscovery of his father is often seen among the mentally healthy boys who have developed many of their interests through association with the mother.

Laura, too, was briefly mentioned in chapter 4 (drama). Of the influence of her mother, she pointed to her mother's avid interests in reading. "We read the same novels. . . . She'd reread the books I'd bring home."

The contagion of enthusiasm can work in almost any field in which the child is able to share with the adult. Sally's absorbed interest in nature—just drinking it in, not being scientific about it—she got in association with her father (chapter 6: sensory stimulation). Here again we have the cross-sexed identification that has turned up so frequently.

The developmental history of interest in adventure has already been discussed in chapter 9 (adventuresomeness). For Sidney, his exploits can be traced to his father's adventurous flying; Victor is a flyer who grew up in a family of flyers; Donald, who became avidly interested in science fiction, owes his reading interests to his mother. The case of James was a little different; his interests apparently arose out of loneliness.

This review of earlier cases suffices to show how frequently the involvements have developed in close association with one or the other parent, of either sex, or with both parents. Typically the involvements begin early, well before the onset of adolescence. For completion of the picture of the development of involvements, however, we need to examine some additional problems. Three questions are of particular interest here. First, if the involvement is developed in childhood, does it automatically persist, or can it be lost? Second, if it does not develop in childhood, can circumstances lead to its development later? Third, how do involvements develop in the absence of parental contagion?

The answer to the first question is that an involvement developed in childhood may indeed be lost, and when it is lost the correlative hypnotic ability is also likely to be lost. Something of this sort may indeed be rather widespread and thus account for the decrease of hypnotizability in adolescence and beyond. The case of Ward, who scored at the bottom on the hypnotic scale (0 on SHSS-C) as a senior in college, can serve to illustrate what may happen.

We made a serious mistake in judging Ward's hypnotizability on the basis of his interview prior to hypnosis because, at the time, we did not know as much about these matters as we have learned from the review of all of the evidence. Having been rather impressed by the frequent suggestion that hypnosis was a regressed state, we then thought that if the appropriate childhood experience had been there it would probably be reinstated during hypnosis and capitalized on as a basis for hypnotic performance. We have since learned that the capacity for deep emotional involvement can be destroyed through the intellectualization of interests, and once destroyed it apparently removes with it the capacity for hypnosis that may have been there earlier.

As a child Ward was deeply involved in reading. "I always identified. I was the character in every book I read as a child. I lost this in adolescence. I no longer do this."

In an interview subsequent to hypnosis we learned more about this shift. As a child he was richly imaginative; he would lie in bed and dream of a desert island, with himself as a Robinson Crusoe. His reading habits changed dramatically around the age of twelve. Before that time he had been greatly involved in novels and adventure stories, putting himself easily into the character parts. He had felt himself one of the characters in the *Count of Monte Cristo,* one of *The Three Musketeers.* The last book he remembers becoming involved in is *The Grapes of Wrath,* which he read at age eleven or twelve. Then all such involvement disappeared. He thought it was due to the fact that at age thirteen he had reached puberty (he was already six feet tall then). At any rate his reading pattern changed. He stopped reading all novels and romances and instead read objective literature such as science and history. He added that his father was the science type in college and had never been interested in novels.

The early reading interest had been developed through close affiliation with his mother. She began to read to him when he was three years old. She read *Robinson Crusoe, Black Stallion,* and *The Three Musketeers,* among others, up to his eighth year, when he began to read for himself. At twelve we have a shift of identification away from the romantically involved mother to the objective and scientific father. Ward is following his father's footsteps by planning to go into medicine. His father is a physician who devotes himself to his work. The older brother apparently made a shift similar to Ward's: he had majored in English in college (showing a residual influence of their mother) but has since gone to medical school and is now described as an "objective" person like the father.

As a consequence of the shift, Ward now describes himself as a skeptic, a scoffer—always pleasant, but with *no emotional involvement in anything.* He is particularly doubtful about the influence of words: he believes neither that his words can influence others nor that the words of others can influence him. We believe his lack of hypnotic susceptibility is predictable from the kind of person he is now, not from the kind of person he was as a preadolescent. We use him, then, as an illustration of how involvement can be lost, and with it, probably the susceptibility to hypnosis. Ward might be an interesting case for study in techniques for enhancing the hypnotic susceptibility of those whose histories suggest that they were once hypnotizable. There need be nothing *absolute* in the loss of hypnotizability that he shows in the standard testing situation.

A somewhat similar shift was noted for Parker (chapter 3: reading), again from identification with a literary mother to a literal-minded scientific father. Earlier he had been interested almost exclusively in science fiction, and he expressed a certain wistfulness about experiences now lost, as when he used to imagine sequels to a story days after reading an exciting tale. In high school he began to shift. As he put it, no magic sweep of the hand would bring admission to medical school. He had recently tried to immerse himself in science fiction again but found that the relaxed enjoyment of the old fantasies could not be recaptured. He scored two on SHSS-C.

The second question raised earlier was whether or not involvements not developed in childhood could be developed later. There is some reason to be uneasy about this, as pointed out in the cases of the religious converts, but the failure for the later-developed interest in religion to be related to hypnosis was interpreted as owing to a different function of religion for the convert than for the religiously nurtured. The hypothesis that has gradually emerged is that a *new* involvement may develop later in life (e.g., in adolescence) *provided* that there has been a pattern of involvement laid down in some other area earlier. That is, the new involvement is in some sense grafted upon the old one. George, whose reading interests developed late, was described in chapter 3 (reading). For him there had been an intense involvement in TV and movie watching, and it was inferred that the reading interest, evolving from these, had a relationship to hypnosis similar to that which it would have had if the reading had developed earlier.

The third question is, How do involvements develop in the absence of parental contagion? We have mentioned that for James (as for others) an involvement may develop when there is lonesomeness that is filled by reading or other activities unrelated to the parental interests. In the absence of the parents there are others who can serve as models: siblings, peers, athletic coaches. *Provided the involvements that develop are free of conflict with the parents,* they need not be guided by parental interests.

## Concluding Remarks on Identifications and Hypnotizability

Our study of the relationships of our subjects to their parents have suggested some aspects of the identification found in this university population and have given us some hints about how these identifications are related to hypnosis. The following points are deserving of mention:

1. Among those subjects who are predominantly normal in their sex-typing, there are important ways in which they resemble parents of the opposite sex. For example, 23 percent of our male subjects and 26 percent of our female subjects reported that they had picked up their work habits and attitudes from the parent of the opposite sex; 30 percent of the males and 35 percent of the females felt they were more similar in temperament to the parent of the sex that differed from their own.

2. A thread running through the relationship between hypnotizability and identification is that higher hypnotizability is associated with identification with the parent of the opposite sex rather

than with the parent of the same sex, although this difference reaches statistical significance only in the case of temperamental similarity. A plausible interpretation is that the child selects as an opposite-sexed parental model of temperament a parent whose attractiveness to the child is based on the kinds of qualities that make the parent (and ultimately the child) susceptible to hypnosis. An alternative explanation is that cross-sexed identification favors the kinds of dissociative experiences on which hypnosis is based.

3. There is little likelihood that the child who is identified with neither parent in work or in temperament will develop or retain the qualities that would make him hypnotizable as a young adult. This is less true for recreation, perhaps because recreational models can be found among siblings or peers who keep the appropriate qualities alive without parent participation.

# 14

# Childhood Development:
# The Role of Punishment

Our developmental-interactive interpretation of hypnotic susceptibility is based on the belief that early childhood experiences either
maintain or enhance whatever abilities distinguish the more hypnotizable person from the less hypnotizable. There have been a number of hints at these developmental aspects in earlier chapters,
particularly concerning how the involvements of children grow in
activities shared with parents. One aspect of development is the
kind of discipline parents use with their children. We find in our
study a correlation of $r = .30$ ($N = 187$) between severity of punishment in childhood and later susceptibility to hypnosis. This is as
high a correlation as is found with any single predictor, and its understanding becomes the theme of this chapter.

The role of punishment in childhood is incompletely understood. With the development of more sensitive attitudes toward
child rearing, a general diminution of physical punishment has occurred. Support for this attitude comes from scientific sources, with
learning theorists as far apart in general viewpoint as Thorndike and
Skinner pointing out the ineffectiveness of punishment (or aversive
stimulation) in the strengthening of desirable behavior. Correspondingly, a psychoanalyst such as Erik Erikson points to the need
for a development of "basic trust" through warmth of handling and
assurance for the child that the world is a friendly place. Careful
studies of the effectiveness of punishment show, however, that
punishment may be informative and that it may set limits for the
benefit of the child's personality development in the areas of conscience and self-control. Therefore, it is important not to treat all
punishments alike but instead to make some distinctions.

We began our studies with the thought that a strong supportive role from adults would be useful in making the subject trustful of adults, and hence more hypnotizable, and that probably high punishment in childhood would be a negative influence. But our quantitative findings were quite the opposite, and year after year we have found a relationship—always in the same direction, occasionally highly significant statistically—associating severity of punishment in childhood with high hypnotizability. These findings provide the background for this chapter.

## Punishment in Childhood as Predictive of Later Hypnotizability

Punishment was rated by our interviewers on a seven-point scale similar to that used for rating other dimensions of experience thought possibly related to hypnosis. A high rating meant a high severity of punishment. The results for the 187 subjects of the 1962–63 and 1963–64 samples are given in table 39. As we have

TABLE 39

*Severity of Punishment as Related to Hypnotic Susceptibility*

| Severity of Punishment | Susceptibility (SHSS-C) | | |
|---|---|---|---|
| | Low (0–5) | High (6–12) | Total |
| High (5–7) | 22 | 41 | 63 |
| Medium (4) | 36 | 30 | 66 |
| Low (1–3) | 37 | 21 | 58 |
| Total | 95 | 92 | 187 |

Significance test: $\chi^2 = 10.62$; $df = 2$; $p = .01$.

found throughout, relationships are not high, though they are statistically significant and warrant some further inferences from the case studies. Expressed as a correlation, the relationship between rated severity of punishment and hypnosis is $r = .30$; with $N = 187$ this correlation is significant, as is the chi-square represented in the distributions of table 39. It is to be expected that the correlation is clearer when extremes are compared; thus, of those rated high in punishment, 41/63, or 65 percent, fall in the upper half in hypnotizability, while of those low in punishment only 21/58, or 36 percent, fall in this half.

We can look at the figures from the opposite side, by beginning with the highest-scoring hypnotic subjects. Of the 24 subjects among the 187 who scored ten, eleven, or twelve on SHSS-C, 13, or 52 percent, were rated high in childhood punishment (ratings of five, six, or seven). This is to be compared with the 50 among the other 163 subjects, or 30 percent, who were rated this high in punishment. There is no doubt that within this sample some relationship exists between severity of punishment and high hypnotizability.

It is of interest that this rating, made by the same interviewers in the same interview in which other ratings were made, failed to correlate significantly with any of the other ratings, with one exception. The exception was a correlation of $r = -.27$ with reasoning as a method of discipline—a negative correlation that is clearly to be expected. Because the correlation of rated punishment with the various involvements found related to hypnosis is not significant, it becomes virtually another "factor" in the prediction of hypnotizability. That is, it is almost as highly correlated with the criterion (hypnotic-susceptibility scores) as the sum of the individual involvements, but it is uncorrelated with the involvements (correlation with the sum of involvements is $r = .12$).

Punishment has been selected for discussion because it was the mode of discipline that correlated with hypnosis. There were other kinds of discipline rated in the interviews, and the comparative frequencies are summarized in table 40. The three kinds of disci-

TABLE 40
*Kinds of Discipline Experienced in Childhood*

| Rating | Reasoning | Punishment | Reward |
|---|---|---|---|
| | % | % | % |
| High (5–7) | 42 | 34 | 12 |
| Medium (4) | 29 | 35 | 27 |
| Low (1–3) | 29 | 31 | 58 |
| Mode indicated but not rated | — | — | 3 |
| Total ($N = 187$) | 100 | 100 | 100 |

pline were separately rated, and the table does not show the overlap of the various kinds. What it does show is that, in retrospect, more of our student subjects remembered that they had been reasoned with than reported the other kinds of discipline, with punishment second, and reward a poor third. Nearly three-fifths (58 percent) reported a very low frequency of reward in their training, despite the preference for reward (positive reinforcement) found in much of our current psychological literature on training. The significant correlation between severity of punishment and hypnotic susceptibility has already been given ($r = .30$); the other two types did not yield significant correlations with hypnosis (reasoning, $r = .00$; reward, $r = .09$). The predominant mode was reasoning ($N = 72$); punishment ($N = 53$); or reward ($N = 6$). The predominant mode omits those subjects who rated two modes of discipline as equal. While those with punishment as the predominant mode had numerically higher mean hypnotic scores than those in the other groups, the difference did not reach statistical significance for subjects selected as reporting one mode of discipline as predominant. What this may mean is that punishment affects the hypnotic susceptibility of the subject, even when it is not the predominant mode of discipline.

### The Disciplinary Histories of Highly Punished and Highly Hypnotizable Subjects

Individual cases have the advantage over statistical trends in that they are the stories of real people whose disciplinary histories are coherent with the fact they are highly hypnotizable; the causal relationships may be uncertain, but the facts are in context. For the purposes of the present analysis, cases have been chosen who score in the highest range of our hypnotic sample (scores of ten to twelve on SHSS-C) and who have been rated as high in severity of childhood punishment.

The first case is that of Irene. She was punished by both her mother and her father, but their types of punishment differed. Her father spanked her, not infrequently, through the age of seven. Her mother tended to hurt her with words, telling her for hours how much she did wrong and how she had no manners. She was then made to stay in her room for long periods or had things she liked taken away from her. She considered the discipline irrational and inconsistently applied.

It was often revealing to ask the subject whether or not the discipline was the kind that would be used with his or her children, on the assumption that "successful" discipline, however described, might be recommended for the next generation, but it was not so for Irene. She said she would be more lenient with her children and would use supporting love instead of pounding the child into a mold, as she felt herself to have been pounded. "I was repressed

rather than made confident. Little things were too much emphasized. If I said 'Yes' instead of 'Yes, Mother,' all sorts of hell broke
loose." When asked whether this treatment made her alert, she
replied, "I was forced to be very aware of my environment. I wel-
comed opportunities when I didn't have to be so alert. Hypnosis is
such an opportunity."

The remarks so far would lead to the inference that Irene's
punishment might be contributing to hypnosis in two ways: first, by
establishing the habit of strict and prompt conformity to the commands of an authority, even when the commands are somewhat
irrational, and, second, by providing some kind of escape from the
responsibility for alert self-control.

We might leave it at this, except that Irene also developed the
kind of involvements that we have found important in hypnosis,
particularly reading, but also other creative activities—music, art,
poetry, and the appreciation of nature. It will be recalled that there
is no significant correlation between these rated involvements and
punishment, which, taken at its face value, means that there is
no overall causal relationship between punishment and involvement, although they are not antithetical. (If they were in conflict,
the correlation would be negative). A subject who has *both* a history of punishment and involvements (as in Irene's case) is more
likely to be highly hypnotizable than a subject with the history of
only one of these; this is the meaning of the multiple correlation to
be presented in chapter 16. It is necessary to be cautious, however,
in interpreting an individual case according to a statistical relationship, for there may be subtle combinations of discipline and involvements that do not leave them as distinct as the low correlation implies.

Despite the unsatisfactory disciplinary handling by Irene's parents, the personal relationships were by no means negative, especially those with her father. She respected him as a man of excellent
judgment who made good decisions. He was both gentle and
tough, a good conversationalist, and basically serious but with a
sense of humor. If she could change him she would make him "less
serious and more relaxed," but she shared many interests with him,
particularly work interest, and her choice of career has been much
influenced by his.

The involvements she developed were genuine, as some of the
following quotes indicate. "I like listening to classical music; it
affects the mood I am in, tremendously. I like singing for fun, and
am in the chorus here. . . . I prefer reading for enjoyment rather
than for analysis. . . . [On enjoyment of nature] I stop and stare and

fix images in my mind, so that I can call them up later . . . the beautiful views, so beautiful I catch my breath . . . I drink in the view of sun on the oak trees . . . I get absorbed in movies. I became the heroine of *Breakfast at Tiffany's* . . . I get carried away and absorbed. . . . My mood gets carried along and I don't analyze. I get the *feeling.*"

This kind of absorbed involvement carries over into her experience of hypnosis. "Hypnosis is similar to reading. I concentrate so hard on a book. I'm terribly immersed and won't be able to put it down. When you read you get outside yourself. In your reading you become involved in another set of circumstances, so temporarily you can liberate yourself from your environment and put yourself into one of the characters. You escape yourself. When you're by yourself, with a book or with the hypnotist, your environment is blanked out. In hypnosis it is by your intense concentration on the voice of the hypnotist which says you're being liberated from your environment. As it goes deeper you may tend to escape your personality temporarily."

When asked about her use of the word *temporarily,* she went on, "In reading, the book is going to come to an end. So in hypnosis—the idea of escape, of not having to control yourself. As when you go to sleep, you've needed a release. You may dream. You wake when it's time to wake up."

It may be noted that in her account there is little reference to the authority of the hypnotist; it is rather that he provides an opportunity for her to concentrate and thus to lose the requirement of alertness to the usual environment. She may have used reading as such an escape. Hence the assumption that the voice of the hypnotist is the voice of the parents demanding conformity is not the way it feels to her. In fact she differentiated the hypnotist from her parents. "I trust doctors, and I associate the hypnotist with a doctor. I've had doctors who were wonderful to me." Of course this does not mean that her habit of obedience to parents had little to do with her hypnotic responsiveness, but the parallels she draws are with escape (as in reading) and pleasant experiences (as with doctors). Her combination of the involvements that we have found associated with hypnosis, along with severity of punishment, we shall find in other cases of the highly hypnotizable; the causal sequences remain obscure.

Another case is that of Maude. We have met her before, in chapter 3, where she illustrated the development of reading involvement in relationship with her parents. At that point, nothing was said about the kind of discipline in the home. In her account of discipline she explained that it was a combination of punishment and reasoning—the kind of combination which accounts in part for the fact that the negative correlation between punishment and reasoning, while found, is a low one. Her father was very severe about small infractions of the rules. He created a grim, solemn atmosphere over little things. "Dad was the main disciplinarian. If he was angry he'd lecture and scold us. He could make us feel like withering up and crawling into a hole—just by a look. He has an intense type of temper, though he's not violent and he does not shout. He'll say things that are very emotional and can cause hurt feelings." Maude went on to say that he was prone to inconsistencies. If she came home late from a show sometimes he wouldn't be upset at all. At other times he would be upset and imply accusingly that she hadn't used good sense. At the dinner table her father was always drilling good manners into the children, accomplishing this by a look. In reply to questioning, Maude indicated that she would not use her father's kind of discipline with her children; it was too severe. One consequence, she thought, was that it made her exceedingly alert to what she should do, both in relation to her father and to others. She tended to watch others to see what they wanted.

In some respects Maude has reacted to her discipline in much the same way as Irene, with some disapproval of its severity and inconsistency, with the consequence of alertness to the environment, and, perhaps, with some satisfaction through the escape in reading.

Maude is closer to her father than to her mother, as Irene is, though their relations to their mothers are quite different. Maude describes her mother as warm and comfortable, "tolerant, understanding, keeps the family running smoothly, takes responsibility easily." Still, Maude is more like her father. She says she resembles him more than her mother, in both temperament and personality. She used to take offense when people said that she was like him, for she disliked his intolerance and dogmatic attitudes. At the same time, he was independent and intelligent, and she, like Irene with her father, shared work interests with him.

Like Irene, Maude found hypnosis a state of "complete peacefulness and relaxation." Perhaps the relationship to her discipline in childhood also combines the compliant responsiveness to one in authority with the desire to escape the need to be ever on the alert. Because the reading interest is the nearest parallel to hypnosis, and the reading interest developed in close relationship with the parents, it may be appropriate to think of the discipline as accentuating the hypnotic responsiveness based upon the involvement in reading.

Roger was mentioned briefly in chapter 5 as a high-scoring hypnotic subject who was religiously devout, following his mother and (in part) his father. Questioned about discipline, he said he was raised on "good spankings" to the age of twelve, much scolding, little reasoning, and few material rewards. Because his only area of deep involvement was religion, it would require some speculative interpretation to relate this involvement and his acceptance of punishment. One might assume that a watchful, punishing God might be related to a powerful, punishing parent, and in turn to a powerful hypnotist—but the opposite is equally plausible: a loving God providing relief from punishment, and the hypnotist providing escape from responsibility. We do not have enough evidence to follow the causal strands, but his case illustrates a history of continued spanking in childhood associated with high hypnotizability.

A fourth case is that of Earl, described in chapter 8, where emphasis was upon imaginary companions. He was spanked "with a big black belt" until the age of ten. In his case, the punishment was not resented in retrospect for "it had served its purpose." We do not know whether his imaginary companion provided something of an escape from the environment. In any case, he was among the higher-scoring subjects (score of eleven on SHSS-C) and combined punishment and the imaginary companion with other involvements, particularly fiction and music.

A fifth and final illustration of this group of highly punished and highly hypnotizable subjects is provided by Anna. Rules in her home were very strict, and disobedience was punished. Father made the rules and there were many of them. When the children were young these rules required no explanation, for the father was clear: "Do it because I say so." As she grew older there were some reasons given for the rules, and the discipline worked well: Anna feels that she had "wonderful" parents and is grateful for them. She described her mother as vivacious, an optimist, unwilling to look at the unpleasant, full of fun, generous, doing for everyone, enthusiastic in her interests. Her father she said was very strong, intelligent, successful, quiet, always a good father but waiting for the children to be old enough so that he could communicate comfortably with them. In a reserved way he was enthusiastic about his interests, but they were rather autonomous and little shared. Anna identified more with her mother in temperament and interests. In work both she and her mother took short cuts unless interested; despite what she characterized as "laziness" about work, they had a sense of responsibility which carried them through.

Anna, like the others we have discussed, combined imaginative involvements with punishment; if all cases were like these we would expect a positive correlation, but we are dealing with one portion of a distribution, and the correlation does not hold overall. She was rated high in involvement in reading, in movie watching, in adventurous activities, and in appreciation of nature. We would have predicted her hypnotizability on the basis of these involvements, disregarding the punishment, but the correlation with punishment is there to be explained. She communicated well in the interview and was rated as normal and outgoing. The interviewer described her as a warm, enthusiastic person. It was not surprising that she looked forward to hypnosis and enjoyed it when she experienced it.

We have reviewed in capsule form the childhood punishment of five highly hypnotizable subjects. It is significant that they also were rated high on involvement of one sort or another and that their involvements were not inhibited by punishment.

### Highly Punished Non-Hypnotizable Subjects

When we reviewed our cases we looked also for the exceptions to the rule. There are some high-punishment subjects who are not hypnotizable. The following two illustrate these.

Dave is a competitive athlete, the kind of athlete described in chapter 10 as not hypnotizable. His punishment seems to classify with the kinds already described. While his father used a strap on him and was very strict, particularly in the early years, when Dave became self-reliant enough to deserve freedom he was given it. Although he did not think that his father's demands for conformity were always reasonable, he always knew why he was being punished. He talked about having had to earn his freedom; his parents were strict, with spankings as part of the discipline, until both felt that he had taken over the parental standards and could be trusted on his own. He has been "on his own," making all his own decisions, since the age of thirteen or fourteen. The situation earlier was quite the reverse; for example, his parents always took the teacher's side, and if he got a "lick" at school, he got three more at home. He believes that he grew up to have an exceptional respect for authority, while at the same time being very independent.

Dave's only area of involvement, as described earlier, was in competitive athletics, wherein he made his way to the varsity teams. He felt that he was like his father in temperament and in athletic interests. He was a natural competitor, had been one all his life; the form the competition took was athletics, and in this, too, he was like his father. If punishment is positively correlated with hypnotizability, why was Dave not hypnotizable? The position taken earlier was that the realistic alertness to the actual situation in competition tells against accepting the reality distortions of hypnosis. If this is the explanation, then whatever punishment does is not enough to produce hypnotizability by itself. It might turn out that punishment is an energizer of other trends and thus enhances hypnotizability for those whose involvements favor hypnosis and enhances competitiveness for those who move in that direction; if that is the case, punishment alone cannot be expected to account for hypnotizability, although in interaction with other trends it doubtless has an influence.

A second illustration of the nonhypnotizable, highly punished subject is provided by Susan. Like Dave, her only area of involvement was competitive athletics; her history of punishment in childhood, rated at a severity of five on a seven-point scale, did not enhance hypnotizability, which was represented by a score of three on the SHSS-C. Both parents were athletic and the father was a professional competitive athlete. She had been on basketball and hockey teams in high school and was continuing her athletic career in college. Her failure to be hypnotized could not be due to a rejecting attitude, for she wanted very much to be hypnotized. Before trying hypnosis she said, "I think it would be *really* interesting . . . I've always wanted to be hypnotized . . . I think I'll be a good subject."

### Parental Warmth of Punishing Parents

The stereotype of the punishing parent is that he is colder and more forbidding than the parent who uses punishment less. Since many of our case studies of punished subjects showed them to be admiring of their parents, and ready to emulate them, with many developed enthusiasms shared with their parents, it seemed wise to analyze what the subjects themselves had to say about parental warmth in relation to punishment. It was somewhat easier for the subjects to characterize the warmth of their mothers than of their fathers, and thus the following analysis is based upon mother warmth.

If one groups the subjects according to the rated severity of punishment in the home and then studies the reported mother warmth, the relationships shown in table 41 emerge.

TABLE 41

*Mother Warmth Related to Severity of Punishment in Childhood*

| Mother Warmth | Severity of Punishment | | | Total Cases |
|---|---|---|---|---|
| | Low (1–3) | Medium (4) | High (5–7) | |
| High (6–7) | 19 | 12 | 21 | 52 |
| Medium (3–5) | 39 | 51 | 31 | 121 |
| Low (1–2) | 0 | 3 | 10 | 13 |
| Total | 58 | 66 | 62 | 186* |

Significance test: $\chi^2 = 19.47$; $df = 4$; $p = .01$.
* One case not ascertained.

One point to be made about punishment in our student-population sample (which we have described as punishment with a successful outcome) is that it is commonly associated with parental warmth. There is fully as much punishment in the homes where the mother is rated high in warmth as in the sample as a whole; it is only with the mothers of extremely low warmth (7 percent of the mothers) that we find any disproportion in the amount of punishment (table 41).

## Conformity Developed without Punishment

If we make the assumption that part of the development toward hypnotic susceptibility rests upon an acquired conformity to the demands of a situation which has within it something in common with hypnosis, this provides us with one interpretation of punishment. But perhaps this role can be played by other experiences which are not punitive in nature; if that is the case, the understanding of punishment has given us a hint about how to look at other developmental experiences that might lead to hypnotizability. We have many hypnotizable subjects who were not punished in childhood, which leads us to ask, How did they acquire the kind of conformity to environmental demands that made them hypnotizable?

There are some subjects who, though not punished, learned conformity through strict home discipline. This is the kind of home in which the rules are very clear, and obedience to them is expected: in such a home the child may conform without need for overt punishment and, when asked about punishment as a young adult, will report that it was at a low level or absent. Some of these subjects will recognize, however, that they were indeed manipulated by their parents; such manipulation may provide a background for hypnosis that is almost indistinguishable from the effects of punishment.

Mabel represents one such case. We are acquainted with her as one of those reporting imaginary companions in chapter 8. Her voice of conscience, which may have been related to the developing of her imaginary companion as an alter ego, was not developed through punishment, as such, but through an essential strictness in her home to which she conformed. Mabel said she never had much discipline because she never strayed very far from what she considered right, though occasionally she was sent to her room when she did not measure up to the home's strict standards. The strictness was implied in part by her assertion that her mother won all the arguments, and thus manipulated her by *words,* making corporal punishment unnecessary. The consequences for her were about the same as the punishments we have reported for the others. As in the other cases of the highly hypnotizable, she had a number of involvements, especially reading and drama.

Another group of low-punishment cases (among the highly hypnotizable) is represented by those whose childhood discipline emphasized reasoning instead of punishment. Reasoning was an alternative to punishment frequently enough to produce a negative correlation between the use of punishment and the use of reasoning. These children tended to derive their conformity not so much from the logical talk of the parents—although words are of course involved in reasoning with a child—as through the kind of contagion of shared interests, a parent-child relationship already much discussed in earlier chapters. We may turn to a couple of cases as reminders, but with particular attention to the reasoned discipline.

Sally was described in chapter 6 as one whose hypnosis appeared related to her aesthetic appreciation of nature. Unlike many of the highly hypnotizable subjects, she was disciplined in childhood more by reasoning than by punishment. Asked about discipline, she felt that reasoning had been used the most, "more than was usual in the families of my friends." There were no tangible rewards that she could recall. She had generally conformed at home, and discipline had not been much of an issue. She would try to use the same methods with her children. If, then, conformity is the key to the relationship between discipline and hypnosis,

Sally has come to this through reasoning just as some of the others have come to it through punishment. As in the other cases, there were a number of imaginative involvements, and these had been developed in close relationship with her parents, whom she greatly respected. In addition to her interest in nature she had developed involvements in reading, drama, religion.

A second subject whose conformity arose from a reasoned discipline is Jack, again a high-scorer in hypnosis, ten on SHSS-C.

He had seldom been punished. The rules were explained to him, and they seemed reasonable. As a child he had sometimes disobeyed, but he was never considered to be a problem by his parents. His parents had shown great confidence in him—had never pushed him but rather had let him make his own decisions as he grew older. He was satisfied with his handling and hoped to use the same methods with his children. Here again we have a picture of "successful" discipline, with scarcely any punishment.

I believe that his remark "We do most things as a family" was the key to the development of the interests which appeared in his case to be related to his hypnotizability. The whole family had together learned how to ski. He and his father worked together on a sports car; earlier they had worked together constructing model trains. He gets very involved in his skiing. He forgets everything when he is skiing, and in other athletic events he participates for the enjoyment rather than to win a victory over an opponent.

It becomes abundantly clear why it is difficult to find high relationships between particular background experiences and hypnotic susceptibility, for the features that are important are likely to be derivative from the described experience rather than represented by the experience itself. Thus the derivative of punishment may be conformity to parental standards, in which case the equivalent can be obtained in other ways, as through strictness without punishment, or effective use of reasoning. At the same time not all punishment, not all strictness, and not all reasoning lead to conformity and acceptance of parental rules: sometimes they lead to defiance and rejection. Unless distinctions are made very carefully, it is easy to go wrong in grouping together things with common names and different significances, and separating things with different names but a common significance.

## Inferences on Punishment and Hypnotizability

Both the quantitative material and the case material support a relationship between childhood punishment and later hypnotizability, an unexpected relationship that is deserving of further study and interpretation. The following conjectures represent an attempt to summarize the cases which have just been presented and to make some tentative generalizations on the basis of them.

1. *The consequences of the punishment are not incompatible with the development of imaginative involvements.* Although across the board there is no correlation between rated involvements and rated punishment, a zero correlation differs from a negative one in that there is no incompatibility between the two variables; the cases of unusually high punishment and unusually high hypnosis typically show the two factors present together. When the high punishment is associated with high achievement motivation, and little imaginative involvement, as in the cases of competitive athletes, then one finds low hypnotic scores. It is not altogether clear when punishment is likely to be associated with imagination and when with achievement; we looked for differences in the patterns of punishment, but it did not seem to matter whether the punishment was high and predictable (that is, consistent), or high and unpredictable (inconsistent).

A possible tie between punishment and hypnotic involvement might come by way of dissociation. Although we have no direct evidence, some of our case material (such as in the case of Irene, described earlier in this chapter) suggests that reading or other involvements may sometimes be an escape from the harsh realities of a punitive environment. It will be recalled that Irene was punished by being forced to spend much time alone in her room. Some dissociative elements may be found in her identifying the hypnotist with a doctor rather than with her parents. In the case of Maude (described above, this chapter) there is some indication that hypnosis, like reading, provided an escape from being ever on the alert lest some trangression might provoke her punitive father.

2. *The illogicality of strict discipline may be reflected in the illogicality of hypnotic response.* Strict discipline, which requires a child to toe the mark set by an adult code of conduct, must appear to the child to be arbitrary, and he learns to conform in some cases *because an authority insists upon it*. This habitual conformity may have something to do with the ready conformity in the hypnotic situation, in which the subject does indeed place himself in the hands of an authority figure who also asks of him things that are arbitrary. This belongs to the category of transference rather than identification.

3. *Strict discipline may reflect a well-structured home environment, in which discipline and warmth are combined.* It was earlier

pointed out (table 41) that mother warmth was often rated as high. We may suppose that in these circumstances a strong ego develops, so that the child knows what is expected and accepts the consequences of failure to live up to expectations. To the extent that a strong ego, characteristic of a normal-outgoing person, is favorable to hypnosis, punishment may in some cases produce its effects via this route.

4. *It is not essential that the childhood discipline should be unconditionally accepted,* but it is important that it be successful in its outcome. Some subjects reported that they got "only what they deserved" when they were punished, so that there was a general conformity to the discipline, without later resentment. These subjects tended to report that they would discipline their children in the same way. Others, however, were resentful and thought the powerful adult made them conform; they had a desire to rebel, and these tended to say that they would not use the same practices with their children. Even so, there was little difference in the hypnotizability of these two groups. It may be inferred, therefore, that both types of discipline were successful in achieving respect for order and control. It should be noted that our subject population consists of successful products of the educational system, who meet the standards of admission to a highly selective university; if the punishment had produced the kind of rebellion that leads to a total defiance of the parents, we would probably not have found the subjects in our sample. Hence we infer that from the point of view of personality development, identification with parents, and acceptance of the ideal of a higher eduation, the punishment occurred in a context of successful child-rearing practices.

While to our knowledge the relationship between childhood punishment and hypnotic susceptibility is reported in our studies for the first time, there is added plausibility to the findings on the basis of some quite independent work by Nowlis (1969). He made use of a number of subjects who had been studied while in kindergarten in 1951–52, as reported by Sears, Maccoby, and Levin (1957). They were located twelve years later, in 1963–64, by which time they were seniors in high school. Thus a developmental study was possible in which the childhood data were obtained from young children, rather than as a retrospective account. The high school seniors were invited for a group hypnotic session in which the Harvard Group Scale of Hypnotic Susceptibility (Shor and Orne 1962) was used, a form closely paralleling the Stanford Hypnotic Susceptibility Scale, form A. More of the high school seniors later completed the Personal Experiences Questionnaire, form L, a questionnaire designed to find experiences from everyday life similar to those in hypnosis, and thus predictive of hypnotic susceptibility (Shor 1960). The later sample also took the hypnotic test.

The relationships between the variables recorded at kindergarten age and later hypnotic susceptibility proved disappointing; only one variable met satisfactory criteria of significance in the two halves of a divided sample. This variable, however, was "pressure for conformity to table standards," and it correlated $r = .31$ with hypnotic susceptibility in Sample A ($N = 37$) and $r = .25$ in Sample B ($N = 44$), yielding a combined $p = .01$. It is of interest that this one significant variable shows a relationship of conforming discipline to hypnosis, which is coherent with our findings.

Some further support is given, albeit somewhat indirectly, by the results of the Personal Experiences Inventory. While the correlations between the experiences inventory and the scores on hypnotic susceptibility were lower than anticipated (significantly positive in Sample A, but not in Sample B), there were some significant relations between the experiences inventory and the earlier kindergarten variables. Significant positive relationships were found, for example, between the experiences inventory and frequency with which the mother spanks, extent of use of physical punishment, pressure for conformity with table standards, severity of punishment for aggression towards parents. Thus we find that childhood punishment studied at kindergarten age is predictive of experiences known to be somewhat related to hypnosis as they are reported in high school. The relationships are all so weak they do not establish firmly a connection between the experiences and hypnotic susceptibility in this study, but they point in the same direction as the results we have found.

## Punishment, Identification, and the Subject's Relationship to the Hypnotist

Our findings on the relevance of punishment (and probably other forms of strict discipline) in relation to hypnotic susceptibility may bear on the long history of speculation about the relationship of the hypnotized subject to the hypnotist.

In the psychoanalytic literature, the observations on which the theories rest have been made on patients coming for treatment, so that the attitudes toward the analyst as hypnotist and as psychotherapist are inseparable. Freud (1905), while emphasizing the erotic component in the relationship, also noted the "credulous submissiveness" of the hypnotized subject, a submissiveness with masochistic components. In a later paper, Freud (1921) considered the paralytic helplessness of the patient—who acts as though he were in the hands of someone of superior power—a major unexplained element of hypnosis. Freud thought it was probably due to a heritage of childhood subservience toward parents.

In the meantime, Ferenczi (1909) had described hypnotic induction as of two types, an authoritarian type which he called "father hypnosis," and a gentler type called "mother hypnosis." He believed some subjects more ready for the first kind of induction, others more prepared for the second kind. Presumably the more masochistic would welcome the authoritative "father hypnosis." Thus Ferenczi had sensed that the child's relationship with his parents may be reflected in his behavior within hypnosis.

Kubie and Margolin (1944) state that the incorporated image of the hypnotist "plays the same role as does the incorporated and unconscious image of the parental figure in the child or adult." It would take very little supplement to state that the incorporated image of the hypnotist is possible because of the manner in which parental images have been incorporated. Somewhat along the same line, Erika Fromm (1968b) points out that the patient sees the hypnotist as the omnipotent parent.

We face the problems of how punishment is related to identification with parents, on the one hand, and to the hypnotic relationship on the other. The previous discussion suggests that the relationships with parents may carry into the hypnotic relationship, but the detailed connection with punishment remains to be worked out. Modern identification theories tend to distinguish between identification with the warm or hurturant parent, through a process of modeling or imitation supported theoretically by social learning theory, and a defensive identification, in which the child incorporates the standards of the powerful and punitive parent in order to achieve some sort of mastery. The concept of defensive identification derives from the psychoanalytic theory of the manner in which the Oedipus complex is resolved, particularly in the male. These concepts are reviewed, in relation to the appropriate experimental evidence, by Kohlberg (1963) and by Sears, Rau, and Alpert (1965).

In the light of our previous discussion some of the effects of punishment in a home where warmth exists will serve the nurturant (anaclitic) type of identification because punishment may reflect a well-ordered home in which ego strength may develop. Where the punishment is authoritarian and its results are based on the acceptance of the role of the powerful adult, the appropriate concept may be transference instead of defensive identification. The hypnotist becomes the powerful parent. We have no evidence for or against the theory of masochistic surrender in accepting this authority.

## Conclusions regarding Punishment and Hypnotizability

We have in punishment clear support for a developmental contribution to hypnotic susceptibility, for punishment begins in the years before hypnotic susceptibility can be tested and still correlates significantly with hypnotic-susceptibility scores in a college sample. The correlation is established, and it gains some support from a follow-up study of children tested first in kindergarten and later as seniors in high school.

The causal relationships are more obscure. Most of our punished subjects appear to have established good relationships with one or both parents, and many have developed the imaginative involvements already reported as bearing upon hypnotic susceptibility. Because severity of punishment does not correlate with involvements, but both involvements and punishment correlate with hypnosis, the punishment makes a separate contribution, probably through the habits of conformity that it engenders, through a structured home as much as through an authoritarian one. Those non-punished subjects who score high on hypnosis also appear to have learned conformity, possible through a different but equally successful identification with parental figures. The possibility of some contribution by way of escape from responsibility through fantasy (or hypnosis) cannot be ignored, and perhaps there is some relationship of punishment to dissociation.

# 15

## Motivation and Hypnotizability

It has long been felt that a person's desire to be hypnotized has a good deal to do with his success as a hypnotic subject. The motivation to please the hypnotist was taken by White (1941) to be one of the basic considerations accounting for the forms of hypnotic response. There is another aspect of motivation, also, in the pressure put by the hypnotist upon the subject to conform, as through special exhortation, involving instructions, or through other forms of psychological coercion, which may enhance the ordinary coerciveness of the hypnotic atmosphere already rich with suggestions to conform.

In earlier studies from this laboratory, subjects were asked, prior to any opportunity to participate in experiments on hypnosis, how they would view an invitation to participate (Boucher and Hilgard 1962; Melei and Hilgard 1964). It was found that those who signed up for hypnosis expressed more favorable attitudes than those who failed to volunteer, a not unexpected finding. But even among those who did volunteer, there were some differences corresponding to their expressed attitudes. At least for female subjects, the more favorable attitudes toward hypnosis were related to higher scores on the SHSS, forms A and C. The situation was less clear for males, a finding also from the experiments of Rosenhan and Tomkins (1964).

We asked some questions in our interviews, prior to hypnosis, in regard to the way the subject felt about his expected participation in hypnosis and rated his motivation toward the experience on a seven-point scale similar to our other scales, with a low rating indicating negativism or apprehension, and a high rating a strong desire to experience hypnosis, with little anxiety about what might happen.

The rated motivation for hypnosis correlated $r = +.25$ with SHSS-C ($N = 184$), a correlation as high as that with the various involvement ratings. What such a correlation actually means is best illustrated by the distribution in table 42. The correlation is as low

TABLE 42

*Motivation for Hypnosis as Related to Hypnotizability*

|  | Susceptibility (SHSS-C) | | |
| Motivation | Low (0–5) | High (6–12) | Total |
| --- | --- | --- | --- |
| High (6–7) | 9 | 20 | 29 |
| Medium (4–5) | 65 | 64 | 129 |
| Low (1–3) | 19 | 7 | 26 |
| Total | 93 | 91 | 184* |

Significance test: $\chi^2 = 9.86$; $df = 2$; $p = .01$.
* Three cases not ascertained.

as it is because such a large fraction of the cases fall in the middle categories in motivation and turn out to be about equally in the upper and lower halves of hypnotizability. It is only at the extremes that the motivation becomes more diagnostic, with 20/29, or 70 percent, of the high-motivation subjects in the upper half of hypnotizability and but 7/26, or 25 percent, of the low-motivation subjects in the upper half.

We are ready now to look at the cases of those who fall in various parts of the scatterplot of the relationship between motivation and hypnosis, to see if we can discover what this means from the point of view of the subject presenting himself for hypnosis.

### The Highly Motivated Highly Hypnotizable Subject

Subjects who are eager for hypnosis generally support what we already know, that the kinds of people with deep involvements are likely to be the ones enthusiastically ready for hypnosis. A typical case is Anna, whom we met in chapter 14. Discipline in her home was described as strict.

There was no doubt about Anna's eagerness to be hypnotized. "I'm very excited about it. I've been looking forward to it for weeks." She represents a "typical" hypnotizable subject according to the criteria established in earlier chapters: she achieves great involvement in reading, in movies, and in adventure. She has a deep appreciation of nature. "The majestic mountains . . . I'm a nature worshipper . . . I feel puny in contrast to beauty and grandeur." She loves water sports and the water itself, especially the large waves of the seashore: "Somehow I become a part of the ocean." She reported an active imagination as a child. "Mother kept a record of what we did in some baby books, and she put down how I made up songs and poems." Even today Anna likes to write, especially about nature. She is very friendly and outgoing. She has identified more with her mother. She was grateful to her parents for the way they had insisted that she do the right things (their discipline included punishing her when she did not come up to expectations).

There is a problem in the overmotivated subject, a problem that is present in some of the experiments in which the demands upon the subject are so strong that he accommodates himself to the hypnotist's wishes even though his experiences of hypnosis are not very real, as pointed out by Bowers (1966). One such case that came to our attention was Peter, a subject so eager to have the range of hypnotic experiences that he "helped them along," and to such an extent that it was hard to tell what was genuine and what was superficial role playing.

Peter represents a kind of performance very unusual among our subjects, although we were on the alert for the appearance of more who would behave as he did. In advance of hypnosis Peter said he was much interested in being hypnotized, had read extensively on the subject, and had experienced hypnosis in the past, with moderate results. Since then he had worked with self-hypnosis, had hypnotized others, and felt that he was ready and eager to respond to this new opportunity. He expected hypnosis to be useful in medicine, a career for which he was headed. He did respond, making a score of eleven on form C, out of a possible twelve.

By contrast with Anna, Peter did not appear to be the kind of subject who would be readily hypnotizable, on the basis of interviews in advance of hypnosis. He did not become readily absorbed in things, was very cautious and analytical in his remarks. The interviewer expected him to score about five in hypnosis, perhaps a little below the mean. While he showed signs of imagination, there was always some truncation of the experience. He had done little reading because he did not like to sit still. He said he was interested in cars and wanted to drive a racing car, but on further questioning it was found that he had done nothing serious about these wishes.

This puzzling boy, who wanted to be hypnotized, who scored high on the scale, yet who seemed so unlike other high-scoring subjects, revealed some of the answers in the interview following hypnosis. It turned out that he had thought so much about hypnosis that he could well imagine what the experience would be like when it was called for in hypnosis, and he tried to make it come true by describing the experiences he had conjured up as appropriate. Yet when asked about their reality he was unclear: some of the things he had clearly helped along, some seemed real. It was hard to tell where deliberate role playing ended and the more spontaneous experiences of hypnosis began.

The terms *role playing* or *simulation* conjure up pictures of fraudulence, of attempts to deceive the hypnotist. There is a spectrum here, of course, but in the case of Peter, as in the cases of most of the subjects who have his problems, the conflicts are within him, rather than between him and the hypnotist. He discussed frankly what had happened. "I was not completely under the control of the hypnotist. I was cooperating. Whenever I was told to do something, I did what I was told to do. Sometimes I experienced nothing and sometimes I experienced what I was told I'd experience." Some of the items were, in fact, quite vivid. "I'm extremely sensitive to ammonia, yet when I was told I wouldn't smell it, I couldn't smell it at all. I smelled a little tobacco on the hypnotist's hand. . . . When told I would have tastes in my mouth I had to imagine awfully hard, and the results were not vivid. . . . When told I would dream I got one picture in my mind, like a slide projector that wouldn't change. I had to daydream to keep up the action. It was a 'never-changing picture.' A white mountain in the distance, a snowcapped peak; I was standing in a small stream, there was a highway 100 yards away. The white mountain was as though *painted* white. I thought the white mountain was indicative of success in hypnosis."

One difficulty in appraising Peter's performances in hypnosis is that he had experimented considerably with self-hypnosis. He believed his deepest trances had come when he had hypnotized himself. He put up with an external hypnotist for the sake of learning more about hypnosis, and of exploring his own reactions to hypnosis, but it was intrinsically unpleasant for him to have someone else in control. He preferred to go along with the hypnotist's suggestions, even when the results did not occur automatically, first, in order not to break whatever level of trance he had already achieved, and second, in the hope that going through the motions would deepen the trance. Thus his motivation for hypnosis led to some of his role enactments. It appears that he is inherently in the moderate range of hypnotizable subjects and that there are characteristics within him preventing the deeper experiences some others achieve; for him, the scores derived from standardized scales seem to be inflated by his interpretation of what the behavior is that will achieve the most for him.

## The Subject Passively Resistant to Hypnosis

Contrasting with the subjects who are eager for hypnosis are two groups of resistant subjects: those passively resistant, who have little taste for hypnosis but are not openly antagonistic, and those actively resistant, who would prefer to have nothing to do with it, or actively avoid involvement. These two shade into each other, and it is not always clear to what extent the passively resistant are actually more deeply resistant. Some cases will make clear what we meet in these subjects.

Bruce said he came to the hypnosis experiment only because it would satisfy some of the experimental time requirement for the course he was taking, and the hours were convenient. He thought the topic of hypnosis was interesting, but for himself, he said, "I would hate to feel vulnerable. I will cooperate with the directions, and won't resist intentionally."

What Bruce felt about hypnosis had a direct relationship to his relinquishment of involvements in his life outside the laboratory. He had earlier read much, and with high absorption; he had become so involved in tennis playing that he had been teased about it. Now he was trying to be more detached, more intellectual. He wanted to think about what he was reading, instead of being carried away by what he read. He had to struggle *not* to become involved, for he was embarrassed if his involvement showed. The interviewer detected this resistance to involvement and wondered whether the earlier experiences would still produce a high hypnotic score, or whether the fear of becoming vulnerable and losing control would defeat hypnosis. He was predicted to fall just above the mean, at six, and actually scored a five on form C.

Lester had at first indicated on the questionnaire inviting him to participate in hypnosis that he was not interested, but he changed his mind and decided to see what it was all about. He thought he would be difficult to hypnotize. His remarks after attempted hypnosis were as follows: "I had not known what to expect, and it was not successful. They actually did nothing here that

one could object to . . . I had a dubious feeling in general about it
. . . I was paying attention to the directions but was not really absorbed; I was watching what was going on and analyzing all the
time. . . ." It is not surprising that his score was two.

Dennis came in order to fulfill a laboratory requirement. "Except for the convenient time, I wouldn't have chosen an experiment
in hypnosis, for I really don't care much about being hypnotized.
However, I will cooperate, even if I don't think I'll get hypnotized."
After hypnosis he said he had not expected to respond, and he did
not. He was watching throughout the experience. "I really never
forget myself at any time; I'm always aware of my surroundings."
He scored two in hypnosis.

The interviewer described him as solemn, colorless, emanating
no warmth. He did not articulate well, swallowed his words, and
stammered a little. In describing his family and himself he used a
minimum of words, preferring to describe his family and himself as
"average, just like everyone else."

Brent was another rated low in motivation for hypnosis and
scoring low in hypnosis; he received the lowest possible score, a
zero on form C. He said of his attitude toward hypnosis, "I felt
apathetic toward it, but decided it was a quick way to secure credit
to meet the laboratory requirement." He doubted that he could be
hypnotized and was not sure he wanted to be. The interviewer
noted that he came to the interview with a chip on his shoulder.
Throughout the interview he challenged her by asking for an explanation of the purpose for each question. It was obvious that he was
bright and alert and could have understood without his questions.

These subjects who express little interest in hypnosis, but go
along in any case, tend to give some hints of resistance. While many
tend to be openly cooperative with the hypnotist, they do not become involved in the experience and commonly achieve low
scores.

### The Actively Resistant Subject

Not all actively resistant subjects are alike in their resistance. Some
of these are *temporarily* resistant, as they explore a new situation
to see how threatening it may be. When they find it nonthreatening,
they go along comfortably with hypnosis. These disturb the reliabilities of hypnotic susceptibility tests because they score low on a
first day, higher on later days; they also may make the later hypnotist believe that he is a more skilled hypnotist than the one who
tried it first.

Carl is one of those who reduce the reliability of retest hypnosis scores by making substantial changes between a first and a second session. He scored a below-average four on the first day, with form A, the somewhat easier scale; and then scored an eight on form C shortly thereafter. He approached hypnosis with the thought, "Hypnosis is very interesting, but I can't see myself as being unconscious."

In an interview after the second day he described the difference between the two days. "Because I didn't know what was going to happen, I was taking it easy on the first day to see what it was like. I'm always that way." On the second day he was freer and more spontaneous. Carl described similar family attitudes: "Be careful what you try. . . . My parents would first want to find out what something was all about, then if they found it to their liking, they were liberal and did it. It could be something new." Over and over again Carl expressed feeling greater ease on the second day because "I knew what was coming." His typical pattern has been to go slow until he is sure something is all right, then plunge in. He also stated that part of his eventual success in hypnosis was due to the way he had been taught to concentrate by his parents.

There are many variants on resistance to hypnosis, running all the way from religious scruples and fear to open defiance of the hypnotist. The resistance is found in some cases among those who have some awareness of themselves as hypnotizable but fear that submitting to hypnosis may produce a change in them more profound than they wish to face. Very occasionally we find a subject who has an aversion to loss of control to another but who is able to demonstrate hypnoticlike phenomena through autosuggestion. One such case is that of Loretta, whose responses were quite unusual. She was chosen as a nonhypnotizable subject (form C score of two) to serve as an invited simulator in an experiment in which she was asked to simulate hypnotic analgesia to the pain of ice water; her physiological responses under these circumstances were to be compared with those of the "true" hypnotic subject, whose pain would actually be reduced under hypnosis. What happened was that she actually was able to turn off the pain (the only simulator we have found able to do this among many who have served in this way). Usually the subject complains violently if the hand and arm are kept in the ice water for more than a minute, but she kept hers in comfortably for four and one-half minutes. She afterward explained how she had done this. While she was instructed to keep her eyes closed, she had in fact opened them enough to select a spot on her skirt and, focusing on it, diverted her attention from the ice water so successfully that she did not feel it. This response appears very similar to what highly hypnotizable subjects can do; yet, according to our measures, she was not hypnotizable.

The history of this ability to divert her attention came out in an interview following the ice-water experience. Prior to high school she had been quite emotionally involved in music, ballet, playacting, and reading, but all this had changed when she was sent to boarding school at age fourteen.

There were long religious services which she did not like. In order to maintain her calm she developed the practice of "making her mind vacant" by concentrating visually upon a target, such as a pine knot in the woodwork. "My responses became very sluggish. The only thing I was aware of was my head. If someone touched my hand, I wouldn't know it immediately. I wouldn't know it until later." She had practiced this for four years in high school and had tried it recently during a church service which she had found dull.

What Loretta wants most is to be able to depend on herself. She felt that she had developed this trait by working hard at it. "I *made* myself the person I could count on." She dislikes being dependent on anyone else, and despite an expressed wish to be hypnotized, this avoidance of dependence may have been an important part of her low score in the presence of the hypnotist.

There are, however, other aspects of her involvements which differ from those typical of the highly hypnotizable person. Most of our highly hypnotizable subjects look forward with enthusiasm to the involvement they have in various experiences. She now thinks that she went a little far in de-emphasizing feeling and in intellectualizing her experiences; for example, she hopes that her earlier emotional involvement in music can be recaptured. On balance, prior to hypnosis we would have predicted her as more hypnotizable, and under favorable circumstances she may well be susceptible. The uncertainties in a case such as hers keep open the doors to finding out some of the things about hypnotic susceptibility that up to now have escaped us.

There are also kinds of initial resistance to hypnosis that are overcome before the actual hypnotic session, so that scores are not reduced, even in the first hypnotic session.

Bill was such a subject. He scored eleven on form A, his first hypnotic session, and ten on form C, in his second session. Why is he said to be resistant, when his scores were so high? The overt evidence lay in his tardiness and procrastination, both in the interviews and in the hypnotic sessions themselves. He came late for both of the scheduled interviews prior to hypnosis and failed to show up for the first scheduled hypnotic session. Without making excuses he came in for the hypnotic session the next day, without rescheduling. He made an appointment for the second session but again failed to arrive at the appointed hour; eventually a new appointment was arranged, and he scored high. We were not especially surprised when he did not respond to a request for an additional interview after hypnosis.

This tardiness and failure to show when expected might be interpreted as careless irresponsibility if it were not for the content of the interviews prior to hypnosis. It was apparent from the start that he had a strong need to control the interview. He wanted to know the purpose of each question and was watchful throughout. After the second interview was formally terminated, he remained an extra twenty minutes to question the interviewer and to comment on the lack of reaction to the material that he had presented about himself. This material showed him to have many of the qualities we have found associated with high hypnotizability, along with the strong need to control and to get things on his own terms. He somehow managed to turn the hypnotic sessions into his own by having us produce them when he wanted them, rather than when we wanted them. His resistance to the normal procedures took the form of "acting out" against the requirements, but this appeared to satisfy his needs and he could then go ahead with hypnosis.

A second subject, whom we shall call Christine, reported such a consistent and strongly negative attitude toward authority figures all of her life that we doubted that she could be hypnotized. She did, however, express a great desire for the experience, and she had a background of imaginative involvements consistent with hypnotizability. She said that she was sure her parents would not approve of her being hypnotized, and to check this belief she telephoned them the night before her first hypnotic session. They said that in no circumstances should she permit herself to be hypnotized. This was all she needed: she went ahead, in her usual pattern, to negate their authority, and she scored at the top of the scale!

Thus we find the problem of resistance to hypnosis puzzling. Some of the predictions are straightforward, such as that those who dislike hypnosis or are frightened by it turn out to be little hypnotizable. Other predictions break down because we are unable to weigh properly the components in a conflict, one component (such as the capacity for involvement) favoring hypnosis, another (such as the strong need for autonomy) telling against hypnotizability.

## Cases in Which Motivation and Hypnotizability Are Discrepant

When correlations are low, as indeed they are throughout all studies of personality in relation to hypnosis, one can never count on any one determiner to predict hypnotizability. There are a number of subjects eager to be hypnotized who are disappointed in their inability to have the experiences of the more highly susceptible, and, contrariwise, there are those who state that they do not care to be hypnotized and who have a full hypnotic experience.

Karen and Don illustrate subjects with indifferent motivation who turn out to be substantially hypnotizable.

Karen was one of those who came because the hours were convenient for completing course requirements. She had no particular fear of hypnosis, but only a moderate curiosity about it; the interviewer rated her motivation as slightly below average, a three on a seven-point scale. Her score of six on a ten-point hypnotic scale, while not high, was above average for this sample. In the interview prior to hypnosis she was found to have one source of involvement that might well have accounted for her hypnotizability. This was her interest in religion. She was raised as a Roman Catholic, attended Catholic schools prior to coming to college, was still regular in church attendance, and, for her, religion "had real emotional meaning." Both parents were deeply religious, in more than a formal church-attending sense, and religion was a vital part of their lives. She identified with both parents in religion but, in common with many of our more hypnotizable subjects, felt that she resembled her father more than her mother in personality and in her approach to work and play. She was somewhat shy and uncommunicative in the interview and, apart from her religious dedication and identification with religious parents, would not have been predicted as hypnotizable. Her indifferent motivation for hypnosis did not prevent her scoring about where she would have been expected to score had her motivation for hypnosis been higher.

Don was rated low in motivation for hypnosis (one out of seven) but scored a substantial nine in hypnosis on the twelve-point SHSS-C. He came to hypnosis with some apprehension. "I came chiefly because I have to participate in some experiments and this fitted my schedule best. I'm a bit fearful. My parents have urged me to be careful. A friend was hypnotized in public last winter and that was embarrassing. I'm not sure of my subconscious." It is possible to detect a certain ambivalence here, because the fear of hypnosis appears to be based at least in part on the thought that he may be hypnotizable. The experience itself proved somewhat reassuring, as in the case of Carl described earlier; Don's first score, on form A, was only three, but on the later test with form C he made the strong score of nine. Perhaps his motivation had changed in the meantime? Unfortunately, he was not interviewed after that hypnotic experience.

We have met subjects who came to prove that they could not be hypnotized and became·angry in the midst of hypnosis because they began giving evidences of hypnotizability. One such case, whom we shall call Eunice, had a smile on her face when she was told that she would not be able to bend her arm when requested to do so. This smile turned to an angry expression when she found that she was unable to bend her arm when she tried; she continued to score well as a hypnotic subject, and she explained to the hypnotist afterward that she had hoped to prove that she could not be hypnotized and felt weak and disappointed that she had responded so well to the hypnotist's suggestions. The facial expressions are a commentary on what is going on, and within hypnosis they indicate the split within the person; that is, there is an observing ego which notes what is happening even while some other fraction of the personality is responding with a degree of automaticity to the suggestions.

Other cases (and these are more common) have a high motivation for hypnosis and yet are unable to achieve high scores. This is perhaps the most impressive feature of hypnotic experiments with university students such as those in our sample.

Take the case of Stephen. He was all ready for hypnosis. "I am eager to try it. I've really been curious about hypnosis for a long time. I've never had any opportunity to try it before, but my curiosity was stirred up by seeing it one time on the stage. I think I can be hypnotized. I'm fairly suggestible." Despite this eagerness, he scored four out of a possible twelve on form C.

The low score was consistent with his background, even if inconsistent with his motivation. In the interview before hypnosis, when asked about his interests he replied, "Nothing in particular. I just like to keep going and not be stuck in one place too long." His reading had been limited; as an engineer he studied technical books, but he had read very little fiction and had not become deeply absorbed in it. He liked modern music, but chiefly as background rather than for active listening. One area seemed somewhat more promising as a possible background for hypnosis: he reported that he liked to write poetry. However, on probing, he said, "I feel so much like writing but I can't come out with anything that pleases me. I get too diverted by abstract thought."

He described himself as a kind of introvert, and serious, with a fairly even temperament. He said he had a tendency, when discussing something, always to take the opposite side. "I will try to shoot down something I believe in order to test it out." He felt he was more identified with his mother, who was a rather serious person, though he had some longing to be more like his father, whom he admired both because he had clear goals and because he was more playful than his mother.

This description is not that of our highly hypnotizable subjects, and it led to a prediction of low hypnotizability, despite the highly rated motivation for hypnosis.

A few thumbnail sketches will suffice to describe the kinds of things we heard over and over again in our interviews prior to hypnosis from those who turned out to be little susceptible.

Eugene (see chapter on athletics) said he had always wondered what hypnosis was like. "I feel ready to go along with it. I know I won't fight it." He thought he would be "pretty susceptible." Rated a six out of seven in motivation, he scored one out of twelve on form C.

Susan (an athlete whom we met in chapter 14) said, "I think it would be *really* interesting. I've always wanted to be hypnotized. I think I'll be a good subject." Her motivation rated six; her form C score, three.

Elliott (see chap. 9): "I'm kind of a fan of hypnotism. I'm fascinated by it. I've watched hypnotism shows." This was an opportunity he had been waiting for. Motivation rated seven; hypnotic score, two.

Charles (see chap. 9): "I've always wanted to try it as something interesting. I've only seen it in the movies. It's intrigued me. I've read about posthypnotic suggestions." Motivation rated 6, form C score, two.

David (see chaps. 4 and 6): "I want hypnosis as a new and interesting experience." Motivation, six; hypnosis score, one.

These subjects were cooperative and eager to experience hypnosis, but they were unable to achieve other than minimal scores on the hypnotic-susceptibility test. It is important, therefore, to think of hypnotic susceptibility as an ability with a long history of development, and not something easily turned on or off through motivation. These matters are never simple yes-no ones; obviously motivation is important, and negative motivation (resistance) can prevent the experience.

### Motivation of the Clinical Patient

The success of hypnosis in relieving the pains of childbirth, dentistry, burns, surgery, and even terminal cancer leads to the conception that subjects in distress who are convinced that hypnosis can aid them become more hypnotizable because of their high motivation. That they do in fact gain relief is beyond question (e.g., Haley 1967; Kroger 1963; Sacerdote 1965; Schneck 1963).

Clinical observations indicate that intense pain of organic origin, as in terminal cancer, does not interfere with hypnosis, and the hope for its reduction may accentuate hypnotizability. Unfortunately, we have no controlled evidence on the quantitative effect of the high motivation of the patient upon his susceptibility to hypnosis, measured by changes of scores on hypnotic-susceptibility scales. Some clinical work (particularly psychotherapy) may use hypnotic techniques successfully with patients only slightly hypnotizable; we cannot therefore use clinical success as a measure of degree of hypnotizability. While the experience of clinicians that the highly motivated patient tends to be more hypnotizable is plausible, quantitative data would be most welcome.

### Simulation and Deception

Even without practice, a nonhypnotizable subject who chooses to do so can deceive a hypnotist into believing that he is hypnotizable. This is, in the abstract, a serious problem for the hypnotic investigator; in the concrete, however, it turns out to be much less a problem, for several reasons.

1. Most subjects who participate in an experiment for scientific purposes understand the purposes of experimentation and attempt to give honest reports. This does not excuse the experimenter from taking precautions, but it is important. Unless the experimenter himself sets up conditions which invite deception, he can count on honest reporting by most of his subjects. He can have the experiences himself, and he can study them with those who are as deeply committed to science as he is. These circumstances make possible the use of verbal reports, which are often the most precise indicators we have, even though they offer the possibility of falsification.

2. Most subjects do not yield a very high level of hypnotic responsiveness. In practice, this is very convincing to the hypnotist, for the subject shows surprise and excitement over the new experiences that he enjoys, and disappointment at his failures. While, again, with sufficient skill at playacting a subject *might* cleverly fool the hypnotist in these respects, there is little likelihood that there is a widespread conspiracy along these lines.

3. There are ways in which a "true" hypnotic subject performs

that differ from the expectations of a "simulator," particularly when the simulator attempts to act like a deeply hypnotizable person. The simulator commonly overreacts. Orne's use of simulators sometimes gives the reader the impression that he is guarding against a good deal of simulation among his regular subjects. This is not the case; his logic is that he wants to find out what is conditioned upon the expectations created by the experimenter, and what is *different* between the "trues" and the simulators (Orne 1959, 1966).

In our sample we have a very few subjects who score at the top of the scale; it is among these that simulators are most likely to be found. Occasionally we find one, but he may not be trying to deceive the hypnotist so much as trying to place himself in the right attitude to experience hypnosis, as in the case of Peter, previously described.

Burt provided an interesting illustration of a kind of simulation, perhaps better described as role playing. He scored at the top on form A (twelve out of twelve), but when he returned for form C he scored two out of twelve. What happened? He had come much interested in hypnosis and thought that he would score above average. Interviewed after the second day of hypnosis he explained that he wanted very much to be hypnotized. On the first day he was very accommodating, as he put it; he did not wish to protest that the experiences asked for were impossible for him, but tried to go along as if he were having them in the hope that at some point the experiences would feel as he expected hypnosis to feel. "I was not really involved. I was fully aware. Nothing was involuntary. I was watching throughout, because I was interested in the process." By the time he returned for the second experience of hypnosis he decided that he would not go through the motions. When asked about his "passing" of amnesia on the first day, he said that the hypnotist told him he could not remember, so he did not try. He said that he was accustomed to pleasing people. "It's the easiest way to get along." In some sense this is the opposite of those who hold back on the first day, in order to be reassured, and then become hypnotized on the second; he tried for the experience on the first day by role-playing it, was unsuccessful, and then demonstrated his nonsusceptibility on the next day. He was perfectly willing to tell the interviewer what he had done and felt that there was no real effort to fool anyone.

The later score was the one consistent with the interview data prior to hypnosis. He was reported by the interviewer to be bland and inarticulate. From a professional home, he talked about his successful father and generally competent mother but had little to say about affectionate relationships within the family. Burt described himself as easygoing, calm, not easily excited, not impulsive, not competitive, not good at concentrating. He showed little spontaneity of interests. His approach to life was realistic. Majoring in geology, he liked exact facts, the kinds you could classify and describe accurately. His parents were realistic and approached situations analytically. He and his parents, he says, are more cautious than most people. None of this adds up to high hypnotizability, so that his second-day score appears to be the correct one, and the high score the result of his accurately reported role playing.

A very different young man ended up by scoring similarly to Burt. Larry came to the interview prior to hypnosis saying that he was genuinely interested in being hypnotized. He added that he had some doubts about how hypnotizable he would be, however, for a person might want to be hypnotized but might have things on his mind that would interfere. He entered into the experience on the first day and scored a ten out of twelve, but on the second day he, like Burt, dropped down to a two. How did he explain the change when he was interviewed after the second day?

On the first day he deliberately cooperated with the hypnotist, trying to see what it would be like if he went through all the motions. Not having entered into the experience, he felt very critical of the whole procedure on the second day. He added that he was always ahead of the hypnotist, showing that he knew what was coming. When asked by the interviewer if he thought there was anything about him that made him less hypnotizable than some of the other subjects he found it easy to answer. "My pride; it would be hard for me to let go." He pointed out that he does not get drunk, like some of his friends, because he does not want to lose control; he wants to be in command.

While his hypnotic behavior on the two days parallels very closely that of Burt, there the similarity ends. Whereas Burt was quiet and taciturn, Larry loved to talk and he "ran away with" the interview just as he later ran ahead of the hypnotist. Burt had few involvements, while Larry had all sorts of involvements. As a youngster he quit going to the movies because he cried over every injury or death. In high school, as well as being a star athlete in football, track and swimming, he was president of his class and president of the student body. He dominates all the relationships in which he enters, which are numerous, including many friendships with both boys and girls. Although he dates many girls he is serious with none. He describes himself as extremely restless, looking always for new experiences and new excitement. He does not like to conform, and he has a rebellious streak in him.

The contrasting personalities of Burt and Larry again demonstrate the difficulty that besets the interviewer who is trying to find the common features in the background of the hypnotizable and the unhypnotizable. Larry was as little hypnotizable as Burt, but probably more because of his desire to dominate and his resistance against loss of control than because of the lack of deep involvements and the generally cautious outlook that characterized Burt.

### Motivation and Involvement

Despite the many variations that can be played on the theme of motivation for hypnosis, there is a common core that best describes the generality. This core is the relationship between motivation for hypnosis and the imaginative involvements with which we are by now familiar. The generality is that those who have had the experience of deep and satisfying involvements see the possibility of something familiar and satisfying in hypnosis, and therefore, *in general,* they come eager for the hypnotic experience and hence find it easy to interact with the hypnotist in such a manner as to capitalize upon their experiences with involvements. At the other extreme, those who have no deep imaginative or adventurous involvements, who have kept themselves at some distance through caution, an analytical attitude, or a timidity about new experience, are the ones who come with little motivation for hypnosis and tend to be less susceptible. As in other generalizations one can make about personality and hypnosis the association between motivation and involvements is significant, but not high, as shown in table 43.

TABLE 43

*Imaginative Involvements and Motivation for Hypnosis*

| Motivation | Sum of Involvement Ratings* | | Total |
|---|---|---|---|
| | Low (7–25) | High (26–40) | |
| High (5–7) | 36 | 53 | 89 |
| Low (1–4) | 61 | 34 | 95 |
| Total | 97 | 87 | 184† |

Significance test: $\chi^2 = 10.4$; $p < .01$.
* Seven involvements were rated 1–7, hence possible sums, 7–49.
† Three cases not ascertained.

Those with a high "sum of involvements" score tend also to be high in motivation for hypnosis. Thus, those with high-involvement sums are rated high in motivation in 53/89, or 60 percent, of the cases, while those with low-involvement sums are rated high in motivation in but 34/95, or 36 percent, of the cases.

There are always two aspects to motivated behavior, a *motivational disposition* which endures through time and is, in the case of hypnosis, conditioned by the developmental factors that provide a history of involvements congenial to hypnosis; and an *arousal* factor, which is illustrated by the circumstances of the hypnotic induction procedures and conditioned by the interpersonal relationship between subject and hypnotist. The dispositional and arousal factors are related, much as prior habit and present drive are related in learned performances. In the studies which have served as the basis for this book we have been concerned more with the dispositional factors, keeping the arousal factors fairly constant through the standardized hypnotic-susceptibility scales. It is not surprising, therefore, that motivation as we have described it shows a relationship to the persistent involvements of the hypnotizable person.

## Concluding Remarks on Motivation and Hypnotizability

It is difficult to say something plausible about hypnosis that is not partially true, but more difficult to say anything that is universally true. This applies very well to the relationship between motivation and hypnosis. The expected relationship holds, in that the subject eager for hypnosis tends to be somewhat more susceptible than the uninterested or resistant subject, but the exceptions to the rule are in many instances more instructive than those who do what is expected.

# 16

## Implications for Theories of Hypnosis and Personality

The phenomena of hypnosis, after a century and a half of experience with them, are still difficult to characterize in the language of scientific psychology. This is not hard to explain, because the phenomena lie within the areas of psychological understanding that (apart from hypnosis) have been least accessible to experimental clarification: the nature of consciousness and the distinctions between voluntary and involuntary behavior, attention, imagination, dissociation, emotional involvement. We have made some gains in understanding, as the previous chapters have shown, and now we are ready to reflect upon the implications.

### The Facets of Hypnotizability

The aspects of childhood background and present personality that were rated in our interviews and correlated highest with hypnotic susceptibility turned out to be: imaginative involvements, severity of punishment in childhood, temperamental similarity to the parent of the opposite sex, and a number of items reflecting a generally normal and outgoing personality. These normal-outgoing items included ease of communication in the interview, a ready motivation for hypnosis, and a global rating of normality. As a summary of these findings, a correlation matrix is presented in table 44 showing how each of these correlates with hypnotic susceptibility and how they correlate with each other. The multiple correlation of $R = .53$ is about as high as we would expect, in view of the correlation reported earlier (chap. 2) of .62 between two forms of the hypnotic susceptibility scale consisting of unlike items. It was pointed out

TABLE 44

*Intercorrelations of Major Predictors of Hypnotizability
from Interview prior to Hypnosis
(N = 184)*

| Interview Variable | (2) | (3) | (4) | (5) | (6) | (7) SHSS-C |
|---|---|---|---|---|---|---|
| (1) Sum of involvements | 12 | 55† | 27† | 03 | 09 | 35† |
| (2) Punishment | | −03 | −03 | 12 | 08 | 30† |
| (3) Ease of communication | | | 35† | 00 | 24* | 27† |
| (4) Motivation for hypnosis | | | | 06 | 06 | 25† |
| (5) Temperament similar to opposite parent | | | | | −05 | 23* |
| (6) Normal-outgoing | | | | | | 22* |
| Multiple correlation, variables (1) to (6) with (7) | | | | | | 53† |

Note: Three cases of total of 187 not ascertained. Decimal points omitted throughout.
* p < .01.
† p < .001.

there that we can scarcely expect nonhypnotic items to predict hypnosis as well as samples of items within hypnosis can predict each other. Of course a multiple correlation, unreplicated, takes advantage of chance relations within the table of intercorrelations, and it would shrink, if the same regression weights were used on another sample. It must be noted also, however, that the interviewers were hurried in gaining the information that entered into the ratings, and there must be considerable unreliability of the ratings. Thus while the multiple correlation is capitalizing upon chance, it is also being attenuated because it is based on ratings that are of imperfect reliability; it is at once too high (capitalizing on chance) and too low (attenuated by unreliability) to represent what is actually the case. It is in any event well above the chance level, and for our purpose its absolute value is of no great consequence because there is no desire to use it for practical purposes of prediction. Partial replication is provided by considering the sexes separately (table 45). The correlations for the female subjects are for the most part numerically higher than for the males, but with the exception of the last

TABLE 45

*Correlations of Major Predictors with*
*Hypnotic Susceptibility Scores, by Sex*

| Interview Variable | Susceptibility (SHSS-C) | | |
|---|---|---|---|
| | Males (N = 112*) | Females (N = 72) | Both (N = 184*) |
| (1) Sum of involvements | 31§ | 48§ | 35§ |
| (2) Punishment | 26‡ | 35‡ | 30§ |
| (3) Ease of communication | 24‡ | 33‡ | 27§ |
| (4) Motivation for hypnosis | 19† | 35‡ | 25§ |
| (5) Temperament similar to opposite parent | 17 | 31‡ | 23‡ |
| (6) Normal-outgoing | 21† | 22 | 22‡ |
| Multiple correlation, variables (1) to (6) with SHSS-C | 46§ | 67§ | 53§ |

* Three cases not ascertained.
† $p < .05$      ‡ $p < .01$      § $p < .001$.

two items all correlations are significant at least at the .05 level for each sex separately. The multiple correlation turns out to be +.46 for the males and +.67 for the females.

Returning to the body of table 44, we note that the highest correlations are within a cluster that includes the involvements and aspects of the normal-outgoing personality (involvements vs. ease of communication, .55; involvements vs. motivation for hypnosis, .27; motivation vs. ease of communication, .35; ease of communication vs. normal-outgoing, .24). Were a factor analysis to be conducted, these items would doubtless determine a factor, because they are interrelated but do not correlate significantly with any other items in the table (except hypnotizability). These items are of the kind that are generated through contagion with parents, through modeling after them the aspect of identification called *anaclitic*, or *personal*. The item second in importance is severity of punishment, which does not correlate with this cluster but correlates .30 with hypnotizability. This suggests a separate factor.

Punishment correlates significantly with no item in table 44 (other than hypnosis) although the numerically highest correlations (.12) are with the involvements and with the temperamental similarity to the parent of the opposite sex.

The involvements and punishment are sufficient to account for most of the multiple correlation with hypnosis. The two together yield a multiple correlation of $R = .46$, compared with $R = .53$ for all six variables. The involvements and punishment are thus the most influential as determiners of hypnosis, and much of our discussion will be in reference to them.

### Involvements, Punishment, and Identification

The imaginative involvements, as rated in the interviews prior to hypnosis, turn out to be the most substantial of the predictors of hypnotizability, thus giving statistical justification to the emphasis we have given to them. As noted from time to time, these involvements are commonly developed in a kind of contagion with parental interests, and they can be considered in many cases identifications with parents. Since the identification with parents has often been with the parent of the opposite sex, and since the areas of involvement are not highly sex-typed within our culture, we have thought of these as largely non-sex-role identifications. Such involvements, as identifications, are modeled directly upon parental behavior.

The second most convincing of our developmental factors associated with hypnotizability is severity of punishment in childhood. One question that may well be asked is, What has punishment to do with identification? As shown in table 46, 44 percent of those rated high in punishment are identified with the opposite-sexed parent, while but 26 percent of those rated low in punishment are so identified. The explanation of this relationship is unclear, but the possibility of some causal relationship between punishment and identification cannot be ruled out, and it is possible that it is the identification which serves as the intermediary between punishment and hypnotic susceptibility.

Parental influence upon children is partially by way of identification. The child learns not only the *parental* role (stressed in identification) but also learns the *child's* role—that a certain obedience to authority pays off in gratification and reduced conflict. The learned compliance with the rules is important to him as he grows up; thus he knows how to work for a superior without (as in identification) wanting to *be* that superior. It may well be that the

TABLE 46

*Relation between Severity of Punishment in Childhood and Temperamental Identification with Opposite-sexed Parent*

| Parent Most Similar to in Temperament | Severity of Punishment | | Total |
|---|---|---|---|
| | Low (1–4) | High (5–7) | |
| | % | % | % |
| Opposite-sexed | 26 | 44 | 32 |
| Other (like-sexed, both, neither) | 74 | 56 | 68 |
| Total | 100 | 100 | 100 |
| | (N = 123) | (N = 63) | (N = 186) |

Significance test: $\chi^2 = 6.47$; $p = < .02$.

influence of childhood punishment works upon hypnotic susceptibility in this way rather than through (or in addition to) its identification significance. That is, the child has learned prompt obedience through the strictness of the discipline in the home. While we have used rated punishment as the index of strictness, doubtless we could have found other sources of conforming behavior. For example, some of our subjects told us that parental expectations were clear and that they were obedient as children without punishment. In other homes, religion provides a sanction, with trust in the authority of God underwriting the trust in religious parents. Because the strictness of discipline in these homes is orderly, and perceived as just, the compliance becomes relatively automatic and conflict-free. Then, in hypnosis, for the subject who has voluntarily assented to the subordinate role, these old habits take over and he rather automatically accepts what the hypnotist tells him. Note that this interpretation still accepts the importance of childhood experiences and interactions with parents, but the modeling after parents or identification with them is subordinated to responsiveness to them. Because in the correlational analysis punishment seemed relatively independent of involvements, it appears that this interpretation may be more appropriate than the identification interpretation of the effects of punishment.

A third role of punishment, the buildup of dissociated fantasies as a consequence of punishment, remains a possibility in some instances, as when the punishment takes the form of isolating the child in his room.

It has long been thought that the hypnotist is in some sense a parentlike figure in the hypnotic relationship. To the extent that this is true one would look for parental identifications as a background for susceptibility, and for the attitudes toward authority figures that parents engendered. Both the history of involvements in contagion with parental models and the history of strict discipline and punishment as implanting response to authority may provide a continuity between childhood experiences with parents and present experiences in hypnosis.

## Involvements as Bearing upon the Prevalent Theories of Hypnosis

The prevalent theories of hypnosis include psychoanalytic theories, physiological theories such as Pavlov's theory of hypnosis as partial sleep (1923, 1927), learning theories such as Hull's (1933), and role theories including the role-enactment version of Sarbin (1950) and the role-involvement version of Shor (1959). An older theory, dating to Janet (1907, 1919) and Morton Prince (1905), stresses the importance of dissociation. Our data bear more upon the psychoanalytic, the role, and the dissociation theories than upon the physiological or conditioning theories, and discussion will be confined to them. Let us say at the outset that our data give partial support to each of the theories; if there is hesitation in giving full acceptance to any one of them it is based on the incompleteness of any one of the theories in the face of the uncertainty of our present knowledge of hypnosis. We are not ready for a "nothing but" theory—that hypnosis is "nothing but" suggestion, "nothing but" regression, "nothing but" role enactment, or "nothing but" dissociation.

*Psychoanalytic theories.* It is pertinent to recall that psychoanalysis grew out of hypnosis. The psychoanalytic couch is an inheritance from hypnosis, but its persistence in psychoanalysis is not accidental. The couch and the "analytic incognito" serve to facilitate free associations and primary process thinking—circumstances of cognitive activity that have something in common with hypnosis. While Freud and most of his followers rejected hypnosis as a method, they were often interested in explaining its phenomena in psychoanalytic terms, so that we have several variants on psychoanalytic interpretations of hypnosis.

The earliest versions of the psychoanalytic interpretation of hypnosis discussed the parental role of the hypnotist. This was mentioned by Freud (1905) and emphasized by Ferenczi (1909) in his earlier-mentioned distinction between mother hypnosis and father hypnosis. Freud began to suspect an erotic root to the relationship between subject and hypnotist when he saw the hysterical women patients in Charcot's clinic; he had further evidence of this in the studies of hysteria, conducted with the aid of hypnosis, done by him with Breuer (Breuer and Freud 1895). Others following Freud have commented on the tendency of the hypnotic subject to eroticize the relationship (Schilder 1956).

We have found little evidence of the erotic component of hypnosis. Although we did not explore deeply for it, there were plenty of opportunities for spontaneous evidence of it to appear had it been at all prominent. To the extent that the relationship is personalized, most of our evidence points to the hypnotist as a parental figure. As we shall see presently, the hypnotic relationship was often remarkably impersonal, as though the hypnotist were there as a facilitator of an experience for which the subject was ready. This does not mean that the relationship was never personal, nor that it was never sexual. For example, there was an occasion where a young woman dreamed within hypnosis of being led by the hand down a pleasant pathway through a woods by an unknown lover. This could be interpreted as a veiled reference to the male hypnotist.

In another illustration, a subject felt that she actually lived the hypnotic experience. It was so real to her—a kind of "living dream" —that she was unable to have a "dream about hypnosis" when it was called for in the hypnotic session. She talked about her sexual fantasies and sexual life, noting that in adolescence her sexual fantasies stopped when she became involved in actual sexual adventures. She paralleled her not dreaming in hypnosis with her not fantasying sex; hypnosis was as real today as sex was then. The erotic significance of hypnosis was brought out indirectly: "Outside of hypnosis I have never been so submissive and obedient except in a sexual role." Covert or overt sexual references were rare in the Stanford laboratory material.

The concept of a regression has entered into a number of the psychoanalytic interpretations of hypnosis. For example, Gill and Brenman (1959) base their book essentially upon the interpretation that hypnosis is a regressed state, especially in the form of regression in the service of the ego. Imaginative involvements indicate the importance of fantasy, which is significant in primary process thinking and in some sense belongs to childhood. Reality distortion, dreams, acceptance of logical contradictions—these are familiar hypnotic phenomena which can well be interpreted as regressive.

Regression as a characterization of everything that happens in hypnosis, however, may be too inclusive. Some of the subjects have developed their involvements as defensive reactions to ego threats; for example, they may take to reading to shut out the unhappiness of lonesome childhood. This can be interpreted as regressive. There are many others among the normal subjects we studied whose imaginative involvements are part of a continuous, healthy, and natural development. When they seek the new experiences of hypnosis by attaching these to their learned involvements we see no need to call this regressive.

*Role theories.* Instead of talking about subordinate ego structures, as Gill and Brenman do, others have talked about the "roles" the individual is enacting. Role theory has had a long history, particularly in sociology; it has been made specific to hypnosis by Sarbin and his associates (Sarbin 1950; Sarbin and Lim 1963; Sarbin and Andersen 1967). As with regression, role theory is clearly applicable to some aspects of hypnotic behavior. The hypnotized subject can throw himself into dramatic action (flapping wings and crowing like a rooster, as in stage demonstrations of hypnosis; behaving like a member of a different occupation from his own), and much of this behavior has what may be termed a theatrical quality.

The role theory of hypnosis can easily be misinterpreted as implying that hypnosis is sham behavior, performed by the subject in order to please the hypnotist, but essentially deceptive. Such an interpretation has been denied repeatedly by Sarbin, who is the chief proponent of role theory and insists that the hypnotizable subject has an ability to commit himself to roles and to involve himself in them as though they were genuine. Shor (1959) has asserted that role behavior characterizes hypnosis only when it becomes *role involvement,* which includes archaic, unconscious aspects. We would add that involvement is not something that any willing subject can achieve by trying: he must have a history of deep involvement upon which he can capitalize in achieving what Sarbin and Shor have called role involvement.

One objection to the role-enactment theory is that it leads to a facile solution to some difficult problems, especially if it is taken in its "nothing-but" form. One is free to say that all hypnosis is "nothing but" role enactment, and this assertion would be hard to deny, but the assertion would leave many problems unsolved. One of these problems is the significance of different kinds of fantasy as a background for hypnotic involvement. For example, we have found it necessary to make some distinctions between *impulse-incited daydreams,* that is, *more autistic fantasy,* and *stimulus-incited fantasy,* that is, *more directed fantasy.* Daydreaming, arising to solve personal conflicts, does not turn out to be a favorable indication of hypnotizability, while directed fantasy, such as that aroused by the words of the author in a book being read, or the lines spoken in a play, provides a favorable background for hypnosis. One is free to make similar distinctions within role theory, but in its "nothing-but" form there is a tendency not to go on to other distinctions that are required.

Directed fantasy may take different forms. One subject will accept a very precise and constrained suggestion, that is, to see a rabbit sitting in his lap. He will hallucinate the animal and react as if a real rabbit were there. Another, though capable of hypnotic hallucinations, will reject such a specific suggestion because it does not involve him sufficiently. He prefers a suggestion which will open the doors to a broader experience, such as the suggestion that he will dream or will live again in the past. Then he contributes something through his own involvement. This may seem to border on the autistic, but it differs in that there is no neurotic need for the particular experience; affectively it is more like the desire to play or to savor experiences that have been earlier enjoyed. Several subjects whose capacity to enter deeply into fantasy-involving roles in this sense have found it impossible to pass the positive hallucinations of form C (e.g., conjuring up the taste of sweet or sour) or the negative one (seeing only two of three boxes) because the experience called for was too partial, and not adapted to role involvement of the kind they were prepared for and enjoyed.

It should be noted also that some of the imaginative involvements we have found important have very little of role enactment in them, as in immersion in the enjoyment of nature or music listening. Perhaps when a person is lost in these experiences the merging of self and the object of enjoyment is not personal enough to be defined clearly as a role.

*Dissociation.* Dissociation refers to a splitting-off of some aspects of experience, both cognitive and neuromuscular, from the mainstream of awareness and control. Dissociation has some advantages over regression in the interpretation of many of the phenomena of hypnosis. One advantage of the concept of dissociation is its breadth. It covers the whole spectrum, from the normal dissociative activities of talking to oneself to the dissociations of schizophrenia (West 1967).

Let us take a look at some of the familiar experiences outside hypnosis that have dissociative characteristics:

Dreams are dissociative because the events go on more or less out of control of the dominant personality. The subject commonly describes his dream as though it "happened" to him, rather than as though he "produced" it. The dream provides in psychoanalysis the very model of primary process thinking, but it has to be noted that there are also secondary processes evident within the dream, and it is not a regressive experience, pure and simple. In agreement with the position just stated, Fromm and French (1962) in studying the dream as a "cognitive, integrative attempt of the ego to solve a current, here-and-now conflict," believe that they have complemented the classical approach of Freud.

The modern name for hysteria has come to be *conversion reaction* because of the theory that the symptom represents in symbolic form something motivationally relevant for the patient. For example, a paralyzed arm that relieves the housewife of distasteful domestic duties has become "dissociated" from the voluntary control system. Because hypnotic symptoms produced by the hypnotist appeared so much like spontaneous hysterical symptoms, it is not surprising that the connection between hysteria and hypnosis continued beyond Charcot. The point here is that the word dissociation is appropriate to both.

A schizophrenic patient not uncommonly hears "the voices" castigating him or instructing him. These are of course part of himself; to the extent that he fails to recognize these voices as his own thoughts they are illustrative of dissociated activities. Delusions of reference, of persecution, or of grandeur are often called *systematized* because they represent a coherent pattern of thought somewhat isolated from the main thought and behavior of the paranoid patient. While these, too, may be called *regressed* the thought is often quite subtle, and the reasoning good (except for some basic premises that do not correspond to social reality). Such systematized patterns can also be thought of as dissociated.

Cases of multiple personality, of which reports appear from time to time, are somewhat like fugue states, except that the different states tend to alternate with each other over a period of time. The memories are never fully interchangeable, but often personality A knows personality B, even though personality B may not know personality A. To the extent that these reports are accurate, they represent the best evidence of dissociations involving large personality units.

One may also call attention to the dissociations of everyday life, especially the multiple channels of conversation that a person carries on within himself, while talking with someone else; he listens and formulates his answer before he replies; even while he replies part of him is developing the argument beyond what he is presently saying. Were we to understand ordinary waking consciousness better, we would not be so surprised by the dissociations within hypnosis.

We have discussed dissociation at this length to call attention to its prevalence as a psychological phenomenon, and hence to its appropriateness as a concept descriptive of hypnosis. The main features of dissociation are that some mental activity goes on outside of normal controls (e.g., involuntarily) and that the behavior is unrelated to its reality context (e.g., not corrected by ordinary reality testing) and may be isolated from the usually continuous stream of thoughts and memories (e.g., as in recoverable amnesia). These features are all represented in hypnotic behavior.

We have attempted to relate the dissociative activities of the hypnotized subject to his practiced dissociations in imaginative involvements. The imaginative involvements are so absorbing to the truly involved person that he temporarily sets aside the reality testing of his everyday life. It is such practiced dissociation that we have found related to hypnosis.

The experience of dissociation begins in childhood. Children can move readily between the role of fantasy and the world of reality. The childhood flexibility can be preserved if the capacity is kept alive through practice. It involves time-limited experiences, so that a fantasy can be enjoyed and then turned off. Perhaps this time-limiting mechanism is one key to healthy dissociation. A role must not only be adopted, but it must be set aside; this in-and-out behavior is characteristic of hypnosis. A good hypnotic subject, for example, has learned the art of amnesia, which is a temporary forgetting; he can set memories aside but can recover them again when the episode is over.

## Hypnosis as a Communicative Process

The importance of words in hypnosis is very impressive. The subject can enter the trance at a verbal signal; a verbal signal suffices to elicit a dream, or age regression, or a psychomotor abnormality, or a hallucination. We have found fluent communication—a facility with words—one of the predictors of hypnotizability. Many subjects spontaneously commented on the role of the hypnotist's voice—by contrast with the hypnotist as a person—in producing and sustaining the hypnotic experience. The extreme form of separating the hypnotist's voice from his person is represented in the statement by Sarah in chapter 3. She said that she had not noticed the hypnotist, but that it was the voice that was important. Later she added, "The more you know the person [who is hypnotizing you] the more it interferes. . . . This is true of knowing the author of a book as well."

One role of the hypnotist's voice may be to take over the inner voice of the subject. This is the pertinent speculation about hypnosis offered by Miller, Galanter, and Pribram (1960), who assert that "the subject gives up his inner speech to the hypnotist" (p. 105). The general idea is that a subject, in making and carrying out his plans of action (little plans, as well as bigger ones), tends to talk to himself: this self-talk keeps him in control, and if the self-talk is interrupted, or taken over by the hypnotist, the hypnotist comes into a controlling position. The interruption may be by confusion, as in the "double-bind" interpretation offered by Haley (1958); if the subject's plans become confused, the hypnotist's may provide a way out. Whatever the details may be, the importance of words is very great.

Subjects commented on this spontaneously and frequently. A few quotes will help show what hypnosis was like from their point of view.

—"The voice was right there and almost became part of me. The hypnotist did not exist, just his voice."

—"While I listened to the hypnotist's voice I could hear nothing else, only when she stopped talking. I just concentrated on the voice."

—"A great deal hinged on the man's voice. I went along and followed it."

—"The second day I was completely oblivious to everything except his voice—nothing else registered." The subject liked the way the voice sounded smooth and natural. "He knew what he was saying, and it gave me confidence." (This is the first indication in these quotes that there was a person behind the voice.)

—"I let the voice take care of everything. . . . I felt I wanted to let go. . . . I had a desire to enjoy the experience. I couldn't completely enjoy it while I was holding on to a remnant of my self-control."

—"I was able to concentrate and give my will to the hypnotist. He was not a personality to me. The first one was just 'there,' more or less of a teacher. I listened because I was learning. The second one was merely a voice. I could concentrate on it because the technique was then familiar." This subject likened hypnosis to intoxication, in the way the voice in hypnosis was very remote, yet very close.

—"I didn't think of the hypnotist as a person, just as a voice."

If the person is so unimportant, the interpersonal aspects of the relationship, at a surface level, are certainly not prominent; what part they play at an unconscious level or in evoked fantasies is a matter of speculation, for we do not have the associative material that would be necessary to elucidate it. The spontaneous remarks listed in the series of foregoing quotes are based on what the subjects told us, not on what we encouraged them to talk about. In this connection, it may be significant that a voice from a taped induction is about as satisfactory as a "live" one in inducing hypnosis, even though the voice on the tape is totally unfamiliar.

Another aspect of the subject-hypnotist verbal interaction was called to our attention by other subjects, some of whom reversed the Miller-Galanter-Pribram hypothesis. These were subjects who clearly adopted the words of the hypnotists but had to make them their own before the hypnotist's words were effective. Thus, instead of the hypnotist taking over the subject's talk, the subject took over the hypnotist's. Because the words were those originated by the hypnotist, the end result is that postulated by Miller, Galanter, and Pribram. Here are some typical quotes:

—"The hypnotist would say to me, 'Concentrate on the task,' and I would say to myself, 'Concentrate on the task.' His voice being mine, I made myself do it. It wasn't done consciously; it just happened."

—"I talked to myself and gave myself the same directions that the hypnotist gave me. I tried to imagine each task in advance." When asked if this "helping" was a form of simulation, he replied, "My responses were genuine, once I gave myself the hypnotist's commands. I couldn't simulate a stiff arm or locked fingers. I can't consciously mislead another person."

—"I kept repeating to myself what he said, before each of the tasks. When he says I won't be able to name a 'house,' I say in my mind to myself that I'm not supposed to name a 'house' and I don't." When asked what happened in this case, the subject replied, "I see the house, don't recognize it, and show no curiosity about it."

—"When the hypnotist said I was going deeper and deeper I did think of falling gradually into a pit and it was getting darker and darker. I was helping by trying to hypnotize myself. There was conscious effort. I did assume a part and told myself that I was feeling this force and then I experienced it. When I let up on those autosuggestions I did not experience . . ."

The hypnotist's voice, instead of his person, plays an important role in the hypnotic relationship. Kubie and Margolin (1944) early sensed this. Having described the reduction of sensory input in the usual induction (through immobilization and monotony) they propose that this reduction in sensorimotor channels blurs the ego boundaries of the subject, so that there is a psychological fusion between subject and hypnotist; as this stage is reached the hypnotist's words are confused with the subject's own thoughts. They suggest that the subject's apparent suggestibility arises out of this confusion. The implied transference explanation is a partial one only, expressed as "an incorporation of a fragmentary image of the hypnotist within the expanded boundaries of the subject's ego" (p. 620). The rapid transference is somewhat similar to Macalpine's (1950) "transference readiness," a willingness to follow the hypnotist that the subject brings to the session and hence does not have to develop slowly in relation to the hypnotist. Because of this readiness, the hypnotist's voice can quickly take charge of the relationship.

The rapid transference in hypnosis based on transference readiness, just discussed, can, in repeated hypnotic sessions or psychotherapy sessions, be converted to the more familiar individualized transference. As often noted, under these circumstances it is difficult to disentangle what belongs to the hypnosis and what belongs to the psychotherapeutic relationship.

Verbal communication is, of course, not the only communication between hypnotist and subject. The hypnotist may touch or stroke the subject, or communicate by gesture; in emphasizing the voice, we call attention to the usual channel of communication as the subject sits with eyes closed.

### The Developmental-Interactive Interpretation of Hypnotizability

There are separable components to a theory of hypnosis. One component of the theory is required to explain the hypnotic experience as it occurs in the susceptible subject. It is this component that psychoanalytic theories, role theories, and dissociation theories attempt to explain. A second component is demanded by individual differences in hypnotizability, which, in terms of the more general theories, would explain why some people can appropriately regress, why some people can have role involvement, why some people can dissociate, and, conversely, why many people cannot do these things that the theorists say account for hypnosis. Our developmental-interactive interpretation of hypnotic susceptibility (Hilgard and Hilgard 1962; E. R. Hilgard 1965; Hilgard and Hilgard 1967) is proposed to seek the answers to questions about individual differences. Much of our interviewing was directed to this end.

It is unnecessary to restate the major arguments, since they have been repeated in what has gone before. One of the early evidences of the importance of childhood experience in influencing later hypnosis came in our study of sequelae (Hilgard, Hilgard, and Newman 1961). It was found there that some of the unusual hypnotic responses could be related to experiences with anesthesia in childhood, chiefly childhood tonsilectomies. The developmental aspects of hypnotic susceptibility have been stressed in the development of involvements in association with parents, as well as in the significance of early disciplinary practices. The interactive aspects depend upon the characteristics of the present individual who comes to the hypnotic session. He accepts the interaction well if he is normally outgoing, finds communication easy in a face-to-face relationship, and is motivated to enjoy the hypnotic experience.

Once we have accounted in developmental-interactive terms for individual differences in hypnotizability, we have taken steps toward the understanding of hypnosis itself. Hence the two components of the theory of hypnosis are not independent but interrelated. Our reason for favoring the dissociation theory as an explanation for the phenomena of hypnosis in general is supported by the kinds of events that have seemed to us significant in our exploration of the developmental and interactive origins of individual differences.

### Contributions to the Psychological Understanding of Development and Personality

In the course of studying a large number of university students (and some families of children and parents) we have learned about aspects of personality that would not have come to our attention except for our interest in hypnosis. One reason for the usefulness of hypnosis in the study of personality is that as a *criterion* of individual differences among the normal population it is reliably measurable and relatively persistent, and in this respect more satisfactory than most other criteria. Hence it provides a kind of anchorage for the testing of various hypotheses about development and personality. In this section we wish to call attention to some of the ideas we have found to be significant apart from any primary interest in hypnosis itself.

1. *Hypnotic susceptibility as an aspect of child development.* There are many casual references in the literature on early childhood to the richness of children's imagination, the occasional difficulties of children in distinguishing between fantasy and reality, the eidetic imagery of children, and so on, but on the whole the material remains largely anecdotal because of difficulties of measuring and scaling in a manner that can produce clear age trends. It has been known for a century that children are more highly hypnotizable than adults, and this knowledge, combined with the scales available for assessing childhood hypnosis, point to a promising and neglected area of development. While we now have some measures of age trends, as shown earlier in figures 3 and 4, these really indicate important possibilities for using hypnotic susceptibility as a background for the study of imagery, attention, the ability to distinguish between reality and hallucination, and the capacity for imaginative involvement, not only in relation to age but in relation to various aspects of child-rearing practices. We should like to call these possibilities strongly to the attention of those interested in developmental psychology. (A start is being made in our laboratory, and part of the data are presented in figure 4. This study includes a moderate-sized sample of identical and fraternal twins as well as ordinary siblings. The data are not yet ready for publication.)

2. *The importance of the involvements.* Imaginative and adventurous involvements develop early in childhood and, as we have shown, become important in the affective life of the adult. They can be dissociative in that they provide an alternation with the more usual reality- and achievement-oriented behavior. Imaginative involvements have not become part of our standard child psychology, despite their great importance. Such involvements, even though experienced personally by the psychologist, may be "dissociated" also from his scientific perceptions. For example, I recently had a conversation with a psychologist interested in model building in the areas of attention and learning who has a personal hobby of music and possesses rich auditory eidetic imagery. He was surprised to learn, as I talked with him about involvements, that everyone does not have his ability, and he had not related his own deep involvement at all to his scientific studies of attention, even though, in some respects, his ability to hear a whole symphony in imagery is the ultimate in attentiveness.

The possibility that there may be a critical period in childhood in which involvements become most readily established (in accordance with the theories of the ethologist, or of Piaget, or of Erikson, as mentioned in chapter 3) should not be overlooked. Some related evidence is provided by the work on eidetic imagery, which has been said to be more prevalent earlier than later in childhood, although more recent evidence shows that well-established eidetic imagery in elementary school children persists undiminished for at least a six-year period (Haber and Haber 1964; Haber 1969; Leask, Haber, and Haber 1969). The implication is that if involvements become strongly established they may persist, even in the face of the mounting reality demands.

Imaginative involvements also provide an untapped resource for educators. Dewey's early work on interest and effort (1913) called attention to the importance of aroused interest, but motivational psychology got diverted from the role of fantasy in involvement. A psychologist in our laboratory tested the practicality of using involvements in learning by taking two eleven-year old nonreaders and nonspellers for a tryout. He discovered that both of them were fascinated by science fiction in television programs. Building on this fantasy involvement, he arranged a reading program around their science fiction interests and in four months they had made remarkable progress (unpublished cases, courtesy of Errol Schubot). The recent revival of interest in visual imagery as "mnemonic aids" in paired-associate learning is another indication that there is more to be done with fantasy involvement (e.g., Paivio, Yuille, and Smythe 1966). When we discussed the significance of the involvements in chapter 11, it was suggested that these processes were not conflictual or ego-alien but on the contrary might belong in the category that Hartmann calls the "conflict-free ego sphere." This is not to suggest that all involvements are conflict-free but only that those most related to hypnotizability in our college population appear to be coherent with stable patterns of adjustment. They have arisen out of satisfying experiences with parents, rarely out of conflictual ones.

Thus a knowledge of imaginative involvements can be relevant to the work of the psychologist and the educator, not because they are related to hypnotizability, but because they are a significant part of normal personality functioning.

3. *Non-sex-role identification.* One observation that was brought strongly to our attention was the importance of identifications with parents that go beyond the sex role, that is, boys becoming like their fathers or girls like their mothers. The statistics

themselves are of interest (chap. 13, tables 33 and 34) in showing how frequently sons resemble mothers and girls resemble fathers, and how often both parents contributed to the child's development in shared ways. This should be fairly obvious, but much of the literature on identification has been preoccupied with the sex role and the developing of mature sexuality. That the cross-sexed identification is important in work habits and attitudes as well as in recreation and temperament suggests an important field for identification studies.

4. *Successful punishment and ego development.* One of our findings was the significance of early severe punishment in producing the hypnotizable person, but the findings suggest implications beyond hypnosis. Successful punishment—which produces an individual respectful of authority, but without wounds from the punishment—should be better understood. This does not mean that we are advocating punishment, or defending it.

5. *An alternative to the additive assumption in personality measurement.* If one uses hypnosis as a criterion, there appear to be many alternative experiences which serve about equally well as support for hypnotizability, and the presence of several of these is little more influential than the presence of one of them. While our evidence is not as strong as we might wish, it appears that personality theorists might find it useful to look for a logic of prediction that differs from that of the intelligence test, which proceeds by adding up the number of right answers. Personality has a hierarchical structure, and only by finding those features which are high in the hierarchy for the individual will successful prediction be achieved.

6. *Multiple strands within the person.* As soon as one begins to look at the prevalence of dissociations of one sort or another (including the multiple conversations carried on with oneself), it becomes clear that an emphasis upon the unity of the personality may be misleading. There are indeed multiple strands operative at once within the normal person, not unlike those exhibited dramatically in cases of multiple personality. The concept of dissociation, which calls attention to these, deserves to be revived and to find a larger place in personality theory. An unusual place to look for support for this view is in the writings of Kurt Lewin, who, as a Gestalt psychologist, might be thought of as a proponent of unity and wholeness. Yet in his early discussion of personality (Lewin 1926), he makes it very clear that there is considerable segregation between parts of the personality. Whatever psychical unity there may be in the "ego" system, it is a "weak" Gestalt. According

to him, in personality we deal with a number of "strong" Gestalts, that is, highly organized subsystems. They are in part in communication with each other, and in part disclose no genuine unity at all. This testimony, by one committed in general to the holism of Gestalt psychology, in its own way provides support for some kind of dissociation interpretation.

## Relevance to Treatment

Our research was concerned with the normal person, and not with patients, although as a psychiatrist I have been able to test out with patients some of the things learned in the course of this investigation. These remarks on treatment are appended as very tentative suggestions arising from the work, in the hope that they may encourage others to do the kind of research that would make the results of our research with the normal serve as a background for helping those who come as patients. We recognize that the motivation of a patient coming for treatment is very different from that of a subject coming for an experiment, and this doubtless influences not only the relationship to the therapist but the acceptability of the hypnotic experience.

1. *The very slightly hypnotizable person may benefit from a hypnoticlike therapy.* Many of those who regularly use a form of hypnosis in psychotherapy are convinced that all (or nearly all) who come to them for treatment are sufficiently hypnotizable to participate in and profit from this type of therapy. In view of the relatively few subjects who are highly hypnotizable, it must follow that a low degree of hypnotizability suffices. This has long been been recognized, as early as Bernheim (1889). Platonov (1959), who followed the Russian, Bekhterev, in his type of hypnotic therapy, refers to the method of using very light hypnosis as the Bekhterev-Bernheim method. All that is required of hypnosis is that the patient be willing to sit quietly with his eyes closed.

One of our own cases will illustrate success with a patient known to be only slightly susceptible to hypnosis. John, aged forty-one, came to the laboratory with a complaint of headaches which had persisted for six years. Never without a low-grade headache, he had severe ones several times a week. His score was only one (hands moving apart on suggestion) on SHSS-C. Yet one of our colleagues worked with him successfully for four weeks in a daily program aimed at controlling his pain. He received hypnoticlike training, along the lines prescribed by Sachs and Anderson (1967), so that he could sense bodily changes as a result of suggestion. The headaches were gradually reduced as he acquired techniques of doing for himself the things learned in the laboratory. A follow-up six months later showed his headaches still satisfactorily under control. It is doubtful if his hypnotic susceptibility, as tested by our scales, would have been much improved, but the hypnoticlike activities served satisfactorily for the relief of a symptom which had not benefited by other methods.

2. *Something else may happen in the more deeply hypnotizable.* As mentioned several times before, it is difficult to know what belongs to the therapy and what belongs to the hypnosis when the two are used together. The fact that superficial hypnosis is adequate for some types of therapy does not mean that there are no differences when deeper hypnosis is involved. The patient capable of deeper hypnosis could perhaps uncover repressed memories more rapidly (restoring amnesia for them, if therapeutically desirable), and could perhaps make use of preexisting involvements in a therapeutically profitable form. He could profit from types of posthypnotic suggestion that the less hypnotizable could not benefit from.

It is probable that the therapist may have to be more skilled in dealing with the deeply hypnotizable than with the less hypnotizable, for fear that posthypnotic amnesia, excessive regression, or other kinds of reality distortion may interfere with the normal functioning which the therapist is seeking to restore. Unfortunately we do not now have the information upon which to base assertions. The existence of the hypnotic-susceptibility scales will make answers to the pertinent questions possible, provided the therapist is willing to make use of them in classifying his patients according to their degrees of susceptibility.

3. *Transference attitudes typical of intensive therapy may appear within hypnotherapy.* There may be a reciprocal relationship between hypnosis and transference within psychotherapy, and thus hypnosis may in some manner accentuate transference relationships, while the developed transference may also modify the hypnotizability of the patient.

Gill and Brenman (1959, p. 89–91) cite a case of separation anxiety in a young woman patient in long-term therapy for whom hypnosis was used as an adjuvant. When the therapist was about to depart on vacation, the patient's "complete love" expressed for the therapist in hypnosis turned to a predatory and potentially destructive feeling. Gill and Brenman interpret this shift of feeling as an indication that "under the cover of the classic obedience of hypnosis, there lies an intense and hostile wish to turn the tables and to 'devour' the hypnotist, thus stripping him of all power" (p. 91). My own interpretation is that this reaction had not necessarily to do with the hypnotic relationship. It is typical of what patients in intensive therapy may do when the therapist leaves them, particularly if they have serious fears of separation. Anxiety and anger against the therapist, the desire for retaliation against the threatened separation, a wish for power to prevent the separation: these are familiar in intensive therapy *without* hypnosis. All these reactions occurred in the reported patient. Because the prior sessions had been conducted within hypnosis it was to be expected that hypnosis would participate in the negative reactions and the defenses that were stirred up. But whether this behavior *belongs* in any special respect to the hypnotic interaction is doubtful.

What to do about transference manifestations that appear within hypnosis raises the same question of desirable therapeutic practice that comes up in discussions of interpreting the transference. Erika Fromm (1968b, pp. 79–80) compares the analysis of transference in psychoanalysis and in hypnoanalysis: "In ordinary psychoanalysis one analyzes all transference phenomena. . . . In hypnoanalysis it seems that one can do more constructive work by *utilizing* the transference feelings than by *analyzing* them. For instance, in the case of the patient with the need to outshine me, I suggested to the patient in trance that at home, in the evening, she would put herself into a much deeper trance than I could put her into—or than she was in at the time—and that memories or new insights would come to her that would shed light on her major problems (alcoholism and compulsive overeating). What she then brought in for the next therapy hour furnished ample material for further hypnoanalysis."

Presumably the terms of the hypnotic relationship suggest a more active role for the therapist, on the one hand, and a more positive role for the patient, on the other.

4. *The involvements are mostly positive and indicate the desirability of keeping therapy moving along positive lines.* The imaginative involvements that constitute pathways into hypnosis, such as reading, drama, adventure, love of nature, are positive, pleasurable experiences. Because they are, they maintain the ability to experience hypnosis against the inroads of the reality demands that tend to reduce hypnotic susceptibility with increasing age. If, then, hypnosis is to be used to restore confidence, to give hope where there has been anxiety and fear, it is not unreasonable to try to match in affect those experiences that in natural circumstances favor hypnotic involvement.

It is obviously necessary for a patient in conflict to face threatening thoughts and unpleasant experiences, but the question is how to use therapy in such a manner as to reduce the negative affect and to redirect it toward the positive. The problem of dissociative and integrative processes in hypnoanalysis is ably discussed by Fromm (1968a).

We have learned from the experiences of our hypnotizable subjects that they can tolerate sad and distressing experiences of other people as they are portrayed in drama or in writing. The fantasies provoke affective response, but in manageable form. A possibility in therapy, therefore, is to put some distance between the threatening material and the subject by having it presented in imaginative form as though it belongs to someone else. The experience can be examined without its being immediately reexperienced by the person. Bringing in the experience of other people in this way makes the problem a more typical one (generalizes it) and thus reduces the patient's anxiety. A doctoral dissertation from this laboratory (Horowitz 1969) tested hypnotic therapy of snake phobias under several conditions. In one of these, the recall of early experiences of the phobia under hypnosis was done with a full reliving of the affect; under another condition the early scene was revisited, but as though it were happening to someone else, and the unpleasant emotion was *not* reexperienced. The latter condition proved more beneficial in relieving the phobia and is consonant with the idea that sometimes the required relearning takes place better if there is some affective distance from the event.

Once the negative and threatening in therapy have been handled at a distance, perhaps through fantasy, the next step would be to move gradually, with reassurance, to a more direct facing of what has been threatening. There is a temptation within hypnosis to move a little too fast, because it is possible to use uncovering techniques to get at repressed material rather quickly. Such a frontal attack on defenses may interrupt the therapeutic relationship and delay therapeutic gains.

Gill and Brenman (1959) note that when there was an increase in hostility toward the therapist, fluctuations in depth of the trance occurred, and the trance generally became much lighter. In such circumstances, deeper hypnosis may occur as a defense, or the patient may even fall asleep and beome inaccessible for a time. Gill and Brenman say (p. 65), "We can expect a spontaneous change in the depth of hypnosis when there is evidence—accompanied by indices of conflict and anxiety—that an existing impulse-defense balance is being threatened. This threat to the existing balance may occur either as the result of the upsurge of a passive need or as the result of a hostile wish against which the ego is insufficiently defended. The patient attempts to deal with the resultant anxiety by a change in depth of hypnosis."

If it is true that negative feelings weaken hypnosis, this is another reason for stressing positive feelings. One way to do this is to find a patient's sources of strength—particularly any areas in which he can become imaginatively involved—and then to graft positive experiences upon them. This may be done, in fact, without hypnosis, as the next section describes.

When we favor a positive approach, we are not only being supportive but we are also helping the patient to strengthen his ego by learning to cope with his problems, first in fantasy and then in his real-life situation.

5. *The involvements can be used in nonhypnotic therapy.* In a case which I treated, I found I could use what I had learned even though the patient was refractory to hypnosis. A twenty-seven-year-old male graduate student was referred by the medical ward because he was totally unable to eat and was becoming emaciated. There was insufficient medical reason for the condition. He said that his appetite was all right, but that his esophagus was so narrowed he could not get the food down and what little he managed to eat was soon regurgitated. He was already so weak that the act of talking tired him. He was very tense and had difficulty in sleeping even with heavy sedation. According to his wife he had become extremely depressed a month before when told that he had a recurrence of Hodgkin's disease. Repeated Xrays had shown no basis for the eating difficulty.

Hypnotherapy as a method of treatment was ruled out by lack of susceptibility to hypnosis. I searched for areas of involvement, however, and finally came upon one great love of his: waterfalls. As a student from abroad, and widely traveled, he had seen some of the most magnificent falls in the world. I found that he could transport himself to the waterfall, in imagination, and leave behind the hospital and its reminders of his illness. He was not thinking of his troubles as he visited a waterfall, saw it, heard it, walked around it, sat and picnicked beside it. For an hour each day during the first week I helped him to return to the waterfalls, at the same time teaching him how to do the visiting by himself. After the first week, for a period of two more weeks, I saw him three times a week, sometimes merely to talk, sometimes to encourage more variety in his trips to the waterfalls. Anyone watching him could see the relaxation come over him as he went to the falls; his tense expression calmed. He soon began to eat and sleep, and at the end of the three-week period he was able to leave the hospital and soon thereafter to make the long flight home which had earlier seemed beyond the possible.

A few of us working together as a therapeutic team have also made a nonhypnotic application of the concept of involvement in a demonstration project which we have described as affiliative therapy (Hilgard and Moore 1969). Selecting as our patients a group of highly disturbed young adolescent boys, we arranged for therapy sessions in which each boy would be assigned a college student who shared an area of interest and enthusiasm with him. In one case this was swimming, in another case it was science fiction. The essence of the therapy was that the college student (who had no special training as a therapist) would take the boy along with him and share enthusiasm for his hobby. Soon the swimmer was swimming more lengths of the pool than he had ever swum before, and the science fiction enthusiast knew more about science than he had ever expected to know. With this development of ego strength in areas of involvement, something happened to the self-images of these otherwise defeated and discouraged boys. Their school studies picked up (without special tutoring) and their social behavior became more acceptable. The results were so dramatic that we recommend attention to involvements as a therapeutic resource outside of as well as within hypnotic therapy.

6. *Research on specific types of cases is highly desirable.* The many complexities within psychotherapy in general, including those types of therapy which make use of hypnosis centrally or as an adjunct, make it highly desirable that research be focused in such a manner that some conclusions can be reached. At present there are few assertions that can be made about those cases most suited for treatment with the aid of hypnosis, what the limitations are, what the negative indications are, and what belongs essentially to hypnosis as distinct from what belongs in general to the therapeutic interaction.

One very promising area for careful research is the control of pain of organic origin. There is abundant evidence that clinicians using hypnosis are successful in the control of pain in childbirth, in burns, in terminal cancer. These cases have some advantage, for careful quantitative research, over cases involving reduction of pain in migraine or peptic ulcer, where the psychosomatic components are more prominent and the factors contributing to the pain are likely to be less comparable from patient to patient. For careful research, it is desirable to have a large supply of patients with somewhat similar diagnoses, who can then be tested for their hypnotic susceptibilities prior to the beginning of treatment. The intervening treatment can be controlled according to experimental design. It would be desirable to know not only the therapeutic outcome but also what happened to the hypnotic susceptibility in the meantime.

Our own work in the comparative simplicity of a normal college population shows how difficult it is to arrive at clear findings, but we feel certain that we would not have come as far as we have had we tried to do everything at once, with varied populations of normal people and patients. To achieve any precision at all some breadth has to be sacrificed, and this applies to research on therapy as well as to laboratory research on normal populations.

# APPENDIXES

# Appendix 1

FORMS USED IN INTERVIEWING AND RATING

The interview forms and rating scales reproduced here were used in 1962–63, during the period when the interviews covered two hours. In the following year the interviews were collapsed so as to be conducted in one hour.

## Interview in advance of Hypnosis: Day 1

Date _____                     Subject No. _____
Interviewer _____                     Name _____

[The original interview forms have more space for recording replies, but the ordering of questions and general format are as indicated.]

### Introductory Remarks

You have signed up for an experiment in hypnosis, and I want to explain to you why we are beginning with two hours of interviewing. After these interviews you will have an opportunity to experience hypnosis on each of two days.

This research project is concerned with how people respond to hypnosis. We have become aware through our earlier studies that there are areas of hypnotizability that are related to the kinds of experiences a person has had in ordinary life, outside hypnosis. Hence we want to know about your interests, some of your thinking about yourself, and your relationships to your family.

I shall be asking you some direct questions, but I hope that you will feel free to add anything that seems important to you, not waiting for specific questions from me. We appreciate your willingness to cooperate with us in this research. While this material is necessarily personal, your replies will be used in such a way that you will not be identifiable.

269

1. *Present status.* Now just a few questions about yourself:
Age _____ Year in college _____ Major (or intended one)
_____ Vocational plans _____

2. *Re: hypnosis*
How do you feel about being hypnotized?
Have you had any prior experience of hypnosis (seeing someone hypnotized, being hypnotized yourself, trying to hypnotize someone else)?
How hypnotizable do you expect to be? Why do you think so?
Motivation for hypnosis _____
Expectation of susceptibility _____

3. *Composition of the family*
Where do your parents live (intactness)?
Father: Age _____ Occupation _____ Education _____
Mother: Age _____ Occupation (include before marriage)
_____ Education _____
Siblings: List in order of birth, self included; note half-sibs, adoptions, etc.

| Order | Sex | Present Age |
|-------|-----|-------------|
| 1 | _____ | _____ |
| 2 | _____ | _____ |
| 3 | _____ | _____ |
| 4 | _____ | _____ |
| 5 | _____ | _____ |
| 6 | _____ | _____ |

Total number in sibship _____
Birth position _____

4. *Health history of subject and family*
   a. Have there been major health problems in any member of the family?
   b. Have you ever had an anesthetic? Yes/No
   Anything unusual about the experience or the after effects?

5. *Developmental or family crises.* Can you think of any special events or crises in the family that might have affected you as you were growing up? (Illnesses, deaths, separations; unusual experiences; moves from one place to another.)
Impact _____

6. *Participation in activities: Special interests and hobbies*
   a. Now we are especially interested in the things that interest you. What are your special interests and hobbies? (Note duration.) (Note source of intense interests.)
   *Probes*
   Music (playing, singing, listening)
   Reading (adventure, fiction, science fiction, mysteries, biography, history) Absorption through high school? And now?
   Sports (games, swimming, riding)

Space interests (flying, spelunking, skiing, skin diving, mountain climbing)
Nature interests (scientific, aesthetic)
Movies, theater, TV
Work recreation (building and crafts)
Dancing (ballet, tap)
Camping, hunting, fishing
Other

    *b.* Did you have other hobbies that did not continue into the college years? And how long did they last?

7. *Attitudes toward play activities.* (Ask specifically if not already clear.)

    *a. Absorption in activities.* When you are doing something that interests you, such as (specify major interests), how involved or how absorbed would you say you become? (Alternate phrases: Losing yourself, not hearing anyone call you, or finding yourself thinking of other things.)

    *b. Adventuresomeness,* i.e., the new and the different. When the opportunity comes to try something new or something you haven't tried before, are you eager to plunge into it or do you prefer the more familiar? (Do you think you substitute adventure found in books?)

    *c. Curiosity.* How interested are you in the unknown or the mysterious? In the effects of drugs? Have you been interested in extrasensory phenomena? Do you have an interest in philosophy?

    *d. Relaxation in play.* When you play, do you find yourself carefree and relaxed or are you apt to work at it?

    *e.* To sum it up, how important do you think that play is in a person's life?

8. *Religion as an interest or activity*

    *a.* Would you say that religion has played much or little part in your life? In the family life? (What religion?)

    *b.* (If somewhat active) Does church mean to you a kind of dedication or is it more a matter of a Sunday custom?

    *c.* (If dedication) Did you participate in youth groups?

9. *Peer relationships*

    *a. Same sex.* Do you usually share your interests with friends? Are you apt to belong to groups which have shared interests?

        (1) How easy or how difficult has it been for you to make friends?

        (2) How do you get along with other fellows (or with other girls)?

        (3) Would you say you have a lot of friends or that you concentrate on one or two at a time, or that you like to be alone a great deal? Involvement _____

    *b. Opposite sex*

        (1) How about girl friends (or boy friends)?

        (2) How deeply involved do you tend to become? Engaged?

        (3) Do you tend to play the field?

10. In your relationship with others of your own age, have you been apt to take leadership? Have you been apt to be a follower?

11. *Personal characteristics*
    a. How would you characterize yourself? (Probe if needed: calm, nervous, relaxed, worried, impatient, serious, lonely, cheerful.)
    b. What do you think are your strong points or assets? (If needed: what do you like best about yourself or what do you think others like best about you?)
    c. How easily do you find you can *converse* with others? Examples: _____
    d. *Humor*
       (1) Are you apt to employ humor in conversation? What kind of humor do you enjoy?
       (2) Do you actually get funny in the way you behave, i.e., how much do you and others, or you and your family, tend to clown with each other?
    e. *Approach via particulars or via wholes.* When you're faced with a new experience, are you apt to dissect it and look at details or are you more apt to accept the experience as a whole? Does this apply to a new play activity? Work?
    f. *Concentration.* In general? If interested? Examples _____
    g. *Ease in relinquishing control*
       (1) On the whole how easy was it for you to accept your parents' directions? Teachers? Doctors?
       (2) In order to have an experience you are eager for, such as skiing or mountain climbing, would you seek out an expert to guide you, or would you rather try it first on your own?
    h. How do you see yourself in your attitude toward life? As having an optimistic approach, or as being worried, or as being aloof, or perhaps showing some combination of these tendencies?

Tomorrow we can continue this discussion. We prefer that you talk as little as possible about these experiments before next spring when the investigation has been completed.

## Interview in advance of Hypnosis: Day 2

Date _____                              Subj. No. _____
Interviewer _____          Name _____
Yesterday we were discussing your interests and characteristics. Today we can start by considering a few more aspects of your personality.

1. *Personal characteristics (cont.)*
    a. *Rationality*
       How much do you tend to be objective and detached, for example, do you remain aware of both sides of a question, weighing the pros and cons? Some people describe this attitude as characteristic of the

mediator. Would this be just as true when you are doing some leisure time activity?

b. *Analytic*
Do you continue an attitude of questioning throughout an experience, remaining alert to the details? Would this be just as true when you are doing some leisure time activity?

c. *Caution*
Would you see yourself as a generally cautious person?

d. *Have you any particular fears?*

e. *Questioning of authority*
When you were told to do something as a child did you tend to insist on the why's and wherefor's before doing it? (Did you tend to nag when you were told to do something? Or drag your heels?) Do you still see some of this in yourself?

2. *Daydreaming and creative activities*
a. Would you say that your imagination as a child was much stimulated by reading and movies, or did your daydreams develop from within yourself, more from your own thoughts? (Flights of fancy.)
Fantasy from reading and movies _____
Fantasy from within _____

b. Do you still have an ability to daydream?

c. Is your imagination purposeful in planning for the future? True in the past, too?

d. Did you have an imaginary companion as a child? If yes, what was the imaginary companion like?

e. Creative activities such as poetry and other writing, art, composing music, involve the imagination. Have you ever engaged much in these activities?

f. How did these creative interests originate? Parents? School? Reading? Or did they just develop?

Now we want to talk about you in relation to other members of your family.

3. With which parent do you feel you have the most in common

| Father | Mother | Both | Neither | Can't say |
|--------|--------|------|---------|-----------|
| 1 | 2 | 3 | 4 | 5 |

4. *Father*
a. Which of your interests have you shared with your father?

b. What other interests does he have?

c. What is your father like?

d. I am going to read you a list of descriptive phrases and I want you to react to them. Just tell me briefly which of these are descriptive of your father:
(1) Warm and comfortable in relation to the family, or undemonstrative?
(2) Adventuresome?
(3) Rational, weighs pros and cons? True in play?

4. *Father (continued)*
    (4) Analytic? True in play?
    (5) Absorbed in play? Work recreation?
    (6) Humorous in words or action?
    (7) Striving?
    *Examples and clarification of above*
    e. What do you consider your father's strong points?
    f. In what areas does he have difficulties? For example, if you could change some things about your father, what would they be?

5. *Mother*
    a. Which of your interests have you shared with your mother?
    b. What other interests does she have?
    c. What is your mother like?
    d. Now I am going to read you a list of descriptive phrases and I want you to react to them. Just tell me briefly which of these are descriptive of your mother:
        (1) Warm and comfortable in relation to the family? Or demonstrative?
        (2) Adventuresome?
        (3) Rational, weighs pros and cons? True in play?
        (4) Analytic? True in play?
        (5) Absorbed in play? Work recreation?
        (6) Humorous in words or actions?
        (7) Striving?
    *Examples and clarification of above*
    e. What do you consider your mother's strong points?
    f. In what areas does she have difficulties? For example, if you could change some things about your mother, what would they be?

6. *Common activities with parents*
    a. What activities and interests do your parents have in common?
    b. In which ones did you share as a family?
    c. How much conversation took place in your family? How easily could you talk with your parents? (Extent, participation, topics.)

7. *Identification*
    a. Which parent do you think you most resemble in temperament and personality?
    b. What characteristics of temperament and personality do you share with your other parent?
    c. Which parent do you think you most resemble in playfulness and enthusiasm?
    d. Which parent do you think you most resemble in work attitudes?
    e. To which parent do you feel emotionally closer?

8. *Discipline.* Now we have a few questions on discipline.
    a. How were you disciplined as a child?
       Rewards? Punishment? Reasoning?
    b. How well do you think these disciplinary practices turned out? Will you use the same type of discipline on your children?

c. Did you have regular duties as a child? Did you do these without resentment or did you do these grudgingly? Did you learn to conform automatically without thinking about it or arguing about it?

d. Did your parents show confidence in your ability to do what you wanted to do, or become what you wanted to become?

9. *Problems.* Now we've talked about many things, but we haven't talked much about your problems. Everyone has areas of difficulty. What do you feel yours are?

## End of Interview

If discussion of problems at end makes termination awkward, summarize positive points already discussed, and possibly offer another appointment following hypnosis.

*End with:* We prefer that you talk as little as possible about these experiments before next spring when the investigation has been completed. Your experiences with hypnosis will begin in the next session.

## Ratings from Interview prior to Hypnosis: First Hour

[The rating scales as actually used were precoded for IBM analysis, but these details plus spaces for notes and comments have been reduced in this reproduction.]

Interviewer _____    Subj. No. _____  Sex _____

Date of interview _____    Name _____

1. *Data on subject.* Age _____    Year in college _____

   Major _____    Vocational plans _____

2. *Ratings re: Hypnosis.* Prior experience _____

   Motivation for hypnosis:

             Little   1–2–3–4–5–6–7–X  Much

          Unfavorable             Favorable

   Expectation of susceptibility:

           Low   1–2–3–4–5–6–7–X  High

I. Hypnotic susceptibility as estimated from motivation and expectation:

          0–1–2–3–4–5–6–7–8–9–10–11–12

   Comments on rating _____

3. *Composition of the family*

   Together or apart, etc. _____

   Father: Age _____  Occupation _____  Education _____

   Mother: Age _____  Occupation _____  Education _____

   Siblings: Total Number _____

          Birth position _____

4. *Health history of subject and family* (to be coded later)
   Major health problems of:
           Father _____
           Mother _____
           Most affected sibling _____
           Subject _____
   Experience of anesthesia _____
5. *Rating of developmental or family crises*
   Impact of relevant crisis or crises:
           Not severe  1–2–3–4–5–6–7–X  Severe
6. *Ratings of amount of participation in activities: special interests and hobbies*
   Music (playing, singing, listening):
           Little  1–2–3–4–5–6–7–X  Much
   Reading (various kinds):
           Little  1–2–3–4–5–6–7–X  Much
   Absorption in reading through high school:
           Little  1–2–3–4–5–6–7–X  Much
   Absorption in reading now:
           Little  1–2–3–4–5–6–7–X  Much
   Sports (various kinds):
           Little  1–2–3–4–5–6–7–X  Much
   Space interests:
           Little  1–2–3–4–5–6–7–X  Much
   Nature interests (scientific):
           Little  1–2–3–4–5–6–7–X  Much
   Nature interests (aesthetic):
           Little  1–2–3–4–5–6–7–X  Much
   Movies, theater, TV:
           Little  1–2–3–4–5–6–7–X  Much
   Work recreation:
           Little  1–2–3–4–5–6–7–X  Much
   Dancing (ballet, tap):
           Little  1–2–3–4–5–6–7–X  Much
   Camping, fishing, hunting:
           Little  1–2–3–4–5–6–7–X  Much
   Other:
           Little  1–2–3–4–5–6–7–X  Much
   Age and duration of most absorbing interest _____
7. *Ratings of attitudes toward play activities*
   Absorption in activities:
           Little  1–2–3–4–5–6–7–X  Much
   Adventuresomeness:
           Little  1–2–3–4–5–6–7–X  Much
   Curiosity:
           Little  1–2–3–4–5–6–7–X  Much
   Relaxation in play:
           Little  1–2–3–4–5–6–7–X  Much

Importance of play:

      Little 1–2–3–4–5–6–7–X Much

8. *Rating of religion as an interest or activity*
Religious involvement:

      Superficial 1–2–3–4–5–6–7–X Profound

9. *Ratings of peer relationships*
 a. *Same sex*
 Frequency:

      Few 1–2–3–4–5–6–7–X Many

Involvement:

      Superficial 1–2–3–4–5–6–7–X Deep

 b. *Opposite sex*
 Frequency:

      Few 1–2–3–4–5–6–7–X Many

Involvement:

      Superficial 1–2–3–4–5–6–7–X Deep

10. *Ratings of leadership-followership with peers*
 Leader:

Seldom or unsuccessful 1-2–3–4–5–6–7–X Often or successful

 Follower:

     Reluctant 1–2–3–3–5–6–7–X Willing

**II.** Hypnotic susceptibility as estimated from activities and interests:

      0–1–2–3–4–5–6–7–8–9–10–11–12

Comments on rating _____

11. *Ratings of personal characteristics*
Ease of conversation:

      Hard 1–2–3–4–5–6–7–X Easy

Use of humor in conversation:

      Little 1–2–3–4–5–6–7–X Much

Kind of humor enjoyed:

    Hostile, sarcastic 1–2–3–4–5–6–7–X Friendly, sociable

Use of humor in action:

      Little 1–2–3–4–5–6–7–X Much

Particulars vs. wholes (work and study):

      Details 1–2–3–4–5–6–7–X Wholes

Particulars vs. wholes (play):

      Details 1–2–3–4–5–6–7–X Wholes

Concentration, if interested:

      Hard 1–2–3–4–5–6–7–X Easy

Ease in relinquishing control:

Hard to accept directions 1–2–3–4–5–6–7–X Easy to accept directions

Positive mental attitude:

     Negative 1–2–3–4–5–6–7–X Positive

11. *Ratings of personal characteristics (continued)*
   **III.** Hypnotic susceptibility estimated from positive personal characteristics:

   0–1–2–3–4–5–6–7–8–9–10–11–12
   Comments on rating _____

   *Personality ratings based on the first hour's interview*
   Normal _____   Medium _____   Unstable or neurotic _____
   Outgoing _____   Medium _____   Withdrawn _____
   Participation in active interests:
   Low   1–2–3–4–5–6–7–X   High
   Participation in passive interests:
   Low   1–2–3–4–5–6–7–X   High

   **IV.** Hypnotic susceptibility estimated from first hour's overall impressions:

   0–1–2–3–4–5–6–7–8–9–10–11–12
   Comments on rating _____

   *Final comments by interviewer,* including thumbnail sketch of subject during this hour _____

## Ratings from Interview prior to Hypnosis: Second Hour

Interviewer _____   Subj. No. _____   Sex _____
Date of interview _____   Name _____
   1. *Ratings of personal characteristics (cont.)*
   Rationality (work and study):
   Irrational, impulsive   1–2–3–4–5–6–7–X   Rational
   Rationality (play):
   Irrational, impulsive   1–2–3–4–5–6–7–X   Rational
   Analytic (work and study):
   Accepts on faith   1–2–3–4–5–6–7–X   Analyzes, questions
   Analytic (play):
   Accepts on faith   1–2–3–4–5–6–7–X   Analyzes, questions
   Caution:
   Little cautious   1–2–3–4–5–6–7–X   Very cautious
   Questioning of authority:
   Unquestioned obedience   1–2–3–4–5–6–7–X   Always asked why

   **V.** Hypnotic susceptibility estimated from negative personality characteristics:

   0–1–2–3–4–5–6–7–8–9–10–11–12
   Comments on rating _____

   2. *Ratings of daydreaming and creative activities*
   Fantasy stimulated by reading, movies, as child:
   Little   1–2–3–4–5–6–7–X   Much

Fantasy stimulated from within, as child:
      Little   1–2–3–4–5–6–7–X   Much
Present flights of fancy:
      Few   1–2–3–4–5–6–7–X   Many
Purposeful imagination present:
      Free, spontaneous   1–2–3–4–5–6–7–X   Purposeful
Imaginary companion as child:
      Yes, vivid _____ Yes, slight _____ No _____
      Cannot remember whether or not _____
Creative activities:
      Few   1–2–3–4–5–6–7–X   Many
Source of creative activities _____

**VI.** Hypnotic susceptibility as estimated from imagination and fantasy:
      0–1–2–3–4–5–6–7–8–9–10–11–12
      Comments on rating _____

3. *Which parent most in common?*
      Father      Mother      Both      Neither      Can't Say      NA
        1            2           3          4             5           0
4. *Ratings of father's characteristics*
Warmth re: family:
      Cool, aloof   1–2–3–4–5–6–7–X   Warm, comfortable
Adventuresomeness:
      Little   1–2–3–4–5–6–7–X   Much
Rational, in general:
      Little   1–2–3–4–5–6–7–X   Much
Rational, in play:
      Little   1–2–3–4–5–6–7–X   Much, weighs
                                 pros and cons
Analytic, in general:
      Not analytic   1–2–3–4–5–6–7–X   Analyzes a great deal
Analytic, in play:
      Not analytic   1–2–3–4–5–6–7–X   Analyzes a great deal
Absorption in playful play:
      Little   1–2–3–4–5–6–7–X   Much
Absorption in work recreation:
      Little   1–2–3–4–5–6–7–X   Much
Humor in words or actions:
      Little   1–2–3–4–5–6–7–X   Much
Striving:
      Little   1–2–3–4–5–6–7–X   Much
Father's strong points _____
Things would change in father _____
Father's hypnotizability:
      0–1–2–3–4–5–6–7–8–9–10–11–12

4. *Ratings of father's characteristics (continued)*

**VII.** Hypnotic susceptibility estimated from relationship to father (shared interests, attitudes, approval):

0–1–2–3–4–5–6–7–8–9–10–11–12

Comments on rating _____

5. *Ratings of mother's characteristics*
   Warmth re: family:

| | | |
|---|---|---|
| Cool, aloof | 1–2–3–4–5–6–7–X | Warm, comfortable |

Adventuresomeness:

| | | |
|---|---|---|
| Little | 1–2–3–4–5–6–7–X | Much |

Rational, in general:

| | | |
|---|---|---|
| Little | 1–2–3–4–5–6–7–X | Much; weighs pros and cons |

Rational, in play:

| | | |
|---|---|---|
| Little | 1–2–3–4–5–6–7–X | Much; weighs pros and cons |

Analytic, in general:

| | | |
|---|---|---|
| Not analytic | 1–2–3–4–5–6–7–X | Analyzes a great deal |

Analytic, in play:

| | | |
|---|---|---|
| Not analytic | 1–2–3–4–5–6–7–X | Analyzes a great deal |

Absorption in playful play:

| | | |
|---|---|---|
| Little | 1–2–3–4–5–6–7–X | Much |

Absorption in work recreation:

| | | |
|---|---|---|
| Little | 1–2–3–4–5–6–7–X | Much |

Humor in words or actions:

| | | |
|---|---|---|
| Little | 1–2–3–4–5–6–7–X | Much |

Striving:

| | | |
|---|---|---|
| Little | 1–2–3–4–5–6–7–X | Much |

Mother's strong points _____
Things would change in mother _____
Mother's hypnotizability:

0–1–2–3–4–5–6–7–8–9–10–11–12

**VIII.** Hypnotic susceptibility estimated from relationship to mother (shared interests, attitudes, approval):

0–1–2–3–4–5–6–7–8–9–10–11–12

Comments on rating _____

6. *Common activities of mother and father and within family*
   Activities and interests parents have in common _____
   Activities in which family shares _____
   Ease of conversation in the family:

| | | |
|---|---|---|
| Very difficult | 1–2–3–4–5–6–7–X | Very easy |

7. *Identification*
   Parent most resembled in temperament:

| Father | Mother | Both | Neither | Can't Say | NA |
|--------|--------|------|---------|-----------|-----|
| 1 | 2 | 3 | 4 | 5 | 0 |

Characteristics shared with other parent _____

Parent most resembled in playfulness, enthusiasm:

| Father | Mother | Both | Neither | Can't Say | NA |
|--------|--------|------|---------|-----------|-----|
| 1 | 2 | 3 | 4 | 5 | 0 |

Parent most resembled in reality, work ego:

| Father | Mother | Both | Neither | Can't Say | NA |
|--------|--------|------|---------|-----------|-----|
| 1 | 2 | 3 | 4 | 5 | 0 |

To which parent closer:

| Father | Mother | Both | Neither | Can't Say | NA |
|--------|--------|------|---------|-----------|-----|
| 1 | 2 | 3 | 4 | 5 | 0 |

**IX.** Hypnotic susceptibility estimated from appropriate parental identification:

0–1–2–3–4–5–6–7–8–9–10–11–12

Comments on rating _____

8. *Ratings of discipline as a child*
   Use of rewards:
   
   Little   1–2–3–4–5–6–7–X   Much
   
   Use of punishments:
   
   Little   1–2–3–4–5–6–7–X   Much
   
   Use of reasoning:
   
   Little   1–2–3–4–5–6–7–X   Much
   
   Effectiveness of discipline:
   
   Little   1–2–3–4–5–6–7–X   Much
   (No)                         (Yes)
   
   Duties leading to automaticity:
   
   Little automaticity   1–2–3–4–5–6–7–X   Much automaticity
   
   Confidence of parents in subject's ability to achieve:
   
   Low   1–2–3–4–5–6–7–X   High

**X.** Hypnotic susceptibility estimated from type and consequences of childhood discipline:

0–1–2–3–4–5–6–7–8–9–10–11–12

Comments on rating _____

9. *Rating of problems of subject*
   Frequency/severity of problems:
   
   Few or not severe   1–2–3–4–5–6–7–X   Many or enough
                                           to be troublesome

10. *Rating of communication in the interview* (based on total interviewer experience)

   Poor; yes/no answers;                    Good; adds pertinent
   unable to give examples   1–2–3–4–5–6–7–X   material; clear; fluent

10. *Rating of communication in the interview (continued)*

   **XI.** Hypnotic susceptibility estimated from communication in the interview:

                0–1–2–3–4–5–6–7–8–9–10–11–12

       Comments on rating _____

11. *Interviewer's revised estimate of personality*

    Normal_____   Medium_____   Unstable or neurotic_____

    Outgoing _____   Medium _____   Withdrawn _____

    Participation in active interests:

            Low   1–2–3–4–5–6–7–X   High

    Participation in passive interests:

            Low   1–2–3–4–5–6–7–X   High

   **XII.** Hypnotic susceptibility estimated from second-hour interview:

                0–1–2–3–4–5–6–7–8–9–10–11–12

       Comments on rating _____

12. Final comments by interviewer with thumbnail sketch of subject

    _____.

13. Profile of predictions (transcribed from earlier ratings):

|  | Estimated Score | | | | | | | | | | | |
|---|---|---|---|---|---|---|---|---|---|---|---|---|
|  | 1 | 2 | 3 | 4 | 5 | 6 | 7 | 8 | 9 | 10 | 11 | 12 |
| **I.** Attitude and self-prediction | \| | \| | \| | \| | \| | \| | \| | \| | \| | \| | \| | \| |
| **II.** Activities and interests | \| | \| | \| | \| | \| | \| | \| | \| | \| | \| | \| | \| |
| **III.** Personal characteristics: pos. | \| | \| | \| | \| | \| | \| | \| | \| | \| | \| | \| | \| |
| **IV.** Overall, first hour | \| | \| | \| | \| | \| | \| | \| | \| | \| | \| | \| | \| |
| **V.** Personal characteristics: neg. | \| | \| | \| | \| | \| | \| | \| | \| | \| | \| | \| | \| |
| **VI.** Fantasy and imagination | \| | \| | \| | \| | \| | \| | \| | \| | \| | \| | \| | \| |
| **VII.** Father's characteristics | \| | \| | \| | \| | \| | \| | \| | \| | \| | \| | \| | \| |
| **VIII.** Mother's characteristics | \| | \| | \| | \| | \| | \| | \| | \| | \| | \| | \| | \| |
| **IX.** Parental identification | \| | \| | \| | \| | \| | \| | \| | \| | \| | \| | \| | \| |
| **X.** Childhood discipline | \| | \| | \| | \| | \| | \| | \| | \| | \| | \| | \| | \| |

Estimated Score

| | 1 | 2 | 3 | 4 | 5 | 6 | 7 | 8 | 9 | 10 | 11 | 12 |
|---|---|---|---|---|---|---|---|---|---|---|---|---|

**XI.** Communication in
interview | | | | | | | | | | | | |

**XII.** Overall, second
hour | | | | | | | | | | | | |

14. Interviewer prediction of hypnotic susceptibility after examining above
profile and making essential clinical corrections:

0–1–2–3–4–5–6–7–8–9–10–11–12

15. Revised prediction based on consultation after interview but prior to
hypnosis:*

0–1–2–3–4–5–6–7–8–9–10–11–12

Consideration entering into revision _____

* This is the prediction to be entered into the records in the test of success
of prediction.

# Appendix 2

## SYDNEY MODIFICATION OF
## THE BETTS MENTAL IMAGERY QUESTIONNAIRE

### Vividness of Imagery

*Instructions:* The aim of this inquiry is to determine the vividness of your imagery. The items of the test will bring certain images to your mind. You are to rate the vividness of each image by reference to the accompanying rating scale. For example: if your image is "vague and dim" you give it a rating of 5. Record your answer in the appropriate space next to the question. Before you begin, familiarize yourself with the different categories of the rating scale. Throughout the test, refer to the rating scale when judging the vividness of each image. Try to make each rating on its own merits without reference to what has gone before.

*Rating scale:* The image aroused by any one item of this test may be:

| Rating to be given | Nature of the image |
|---|---|
| 1 | Perfectly clear and as vivid as the actual experience |
| 2 | Very clear and comparable in vividness to the actual experience |
| 3 | Moderately clear and vivid |
| 4 | Not clear or vivid but recognizable |
| 5 | Vague and dim |
| 6 | So vague and dim as to be hardly discernible |
| 7 | No image present at all; just knowing that you are thinking of the object |

*Your rating of pictorial (visual) images*

_____ The sun as it is sinking below the horizon (1)

In J. P. Sutcliffe, "The Relation of Imagery and Fantasy to Hypnosis," Progress Report on N.I.M.H. Project M-3950, 1962. See also P.W. Sheehan, "A shortened form of Betts' questionnaire upon mental imagery," *J. Clin. Psychol.* 23:386–89.

Think of some relative or friend. Rate the vividness of the following images:

_____ The exact contour of face, head, shoulders, and body (2)

_____ The characteristic poses of the head, attitudes of the body, etc. (3)

_____ The precise carriage, length of step, etc., in walking (4)

_____ The different colors worn in some familiar costume (5)

*Your rating of sound (auditory) images*

_____ The sound of the whistle of a locomotive (6)

_____ The sound of the honk of an automobile (7)

_____ The mewing of a cat (8)

_____ The sound of escaping steam (9)

_____ The clapping of hands in applause (10)

*Your rating of touch (tactual) images*

_____ The feel of sand (11)

_____ Of linen (12)

_____ Of fur (13)

_____ The prick of a pin (14)

_____ The warmth of a tepid bath (15)

*Your rating of muscular (kinesthetic) images*

_____ Running upstairs (16)

_____ Springing across a gutter (17)

_____ Drawing a circle on paper (18)

_____ Reaching up to a high shelf (19)

_____ Kicking something out of your way (20)

*Your rating of taste (gustatory) images*

_____ The taste of salt (21)

_____ Of white sugar (22)

_____ Of oranges (23)

_____ Of jelly (24)

_____ Of your favorite soup (25)

*Your rating of smell (olfactory) images*

_____ The smell of an ill-ventilated room (26)

_____ Of cooking cabbage (27)

_____ Of roast beef (28)

_____ Of fresh paint (29)

_____ Of new leather (30)

*Your rating of bodily (somesthetic-organic) images*

_____ Sensations of fatigue (31)

_____ Of hunger (32)

_____ Of a sore throat (33)

_____ Of drowsiness (34)

_____ Of repletion (as from a very full meal) (35)

# Bibliography

Ames, Louise B., and Learned, J. 1946. Imaginary companions and related phenomena. *J. Genet. Psychol.* 69:147–67.

Amis, K. 1960. *New maps of hell: A survey of science fiction.* New York: Harcourt, Brace & World.

Ås, A. 1963. Hypnotizability as a function of non-hypnotic experiences. *J. Abnorm. Soc. Psychol.* 66:142–50.

Ås, A.; Hilgard, E. R.; and Weitzenhoffer, A. M. 1963. An attempt at experimental modification of hypnotizability through repeated individualized hypnotic experience. *Scand. J. Psychol.* 4:81–89.

Barber, T. X., and Calverley, D. S. 1963. "Hypnotic-like" suggestibility in children and adults. *J. Abnorm. Soc. Psychol.* 66:589–97.

Barron, F. 1963. *Creativity and psychological health.* Princeton, N.J.: Van Nostrand.

Balint, M. 1959. *Thrills and regressions.* New York: International Universities Press.

Bender, Lauretta, and Vogel, F. 1941. Imaginary companions of children. *Amer. J. Orthopsychiat.* 11:56–66.

Bernheim, H. 1889. *Suggestive therapeutics: A treatise on the nature and uses of hypnotism.* Translated from 2d French ed. New York: Putnam.

Betts, C. H. 1909. *The distribution and functions of mental imagery.* New York: Teachers College Contribution to Education.

Binet, A., and Féré, C. 1887. *Animal magnetism.* London: Kegan, Paul & Trench Co.

Blum, G. S. 1963. Programming people to simulate machines. In Tomkins, S. S., and Messick, S., eds. *Computer simulation of personality,* pp. 127–57. New York: Wiley.

Bond, D. D. 1952. *The love and fear of flying.* New York: International Universities Press.

Boucher, R. G., and Hilgard, E. R. 1962. Volunteer bias in hypnotic experiments. *Amer. J. Clin. Hyp.* 5:49–51.

287

Bowers, K. 1966. Hypnotic behavior: The differentiation of trance and demand characteristic variables. *J. Abnorm. Psychol.* 71:42–51.

Breuer, J., and Freud, S. 1895. *Studies on hysteria.* Reprinted in *Complete psychological works of Sigmund Freud,* Standard Edition, 2:1–305. London: Hogarth, 1955.

Cooper, L. M.; Banford, Suzanne A.; Schubot, E.; and Tart, C. T. 1967. A further attempt to modify hypnotic susceptibility through repeated individualized experience. *Int. J. Clin. Exp. Hyp.* 15:118–24.

Dewey, J. 1913. *Interest and effort in education.* Boston: Houghton-Mifflin.

Ehrenreich, G. A. 1949. The relationship of certain descriptive factors to hypnotizability. *Trans. Kansas Acad. Sci.* 52:24–27.

Erikson, E. H. 1959. Identity and the life cycle. *Psychol. Issues* vol. 1, no. 1.

———. 1963. *Childhood and society.* New York: W. W. Norton & Co.

———. 1968. *Identity: Youth and crisis.* New York: W. W. Norton & Co.

Eysenck, H. J. 1961. Classification and the problem of diagnosis. In Eysenck, H. J., ed., *Handbook of abnormal psychology,* pp. 1–31. New York: Basic Books.

Ferenczi, S. 1909. *Introjection and transference: Sex in psychoanalysis.* New York: Brunner, 1950.

Franz, S. I. 1933. *Persons one and three.* New York: McGraw-Hill.

Freud, S. 1905. *Three essays on the theory of sexuality.* Reprinted in *Complete psychological works of Sigmund Freud.* Standard Edition, 7:125–245. London: Hogarth, 1953.

———. 1911. *Formulations on the two principles of mental functioning.* Reprinted in *Complete psychological works of Sigmund Freud,* Standard Edition, 12:218–26. London: Hogarth, 1958.

———. 1921. *Group psychology and the analysis of the ego.* Reprinted in *Complete psychological works of Sigmund Freud,* Standard Edition, 18:67–143. London: Hogarth, 1955.

Fromm, Erika, 1968a. Dissociative and integrative processes in hypnoanalysis. *Amer. J. Clin. Hyp.* 10:174–77.

———. 1968b. Transference and countertransference in hypnoanalysis. *Int. J. Clin. Exp. Hyp.* 16:77–84.

Fromm, Erika, and French, T. M. 1962. Formation and evaluation of hypotheses in dream interpretation. *J. Psychol.* 54:271–83.

Galton, F. 1883. *Inquiries into human faculty and its development.* Reprinted, 1919. New York: Dutton.

Gill, M. M., and Brenman, Margaret. 1959. *Hypnosis and related states: Psychoanalytic studies in regression.* New York: International Universities Press.

Haber, R. N. 1969. Eidetic images. *Scientific American* 220:36–44.

Haber, R. N., and Haber, Ruth B. 1964. Eidetic imagery. 1. Frequency. *Percept. Mot. Skills* 19:131–38.

Haley, J. 1958. An interactional explanation of hypnosis. *Amer. J. Clin. Hyp.* 1:41–57.

———, ed. 1967. *Advanced techniques of hypnosis and therapy: Selected papers of Milton H. Erickson, M.D.* New York: Grune & Stratton.

Harriman, P. L. 1937. Some imaginary companions of older subjects. *Amer. J. Orthopsychiat.* 7:368–70.

Hartmann, H. 1958. *Ego psychology and the problem of adaptation.* (German original, 1939.) New York: International Universities Press.

Hebb, D. O. 1960. The American Revolution. *Amer. Psychol.* 15:735–45.

Hilgard, E. R. 1964. The motivational relevance of hypnosis. *Nebraska Symposium on Motivation,* vol. 12. Lincoln, Nebr.: University of Nebraska Press.

————. 1965. *Hypnotic susceptibility.* New York: Harcourt, Brace & World.

————. 1967. Individual differences in hypnotizability. In Gordon, J. E., ed., *Handbook of clinical and experimental hypnosis,* pp. 391–443. New York: Macmillan Co.

Hilgard, E. R., and Bentler, P. M. 1963. Predicting hypnotizability from the Maudsley Personality Inventory. *Brit. J. Psychol.* 54:63–69.

Hilgard, E. R., and Hilgard, Josephine R. 1967. The personality background of susceptibility to hypnosis. In Lassner, J., ed., *Hypnosis and psychosomatic medicine.* New York: Springer-Verlag.

Hilgard, E. R.; Lauer, Lillian W.; and Cuca, Janet M. 1965. Acquiescence, hypnotic susceptibility, and the MMPI. *J. Consult. Psychol.* 29:489.

Hilgard, Josephine R. 1965. Personality and hypnotizability: Inferences from case studies. In Hilgard, E. R., *Hypnotic susceptibility,* pp. 343–74. New York: Harcourt, Brace & World.

Hilgard, Josephine, R.; Hilgard, E. R.; and Newman, Martha F. 1961. Sequelae to hypnotic induction with special reference to earlier chemical anesthesia. *J. Nerv. Ment. Dis.* 133:461–78.

Hilgard, Josephine R., and Hilgard, E. R. 1962. Developmental-interactive aspects of hypnosis: Some illustrative cases. *Genet. Psychol. Monogr.* 66:143–78.

Hilgard, Josephine R., and Moore, Ursula S. 1969. Affiliative therapy with young adolescents. *Amer. Acad. Child Psychiat.,* October.

Holt, E. R. 1964 Imagery: The return of the ostracized. *Amer. Psychol.* 19:254–64.

Horowitz, Suzanne L. 1969. Strategies within hypnosis for reducing phobic behavior. *J. Abn. Psychol.* In press.

Hull, C. L. 1933. *Hypnosis and suggestibility: An experimental approach.* New York: Appleton-Century-Crofts.

Hurlock, Elizabeth B., and Burstein, M. 1932. The imaginary playmate: A questionnaire study. *J. Genet. Psychol.* 41:380–92.

James, W. 1890. *Principles of psychology.* 2 vols. New York: Holt.

Janet, P. 1907. *The major symptoms of hysteria.* 2d ed., 1920. New York: Macmillan Co.

Janet, P. 1919. *Psychological healing: A historical and clinical study.* 2d ed., 1925. New York: Macmillan Co.

Jersild, A. T.; Markey, F. V.; and Jersild, C. L. 1933. Children's fears, dreams, wishes. *Child Develop. Monogr.,* no. 12.

Jones, E. 1957. How to tell your friends from geniuses. *Saturday Review of Literature,* 10 August, p. 9.

Kagan, J. 1964. Acquisition and significance of sex typing and sex role identity. In Hoffman, M. L., and Hoffman, Lois W., eds., *Review of child development research*, 1:137–67. New York: Russell Sage Foundation.

Klüver, H. 1933. Eidetic imagery. In Murchison, C., ed., *A Handbook of child psychology*, pp. 699–722. Worcester, Mass.: Clark University Press.

Kohlberg, L. 1963. Moral development and identification. In *Child psychology*. The Sixty-second Yearbook of the National Society for the Study of Education, pp. 277–332. Chicago: University of Chicago Press.

Kris, E. 1952. *Psychoanalytic explorations in art*. New York: International Universities Press.

Kroger, W. S. 1963. *Clinical and experimental hypnosis*. Philadelphia: J. B. Lippincott Co.

Kubie, L. S., and Margolin, S. 1944. The process of hypnotism and the nature of the hypnotic state. *Amer. J. Psychiat.* 100:611–22.

Leask, J.; Haber, R. N.; and Haber, Ruth B. 1969. Eidetic imagery in children. II. Longitudinal and experimental results. Psychonomic Science Monograph Series.

Lee-Teng, Evelyn. 1965. Trance-susceptibility, induction susceptibility, and acquiescence as factors in hypnotic performance. *J. Abnorm. Psychol.* 70:383–89.

Lewin, K. 1926. Vorsatz, Wille, und Bedürfnis. *Psychol. Forsch.* 7:294–385. Translated and condensed as "Will and Needs" in Ellis, W. D., ed., *A source book of gestalt psychology*, pp. 283–99. New York: Harcourt, Brace & World, 1938.

London, P. 1965. Developmental experiments in hypnosis. *J. Proj. Tech. Pers. Assess* 29:189–99.

McBain, W. N. 1954. Imagery and suggestibility: A test of the Arnold Hypothesis. *J. Abnorm. Soc. Psychol.* 49:36–44.

Macalpine, I. 1950. The development of the transference. *Psychoanal. Quart.* 19:501–39.

MacKinnon, D. W. 1965. Personality and the realization of creative potential. *Amer. Psychologist* 20:273–81.

Madsen, C. H., and London, P. 1966. Role-playing and hypnotic susceptibility in children. *J. Pers. Soc. Psychol.* 3:13–19.

Maslow, A. H. 1959. Cognition of being in the peak experiences. *J. Genet. Psychol.* 94:43–66.

Melei, Janet P., and Hilgard, E. R. 1964. Attitudes toward hypnosis, self-predictions, and hypnotic susceptibility. *Int. J. Clin. Exp. Hyp.* 12:99–108.

Miller, G. A.; Galanter, E.; and Pribram, K. H. 1960. *Plans and the structure of behavior*. New York: Holt.

Mischel, W. 1968. *Personality and assessment*. New York: Wiley.

Morgan, Arlene H. 1969a. Decline of hypnotizability with age. (Manuscript in preparation.)

————. 1969b. The reliability of the kinesthetic aftereffect and its relationship to other cognitive style dimensions. M. A. Thesis, San Jose State College.

Nowlis, D. P. 1968. The child-rearing antecedents of hypnotic susceptibility and of naturally occurring hynotic-like experience. *Int. J. Clin. Exp. Hyp.* 17: 109–120.

Orne, M. T. 1959. The nature of hypnosis: Artifact and essence. *J. Abnorm. Soc. Psychol.* 58:277–99.

————. 1966. Hypnosis, motivation, and compliance. *Amer. J. Psychiat.* 122:721–26.

Paivio, A.; Yuille, J. C.; and Smythe, P. C. 1966. Stimulus and response abstractness, imagery, and meaningfulness, and reported mediators in paired-associate learning. *Canad. J. Psychol.* 20:362–77.

Pavlov, I. P. 1923. The identity of inhibition with sleep and hypnosis. *Scientific Monthly* 17:603–8.

————. 1927. *Conditioned reflexes.* London: Oxford University Press.

Platonov, K. I. 1959. *The word as a physiological and therapeutic factor.* Translated from 2d Russian ed. (1955) by D. A. Myshne. 1st ed., 1930. Moscow: Foreign Languages Publishing House.

Prince, M. 1905. *Dissociation of a personality.* New York: Longmans, Green.

Roberts, Mary R. 1964. Attention and related abilities as affecting hypnotic susceptibility. Doctoral dissertation, Stanford University. *Diss. Abst.* 25:4261.

Rosenhan, D., and Tomkins, S. S. 1964. On preference for hypnosis and hypnotizability. *Int. J. Clin. Exp. Hyp.* 12:109–14.

Sacerdote, P. 1965. Additional contributions to the hypnotherapy of the advanced cancer patient. *Amer. J. Clin. Hyp.* 7:308–19.

Sachs, L. B., and Anderson, W. L. 1967. Modification of hypnotic susceptibility. *Int. J. Clin. Exp. Hyp.* 15:172–80.

Sarbin, T. R. 1950. Contributions to role-taking theory. 1. Hypnotic behavior. *Psychol. Rev.* 57:255–70.

————. 1954. Role theory. In Lindzey, G., ed., *Handbook of social psychology,* 1:223–58. Cambridge, Mass.: Addison-Wesley.

Sarbin, T. R., and Andersen, M. L. 1967. Role-theoretical analysis of hypnotic behavior. In Gordon, J. E., ed., *Handbook of clinical and experimental hypnosis,* pp. 319–44. New York: Macmillan Co.

Sarbin, T. R., and Lim, D. T. 1963. Some evidence in support of the role-taking hypothesis in hypnosis. *Int. J. Clin. Exp. Hyp.* 11:98–103.

Saunders, D. R. 1956. Moderator variables in prediction. *Educ. Psychol. Measmt.* 16:209–22.

Schilder, P. 1956. *The nature of hypnosis.* New York: International Universities Press.

Schneck, J. M. 1963. *Hypnosis in modern medicine.* Springfield, Ill.: Charles C. Thomas.

Sears, R. R.; Maccoby, Eleanor E.; and Levin, H. 1957. *Patterns of child rearing.* Stanford, Calif.: Stanford University Press.

Sears, R. R.; Rau, Lucy; and Alpert, R. 1965. *Identification and child rearing*. Stanford, Calif.: Stanford University Press.

Shor, R. E. 1959. Hypnosis and the concept of the generalized reality-orientation. *Amer. J. Psychother.* 13:582–602.

——. 1960. The frequency of naturally occurring "hypnotic-like" experiences in the normal college population. *Int. J. Clin. Exp. Hyp.* 8:151–63.

——. 1962. Three dimensions of hypnotic depth. *Int. J. Clin. Exp. Hyp.* 10:23–38.

Shor, R. E., and Orne, Emily C. 1962. *Harvard Group Scale of Hypnotic Susceptibility*. Palo Alto, Calif.: Consulting Psychologists Press.

Shor, R. E.; Orne, M. T.; and O'Connell, D. N. 1966. Psychological correlates of plateau hypnotizability in a special volunteer sample. *J. Pers. Soc. Psychol.* 3:80–95.

Siegel, S. 1956. *Nonparametric statistics*. New York: McGraw-Hill.

Sjoberg, B. M., Jr., & Hollister, L. E. 1965. The effects of psychotomimetic drugs on primary suggestibility. *Psychopharmacologia,* 8: 251–262.

Slater, P. 1961. Toward a dualistic theory of identification. *Merrill-Palmer Quart.* 7:113–26.

Sperling, O. E. 1954. An imaginary companion representing a pre-stage of the super-ego. *Psychoanal. Study of the Child.* 9:252–58.

Stanislavski, C. 1963. *An actor's handbook*. New York: Theatre Arts Books.

Stein, K. B., and Craik, K. H. 1965. Relationship between motoric and ideational activity preference in neurotics and schizophrenics. *J. Consult. Psychol.* 29:460–67.

Stukát, K.-G. 1958. *Suggestibility: A factorial and experimental analysis*. Stockholm: Almqvist and Wiksell.

Sutcliffe, J. P. 1965. *The relations of imagery and fantasy to hypnosis*. Final report on N.I.M.H. Project M-3950 USPH.

Svendsen, Margaret. 1934. Children's imaginary companions. *Arch. Neurol. Psychiat.* 32:985–99.

Thigpen, C. H., and Cleckley, H. M. 1957. *The three faces of Eve*. New York: McGraw–Hill.

Weitzenhoffer, A. M., and Hilgard, E. R. 1959. *Stanford Hypnotic Susceptibility Scale, forms A and B*. Palo Alto, Calif.: Consulting Psychologists Press.

——. 1962. *Stanford Hypnotic Susceptibility Scale, form C*. Palo Alto, Calif.: Consulting Psychologists Press.

West, L. J. 1967. Dissociative reaction. In Freedman, A. M., and Kaplan, H. I., eds., *Comprehensive textbook of psychiatry*, pp. 885–99. Baltimore: Williams & Wilkins.

White, R. W. 1941. An analysis of motivation in hypnosis. *J. Gen. Psychol.* 24:145–62.

Wingfield, R. C. 1948. Bernreuter personality ratings of college students who recall having had imaginary playmates during childhood. *J. Child Psychiat.* 1:190–94.

Wiseman, R. J., and Reyher, J. 1962. A procedure utilizing dreams for deepening the hypnotic trance. *Amer. J. Clin. Hyp.* 5:105–10.

# Author Index

Tart, C. T. *See* Cooper et al.
Thigpen, C. H., 113, 125
Tomkins, S. S., 225

Vogel, F., 123

Weitzenhoffer, A. M., 8, 9, 16, 17

West, L. J., 250
White, R. W., 225
Wingfield, R. C., 123
Wiseman, R. J., 17

Yuille, J. C., 258

# Subject Index